Ship's Log
USS Hornet

CV-12

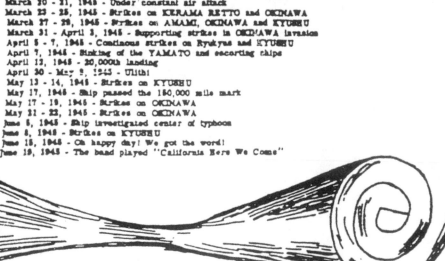

October 10, 1944 - Strikes on Okinawa, Ryukyu Retto
October 11, 1944 - Strikes on Aparri, Northern Luzon
October 12, 1944 - Strikes on Formosa; continous defense against air attack
October 13, 1944 - First plane splashed by ship's gunfire
October 19, 1944 - Strikes on Luzon
October 20, 1944 - Strikes on LEYTE, supporting invasion
October 25 - 26, 1944 - SECOND BATTLE OF PHILIPPINE SEA (LEYTE GULF)
October 29 - November 2, 1944 - Ulithi; recreation parties
November 5 - 6, 1944 - Strikes on LUZON
November 11, 1944 - Shipping strikes, ORMOC BAY, LEYTE ISLAND
November 13 - 14, 1944 - Shipping strikes, MANILA BAY
November 19, 1944 - Strikes on Central LUZON and SUBIC BAY
November 21, 1944 - Strikes on YAP
November 22 - December 10, 1944 - Ulithi
December 13, 1944 - Ship passed the 100,000 mile mark
December 14 - 16, 1944 - Strikes on Central LUZON, supporting MINDORO invasion
December 18 - 19, 1944 - Ship weathered worst TYPHOON ever encountered
December 24 - 30, 1944 - Ulithi
January 3 - 4, 1945 - Strikes on FORMOSA and PESCADORES ISLANDS
January 6 - 7, 1945 - Strikes on LUZON
January 9, 1945 - Strikes on FORMOSA
January 10, 1945 - Passed through Bashi Channel into South China Sea
January 12, 1945 - Strikes on SAIGON, CAMRANH BAY, FRENCH INDO CHINA
January 15 - 16, 1945 - Strikes on HONG KONG, KOWLOON and FORMOSA
January 21, 1945 - Strikes on FORMOSA and PESCADORES; 15,000th landing
January 22, 1945 - Strikes on OKINAWA
January 26 - February 10, 1945 - Ulithi
February 16 - 17, 1945 - Strikes on TOKYO and HACHIJO JIMA
February 18, 1945 - Strikes on CHICHI JIMA
February 19, 1945 - Strikes on IWO JIMA, supporting Marine invasion
February 25 - 26, 1945 - Strikes on TOKYO
March 1, 1945 - Strikes on OKINAWA
March 4 - 14, 1945 - Ulithi
March 18 - 19, 1945 - Strikes on KYUSHU airfields and Jap FLEET at KURE
March 20 - 21, 1945 - Under constant air attack
March 23 - 25, 1945 - Strikes on KERAMA RETTO and OKINAWA
March 27 - 29, 1945 - Strikes on AMAMI, OKINAWA and KYUSHU
March 31 - April 3, 1945 - Supporting strikes in OKINAWA invasion
April 5 - 7, 1945 - Continous strikes on Ryukyus and KYUSHU
April 7, 1945 - Sinking of the YAMATO and escorting ships
April 12, 1945 - 20,000th landing
April 30 - May 9, 1945 - Ulithi
May 13 - 14, 1945 - Strikes on KYUSHU
May 17, 1945 - Ship passed the 150,000 mile mark
May 17 - 19, 1945 - Strikes on OKINAWA
May 21 - 22, 1945 - Strikes on OKINAWA
June 5, 1945 - Ship investigated center of typhoon
June 8, 1945 - Strikes on KYUSHU
June 15, 1945 - Oh happy day! We got the word!
June 19, 1945 - The band played "California Here We Come"

USS HORNET

THE HISTORY OF THE USS HORNET VETERANS

TURNER PUBLISHING COMPANY

TURNER PUBLISHING COMPANY

Turner Publishing Company Staff:
Project Coordinator: John Mark Jackson
Designer: Shelley R. Davidson

Library of Congress Catalog Card No.
97-60754
ISBN: 978-1-68162-488-4

Printed in the United States of America. Additional
copies may be purchased directly from the publisher.
Limited Edition.

Cover photo provided by USS HORNET Club, Inc.
P.O. Box 7189
North Port, Florida 34287
(941) 423-4547

Photos used throughout text courtesy
USS HORNET Club, Inc.
Al Massé – Ships' Store
P.O. Box 7189
North Port, Florida 34287
© 1985

TABLE OF CONTENTS

USS Hornet History 6

History of Carrier Air Group 11 30

Special Stories 34

Veterans 54

USS HORNET Club, Inc. 93

Index 95

Past Executive Director's Message

This book is dedicated to all of the crew members and personnel who were associated with HORNET and paid the ultimate price. In order to continue to acknowledge and perpetuate the memory of our shipmates in continuing peace, this book is being published in their honor. GONE BUT NOT FORGOTTEN.

It has been a great privilege and honor to participate in the production of this book. I would like to thank all of you for your time, memories and submission of notes and articles so that this book could come to fruition.

When I became associated with the HORNET CLUB several years ago, I did not realize the amount of time and effort that was devoted to the Club by so many people. In attending the reunions, it became readily apparent that even after so many years since our active days aboard, that a special bond had developed that cannot be overcome by time or distance. This special bond is manifested throughout the organization and reflected from the CV8 hands to the CVS personnel. It is something that only we have, and I am pleased that I have had the opportunity to be a part of it.

Our families, friends and supporters have provided us with a great deal of backing, enthusiasm and help in seeing that the HORNET memory lives on. We thank each and every one of you for your devoted efforts.

HORNET has been saved and is now in the process of being converted into an air, sea and space museum. It is located at the former NAS Alameda pier. We wish to thank all of the people that made this possible. Through your efforts, our legacy will continue to live on.

May the proud HORNET heritage and tradition be upheld for future generations.

Lyn A. Svendsen
Past Executive Director (1995 - 1997)
USS HORNET Club, Inc.

USS HORNET HISTORY

Ships named "*Hornet*" throughout history

Since the beginning of the United States Navy, eight ships have proudly carried the name *Hornet*. Although little detail is known about the exploits and missions of the early *Hornet*s, available information and accounts acknowledge them as some of the most distinguished fighting ships in American Naval History.

The first ship to bear the name *Hornet* was originally a merchant sloop. She was fitted out with nine ten-pounder guns by the Continental Marine Committee at Baltimore, Maryland in the fall of 1775. Under the command of Captain William Stone, she became part of Commodore Esek Hopkin's fleet and patrolled in the Delaware Bay area for nearly a year. In December of 1776, she was ordered to the West Indies, but the presence of overwhelming British forces in the Delaware Capes prevented her from beginning her mission.

Commanded by Captain John Nicholson, *Hornet* was ordered in January 1777 to escort a convoy of merchantmen safely out to sea through a British blockade. She managed to evade the blockade and accomplished her mission. Upon her return, she was attached to Commodore Saltonstall's squadron in the Delaware River. This assignment would be *Hornet*'s last, for the forts guarding the approaches to Philadelphia were captured by the British in November leaving Saltonstall's vessels without protection. As a result, Captain Nicholson was ordered to destroy *Hornet* to prevent her from falling into British hands.

The merchant ship T*raveller* was purchased at Malta in 1805 and became the second *Hornet*, a 71-ton ten-gun sloop. Under the command of Lt. Samuel Evans, she attached to Commodore Rodger's squadron in the Mediterranean in March and took part in the American blockade of Tripoli. In April, she and two other ships (*Argus* and *Nautilus*) anchored within range of shore batteries at Derne and opened fire. *Hornet*'s sting was too much and the Turks were driven from their guns within an hour, clearing the way for the landing of General Eaton's party and the subsequent capture of Derne. This prompted the Bashaw of Tripoli to agree to Commodore Rodger's terms for peace. *Hornet* aided in the evacuation of Eaton's troops from Derne then participated with the fleet in a show of force off Tunis and other Barbary ports intended to quell the action of pirates against merchant shipping in the Mediterranean. She patrolled the Mediterranean insuring the safety of American commerce until June 3, 1806 when a severe gale tore away her top mast. She arrived in Philadelphia on August 9th and was decommissioned a short time later and sold out of service.

The third H*ornet* was a 440-ton brig-rigged sloop of war, launched at Baltimore on July 28, 1805 and commissioned on October 18th under the command of Master Commandant Isaac Chauncey. Designed in the style of British warships of the time, she carried eighteen 32-pounder carronades and two long nine-pounders. *Hornet* patrolled the East coast until March 1806, then patrolled with the Mediterranean fleet in anti-piracy operations until November 1807 when she was decommissioned at Charleston.

Hornet recommissioned in December 1808. After transporting Gen. James Wilkinson to New Orleans, she cruised coastal waters enforcing the Embargo Act until November 1810, when she was rebuilt and re-rigged at the Washington Navy Yard. While deployed with Commodore John Rodger's squadron during the War of 1812, including *President*, *Congress* and the *United States*, *Hornet* captured the British privateer *Dolphin*. In 1813, while participating in the blockade of the Brazilian port of Bahia, she captured HMS *Peacock* after an engagement off British Guiana.

In 1818, *Hornet* made a patrol to the West Indies and a cruise to Copenhagen followed by a second sortie to the Mediterranean in 1819. She then moved her home base to Pensacola, Florida to begin anti-piracy operations in the Caribbean Sea. She would patrol this region for the next nine years. On September 29, 1829, under the command of Master Commandant Otho Norris, *Hornet* lost her main mast in a heavy gale off Tampico with the loss of all hands.

The fourth H*ornet*, a five-gun schooner, was acquired at Georgetown, D.C. in 1813. She was decommissioned on March 15, 1814 and mounted one long eighteen-pounder and four eighteen-pound carronades. She was employed primarily as a dispatch ship sailing the East coast. Her duties also included utility work such as

The first Hornet.

The sixth Hornet.

harbor and coastal survey and mapping work. She was sold out of service at Norfolk in 1820.

The fifth H*ornet* had been built at Blackwell England in 1864 as the Confederate blockade runner *Lady Sterling*. An 835-ton iron side-wheel steamer, she was captured later that year by the *USS Eolus* and *USS Calypso* of the Union Atlantic Blockading Squadron 28 and set afire off Wilmington, North Carolina. She was purchased by the Navy, recommissioned on April 24, 1865 and renamed *Hornet* on June 17th.

Hornet fitted out at the Washington Navy Yard and, under the command of Master Joseph Avant, carried President Andrew Johnson and his party to Point Lookout in July. In October, she departed the Washington Navy Yard, rendezvoused with *Rhode Island* off Norfolk and sailed to Havana to escort the Confederate ram *Stonewall* to Washington. On the return trip, *Hornet* was separated from the other two ships in a withering gale and 7arrived two days ahead of them in Washington. She then served as a transport, hauling 115 men from Norfolk to New York before putting in at Philadelphia where she was decommissioned on December 15, 1865. After four years in storage, she sold to private interests on June 26, 1869 for $33,000.

Purchased on April 6, 1898 from Henry M. Flagler (for $117,500), the sixth H*ornet* was originally the steel steam yacht *Alicia*, built at Wilmington, Delaware in 1890. Her "vertical inverted triple-expansion" engines of 800 horsepower gave her a very capable speed of 15 knots. After fitting out at the New York Navy Yard, she sailed on April 12, 1898 under the command of Lt. James H. Helm to join Admiral Sanson's fleet blockading Spanish Cuba. Arriving on April 24th, she patrolled Cuban waters, periodically retiring to Key West.

On June 30th *Hornet*, sailing with *Hist* and *Wompatuck*, was ordered to scout the waters off the Spanish fort at Manzanillo. That morning she seized the English schooner *Nickerson*, loaded with provisions and manned by a Spanish crew, trying to enter the blockaded harbor. A short time later, a Spanish gunboat was spotted anchored under the protection of an army blockhouse. The American vessels pressed the attack and, despite extremely heavy fire from shore batteries and Spanish troops, fired on and sank the gunboat, retiring with no casualties. Later that day the three ships entered the harbor and soon found themselves in an intense battle, with shells splashing in the water all around. *Hornet*'s primary steam pipe was pierced by a Spanish shell and the ship filled with boiling steam.

Although disabled, *Hornet* continued to fire on the enemy positions, her crew passing ammunition through the scalding steam as they drifted in close to the shore batteries. A small Spanish sloop approached *Hornet*'s port side, assuming that her attention was entirely on her starboard gun batteries which were pounding the enemy. *Hornet*'s alert crew quickly shifted to port and, with one well-placed shot from the six-pounder, sent the sloop to the bottom. In the meantime, *Hornet* had drifted dangerously close to the shoals. *Wompatuck* steamed over to tow her from the area, all guns still blazing. Despite the heated battle, not one American sailor was lost.

On July 11, 1898, *Hornet* sailed, again with *Hist* and *Wompatuck*, on a mission near Santa

Sailors wave to Hornet at Norfolk.

Cruz del Sur to sever the cable between Manzanillo and Havana, ending all telegraphic communication between them. Days later, the American squadron again pushed into Manzanillo harbor to engage Spanish forces. In a bitter exchange with Spanish flotilla which lasted little over 90 minutes, *Hornet* and her sisterships destroyed nine Spanish ships and four gunboats while withstanding murderous fire from numerous shore batteries and harbor defenses. She was decommissioned on October 18th. She then served with the North Carolina Naval Militia until 1902 when she was assigned as a tender to the receiving ship *Franklin*. The 301-ton *Hornet*'s name was struck on March 18, 1910 and she was sold out of service on July 12th of that year.

The *USS Hornet* (CV-8)

The keel for the seventh *Hornet* (CV-8), authorized by the Naval Expansion Act of May 17, 1939, was laid on September 25, 1939 at the Newport News Shipbuilding and Dry Dock Company, Newport News, Virginia.

Launched on December 14, 1940 as Hull No. 385, she was christened by Mrs. Frank Knox, wife of the Secretary of the Navy. *Hornet* was placed in commission at the Naval Operating Base in Norfolk on October 20, 1941 under the command of then-Captain Marc Andrew Mitscher. He would later be succeeded by Captain Charles P. Mason.

USS Hornet (CV-8).

CV-8 under attack at the Battle of Santa Cruz.

The new carrier was built as one of three ships of the YORKTOWN-class. As her sisterships *Yorktown* (CV-5) and *Enterprise* (CV-6), she was 827 feet in length with a draft of 22 feet. Her flight deck was 114 feet wide and the beam of her hull measured 83 feet. Her geared turbines produced 120,000 shaft horsepower to drive the four screws and propel the 20,000-ton carrier at up to 33 knots. With a capacity to carry over 100 contemporary aircraft, *Hornet's* standard Air Group complement of fighters, torpedo planes and dive bombers was 84. Built at a cost of approximately $32,000,000, the increase of thirteen million over her sister ships (CV-5 and CV-6 cost $19,000,000 each) was indicative of a changing economy, particularly the rising costs of raw materials and technology.

Hornet was at sea off Norfolk on her shakedown cruise when the Japanese attack on Pearl Harbor signaled the start of the war. Air Group Eight, assigned to *Hornet*, immediately began intensive training and preparations for the orders to the Pacific and combat operations which everyone aboard knew were soon to come. A hint that those orders would be delayed came on February 2, 1942 when two Army B-25 Mitchell medium bombers were hoisted onto *Hornet's* deck at Norfolk. *Hornet* put to sea a few hours later and, to the surprise of her crew, the B-25s were launched to evaluate the feasibility of these large land-based planes to take off from the deck of a carrier at sea.

Hornet departed Norfolk on March 4th enroute to the West coast by way of the Panama Canal, Arriving San Francisco on March 20th. On April 1st, with *Hornet's* own aircraft stored on her hangar deck, sixteen B-25s were towed

to the Alameda Naval Air Station dock alongside *Hornet* and hoisted aboard. Lt.Col. James H. Doolittle and the officers and men of his hand-picked squadron reported aboard. With her escorts, *Hornet* departed Alameda on April 2nd, sailing with sealed orders. *Hornet's* crew assumed the ship was transporting the bombers to Hawaii or some other forward base. That afternoon, Captain Marc Mitscher came over the ship's public address system and informed the crew that *Hornet* would transport the Army pilots across the Pacific Ocean where they would takeoff to bomb Tokyo. Shouts could be heard throughout the ship and aboard the escorts when the word was signaled to them.

Hornet's group (Task Force 16.1) was joined on April 13th by *Enterprise* (CV-6) and her escorts (Task Force 16.2) who would accompany *Hornet* and provide aerial patrol since *Hornet's* aircraft, tucked away below on her flight deck, were not useable. Besides the Task Force ships, two submarines, *Thresher* and *Trout*, were patrolling of the Japanese coast keeping tabs on weather and Japanese fleet movements.

Although the original plan was to launch the B-25s on the afternoon of April 19th (400 miles from Japan), the sighting of a Japanese picket ship on the morning of the 18th meant that the element of surprise was gone. Doolittle conferred with Admiral Halsey and the decision was made to launch immediately even though the Japanese coast was still 650 miles away, as the carriers could not be jeopardized. In spite of gale-force winds of 45 knots and 30-foot swells which pitched the ship furiously, the sixteen bombers launched with but two incidents - a flight deck crewman lost his arm when he slipped on the wet rolling deck and fell into the arc of a turning propeller and one of the B-25s smashed its plexiglass nose against the tail of the bomber ahead of it. Both aircraft were launched successfully, however.

The raid caused only superficial damage to Tokyo but the boost to American morale in the aftermath of Pearl Harbor was immeasurable. Of the 80 pilots and crewmen, 73 survived the raid. Three of the seven men who died were executed by the Japanese.

For security, *Hornet's* role in the mission was kept secret for over a year. Presi-

dent Roosevelt told the American people that Doolittle and his flyers took off from a "Shangri-La" somewhere in the Pacific. Unknown to the rest of the world, this "Shangri-La" was the flight deck of *Hornet*. The *USS Shangri-La* (CV-38) was later named to commemorate this event and the gallant *Hornet*. For his part in the raid, Jimmy Doolittle was given a jump promotion to Brigadier General.

Following the rushed launch, *Hornet* brought her own aircraft up to the flight deck and proceeded to Pearl Harbor at flank speed, arriving there one week to the hour after launching the B-25s.

Hornet departed Pearl Harbor on April 30th to assist *Lexington* (CV-2) and *Yorktown* at the Battle of the Coral Sea but she arrived too late to take part. She returned to Pearl Harbor on May 26th with the damaged *Yorktown* and sailed 48 hours later with her sister carriers to defend the island of Midway against an expected Japanese assault.

Carrier-based Japanese planes attacked Midway early on June 4, 1942. A Navy PBY Catalina had sighted the enemy carriers 200 miles northwest of Midway shortly after they had launched their bombers and fighters against the atoll. *Hornet*, *Yorktown* and *Enterprise* launched strikes which arrived over their targets just as the Japanese carriers were rearming and refueling their aircraft. Due to a course change by the enemy flattops, the American fighters and dive bombers initially missed contact, but Torpedo 8 from *Hornet*, a squadron of 15 aging TBD Devastator torpedo planes, found the carriers and, without fighter cover, courageously pressed home their attacks. The slow and cumbersome Devastators were met by enemy fighters several miles from the carriers and followed all the way in to their targets, being shot down one by one. The entire squadron was lost. Ens. George H. Gay, the sole survivor, escaped from his stricken plane and found himself bobbing right in the middle of the Japanese carrier force. Using a dark seat cushion to avoid detection from the ships, he had a ringside seat to the systematic destruction of the carriers *Akagi*, *Kaga*, *Hiryu* and *Soryu* (four of the six carriers from which the attack on Pearl Harbor was launched). *Yorktown*, still nursing her wounds from the Battle of the Coral Sea, was sunk by a combined aerial and submarine attack. The sinking of the four carriers was a significant loss from which the Japanese navy did not recover.

The loss of *Wasp* (Sept. 15th), bomb damage to *Enterprise* (Aug. 24th), and torpedo damage to *Saratoga* (Aug. 31st) left *Hornet* the only American carrier in the South Pacific until she was rejoined by *Enterprise* in October. On Oc-

Hornet number seven is towed away from the scene of battle and sunk by American Destroyers - a gallant death for a fighting ship.

tober 24th, the two carriers (escorted by one battleship, six cruisers, and fourteen destroyers) steamed east of the Santa Cruz Islands to intercept a Japanese striking force of four carriers, four battleships, ten cruisers, thirty destroyers and twelve submarines, which was repositioning south to reinforce Japanese positions on Guadalcanal. The Battle of Santa Cruz took place on October 26, 1942 without direct contact between surface ships of the opposing forces. The intent of this major Japanese offensive was the capture of Henderson Field on Guadalcanal.

While aircraft from *Enterprise* and *Hornet* carried out attacks on the enemy fleet, Japanese planes appeared over the American ships. *Enterprise* was hidden from the sight of the Japanese pilots by a local rain squall and *Hornet* became the focal point of a coordinated dive-bombing and torpedo plane attack. Between 0910 and 0917, *Hornet* was hit by two suicide planes (a Val and a Kate), seven bombs, and two torpedoes which knocked out her boilers, jammed the rudder at an angle, and demolished her generator rooms causing her to lose all electrical power. At the height of the attack, a 1000-lb bomb pierced *Hornet's* deck and entered a room next to the ordnance room but did not explode. The ordnance chief entered the room and disarmed the bomb - in the dark!

The heavy cruiser *Northhampton* took her under tow, making four knots. By early afternoon, over 875 wounded and excess personnel had been transferred to destroyers and the engineering team was working tirelessly to raise steam in the remaining undamaged boilers. The situation was beginning to look up when six Japanese Kate torpedo planes appeared and made runs on the almost defenseless carrier. *Northhampton* cast off the tow lines to get clear, leaving *Hornet* dead in the water. Although five of the attackers were shot down in flames, *Hornet* took a third torpedo hit on her starboard side. The ship's list quickly increased from 7 to 18 degrees and it seemed she might keep rolling and capsize. Captain Mason gave the order to abandon ship at 1625 and was the last man to leave the dying ship.

The destroyers *Mustin* and *Anderson* were ordered to destroy the great vessel to prevent her falling into enemy hands. After taking nine more torpedoes and over 300 rounds of 5-inch shells from the destroyers, *Hornet* remained defiant, refusing to sink. At 2040, radar detected a large Japanese surface force approaching and the destroyers withdrew from the area, leaving *Hornet* blazing throughout her whole length.

Two Japanese destroyers, the *Makigumo* and *Akigumo*, hastening the inevitable, closed in and fired four large 24-inch torpedoes into her

at 2120. At 0135 on October 27th, amid the roaring hiss of escaping air, *Hornet* slipped beneath the surface to an eternal grave under 16,000 feet of water off the Santa Cruz Islands. *Hornet* was only one year and six days old when she went down. A warm breeze blew across the water, the stars sparkled in a clear night sky and the sea was quiet and still again.

In contrast, several thousand miles away on Shipway 8 at the Newport News Shipbuilding and Dry Dock Company, Virginia, things were anything but quiet. The graveyard shift had just completed their night's work and the day shift was arriving to continue where they had left off. The sounds of huge motors and generators ran machinery while towering cranes lifted massive steel beams, girders, and plating. The crackle of a hundred welding machines competed with the echoes of a thousand rivets being driven home. Shipyard workers swarmed over the shipway like ants and engineers in hardhats checked and double-checked measurements and calculations. *Hornet* was built and launched on this shipway 22 months earlier as Hull No. 385. The large structure beginning to take shape, Hull No. 395, is also a carrier. This carrier of the new Essex-class will be designated CV-12. When the keel for this ship was laid almost three months ago, she was to be named *Kearsarge* in honor of the *USS Kearsarge*, commanded by Captain John Winslow, which destroyed the notorious Confederate privateer *Alabama* in the harbor of Cherbourg, France in 1864.

The name of the courageous *Hornet* (CV-8) was officially stricken from the Navy list on January 13, 1943. Shortly after that (on January 21st), Hull No. 395, CV-12, was renamed *Hornet* to avenge the loss of her intrepid predecessor and to keep the proud fighting name in the fleet. Today, in naval and historical circles, few names inspire feelings of pride, tradition, courage, pugnacity, and patriotism like that of *Hornet!*

A New Ship

When Franklin D. Roosevelt, former assistant Secretary of the Navy, was elected to the Presidency in 1932, he was alarmed to learn that the U.S. Navy was considerably inferior to the Japanese navy in combat readiness. The Washington Navy Treaty (Five-power Treaty) of 1922 had imposed a moratorium on the construction of capital ships by the five participating countries (U.S., Britain, Japan, Italy and France). The depression and public apathy brought about severe cutbacks in spending which prevented the Navy from building up to treaty strength. In Japan, by contrast, national policies began to take on a more military orientation, fanned in part by the inferior status imposed by the Washington Treaty ratios.

Roosevelt immediately earmarked $238 million from the National Industrial Recovery Act to put men back to work in warship con-

Adm. Mitcher presenting awards aboard the USS Hornet, June 30, 1944.

struction in naval and private shipyards. Work began on thirty-two new ships including the 20,000-ton aircraft carriers *Yorktown* and *Enterprise*. The Vinson-Trammell Act (1934) authorized sufficient tonnage to bring the U.S. up to levels permitted by the naval-limitations treaties. This would provide 102 new warships by 1942. About this time, the Japanese took the first step on the path that led to the second World War when they gave the required two-year notice in 1934 of their intention to end their adherence to the agreement on naval limitations. The Vinson-Trammell Act-Supplement (1939) made allowances for a 20% expansion program of 40,000 tons to be added to the originally-allowed 175,000 tons. This provided for the new YORKTOWN-class carrier *Hornet* (CV-8) and 20,000 tons for a new carrier that would become the *Essex* (CV-9). In addition to the mandated total tonnage limit, there was also a 23,000-ton limit on individual carriers imposed by the London Naval Treaty (1936). Operational experiences with *Yorktown* and *Enterprise* had identified critical flaws in their design concepts. *Hornet* (CV-8) was laid down to their design not because they were the best possible, but because her completion was considered urgent.

By 1940, it was clear that the Navy needed to embark on a program of much more rapid expansion and the "Two-Ocean Navy" Act of 1940 came into being. This provided funding for three more carriers (CV-10 through 12). With the fall of France, Congress opted for a further 70% expansion by ordering another seven fleet carriers (CV-13 through 19). Two more carriers were funded in December, 1941 after the outbreak of war (CV-20 and 21). Hull numbers 22 through 30 were assigned to the INDEPENDENCE-class of light carriers (CVLs) converted from light-cruiser hulls.

A second war-procurement program in late 1942 ordered an additional ten fleet carriers (CV-31 through 40) from three navy yards. In June 1943, three more were ordered to use up the remaining approved combat tonnage (CV-45 through 47). Contracts for a group of six more were awarded in February 1945 but were disapproved by President Roosevelt a month later. In all, twenty-six Essex-class carriers were approved for construction and all but two were completed.

In 1939, the General Board (a council of senior naval officers) had indicated that a standard tonnage of 20,000 tons provided the most advantageous arrangement of essential features such as speed, armor, storage capacity, and handling characteristics while allowing the greatest percentage of aircraft carrying and operating capacity. Thus the Essex design began with a target displacement of 20,000 tons.

The island size was reduced considerably from that of the YORKTOWN-class as the flight crew ready rooms were moved from the island to the gallery deck suspended immediately below the flight deck (this would later prove to make them extremely vulnerable to Kamikaze and bomb hits on the flight deck itself). The rudder was strengthened and the stern shaped so as to allow cruising astern at up to 20 knots to allow deck launching of aircraft over the stern. Arrestor wires were also provided on the forward portion of the flight deck for aircraft re-

coveries over the bow. The practice of landing aircraft over the bow did not prove successful and was suspended during the war as was the launching of aircraft from the hangar deck catapults which were installed perpendicular to the ship's longitudinal axis. The double-action hangar deck catapults were only installed on the first six ships (CV-10, 12, 13, 14, 17, 18) and they were eventually replaced by a second H-4 hydraulic catapult on the flight deck. *Hornet* (CV-12) was the only carrier to retain her hangar deck catapult until the end of the war.

The Essex class introduced the concept of alternating engine and boiler rooms (as opposed to having all boiler rooms first followed by all engine rooms), an important passive defense against torpedo damage. The first *Hornet* (CV-8) did not have this feature and a Bureau of Ships war damage report indicated that her propulsion system was immobilized, contributing greatly to her loss.

Although the Essex ships possessed some flight deck protection to counter bombs and shellfire (0.2-inch steel plate with 3-inch thick teak wood planking laid transversely across it), they were not large enough to support the topside weight associated with a fully armored flight deck. The hangar deck, as the main deck, was armored with 2.5 inches of Special Treatment Steel (STS) while the 4th deck (three decks below the hangar deck) was armored with 1.5 inches of STS to further protect the ship's vitals. The welded steel hull was protected by 4-inch thick side armor and the steering gear was enclosed by 4-inch side armor on the sides and 5-inches on the top. The commanders of *Yorktown* and *Enterprise* had complained about the poor ventilation in ready rooms for pilots in bulky flight clothing waiting to man their planes and the problems associated with two or more squadrons occupying the same ready room. The Essex design allowed a separate ready room for each squadron and provided much-needed improvements in ventilation including four air-conditioned ready rooms.

The Essex-class carrier required over 9,000 separate plans (including preliminary design, contract design and shipyard working plans). Accommodations were planned for 2,486 men (230 officers and 2,256 CPOs and enlisted men) however, by war's end, that number had increased to almost 3,400. The Essex-class radar assortments were very complex and varied between ships to the point that many ships can often be identified in photographs by their radar equipment.

The 24 Essex-class carriers were constructed at five shipyards over a period of five years (with the exception of *Oriskany*) at unofficial unit costs which varied between $68 million and $78 million. Due to the urgent need for carrier decks, the yards accelerated their construction using a three-shift system which resulted in remarkably short building times. The USS *Hornet* (CV-12) was completed in just 15 months (six months early) by Newport News at an unofficial cost of $69,300,000.

The keel for the USS *Hornet* (CV-12) was laid down on Shipway No. 8 at Newport News Shipbuilding and Dry Dock Company on August 3, 1942. *Hornet*'s massive keel was built up from large steel plates and angles into an enormous 870-foot I-beam which became her backbone and main support structure. Great transverse frames were welded into place, extending from the keel outward around the turn of the bilge and up the sides like the ribs of some giant skeleton. The form of *Hornet*'s voluminous hull began to take shape. Longitudinal frames, running parallel to the keel, were attached along the bottom, bilge and side plating and served to tie the transverse frames and bulkheads together along the length of the ship. While providing *Hornet* with contour, rigidity and strength, these structural bulkheads divided her into hundreds of watertight compartments. The use of welding in lieu of time-consuming riveting did much to shorten her construction time. In addition, the machining of "lightning holes" in deck beams and vertical girders was widely employed as a weight-saving measure.

Hornet was approximately 70 percent complete when launched. The main or hangar deck, flight deck and other levels in the hull were in place and essentially complete and the island superstructure was roughly 40 percent complete.

During her construction, *Hornet*'s towering hull rested on keel blocks which supported the entire weight of the ship. Ten weeks before launch, Sliding Ways were dragged into place on two fixed tracks under the ship called Ground Ways. These were made of Greenheart, a tough wood especially resistant to water. Each of these ground ways would carry a launch load of more than 8,000 tons. The ground ways, lubricated with over 200 tons of heavy grease, were built on a slight incline so that the grease and gravity would ease the big carrier into the water on her first trip. When the sliding ways were in place on the ground ways, a launch cradle was built of wood on the sliding ways to fit the contour of the hull and secured to the ship with temporary fastenings.

CV-12, 1943.

Workmen began the process of "wedging up" or transferring the weight from supporting timbers to the sliding ways. This consisted of driving scores of long wooden wedges under the hull at right angles to force the sliding ways hard up under the ship and hard down on the ground ways. Two days before launch, workmen began knocking out the giant wooden keel blocks from underneath the ship. The shipway was cleared of all tools and equipment including thousands of feet if air, water and power lines. The staging or scaffolding surrounding the hull was taken down in sections. During the construction of *Hornet*, shipwrights used more than 300,000 board feet of lumber (that's over 56 miles of lumber!). The day before launch, ram gangs knocked out nearly 200 enormous timber shores with battering rams to the rhythmic chanting of a gang leader. *Hornet* was now ready to slide down the incline of the fixed ways by her own sheer weight. Holding her back however, were several mammoth triggers whose upper ends were hooked into the sliding ways. The lower part of the shipway was flooded and the water-filled shipway gate was pumped out and towed away. Soundings were taken in the river outside the shipway to make certain the river was clear of obstacles and divers went into the water to blow mud and silt away from the base of the shipway gate to assure a clear path for the hull.

On launch day, tugboats stood by in the James River, ready to pick up the ship and tow her to a nearby outfitting pier. On the sponsor's platform, constructed around the bow, stood the Secretary of the Navy and Mrs. Frank Knox (sponsor of *Hornet*), officials of Newport News Shipbuilding Company, and several high-ranking naval officers including Captain Miles R. Browning, who had been designated to be *Hornet*'s first "skipper". As the planned launch time of 11:36 am approached, the clicking of numerous cameras recorded Mrs. Knox making practice swings with the champagne bottle which was suspended from the towering flight deck by brightly-colored ribbons.

A tremendous crowd had gathered around the bow to witness the historic launching. The happy and auspicious occasion was especially thrilling for the thousands of workmen and women whose labor over the last 12 months had seen thousands of tons of raw materials and components come together to form the enormous vessel.

The air of excitement and anticipation was abruptly interrupted when Newport News Vice-president Woodward came to the podium and announced without explanation that the launching would be delayed. Moments later he returned and announced that the launching would be postponed indefinitely. Newport News officials conferred with the Yard Superintendent and Admiral D.L. Cox, the Supervisor of Shipbuilding. Mr. Woodward again approached the podium and explained that too great a pressure had built up in the hydraulic launching mechanism up forward under the hull, which might endanger the ship were it released at that time. The disappointment was such that no one spoke for several moments and the noises of hammering and welding on neighboring ships could be heard echoing through the vast shipyard. Cameras and newsreels were put away, microphones for

broadcasting the event were taken down and many in the hushed crowd dispersed. The Secretary of the Navy and Mrs. Knox remained with the christening party on the stand, while the scheduled launching time passed.

A short time later, Mr. Woodward came to the podium and proclaimed that his worst fears had been unfounded. He explained that the excessive pressure in the hydraulic launching mechanism had been lowered to the proper levels and that the ship would be launched immediately. Cameras were brought out, microphones were set back up and the air of excitement and anticipation returned to the crowd. On signal from the launch supervisor, Mrs. Knox smashed the ceremonial bottle of champagne across the starboard side of the bow, proclaiming "I Christen Thee *Hornet*". Simultaneously, in the trigger pit beneath the ground ways under the hull (the nerve center of the launch), a lever was thrown releasing the giant triggers, and the ship was off at 12:17pm on August 30, 1943.

Hornet took an estimated 35 seconds to slide into the water amid the deafening cheers of several thousand onlookers. Gaining momentum, she entered the water stern first and floated free of the ground ways. Drag chains immediately swung her bow downstream and when her gliding motion had all but stopped, waiting tugs came alongside and towed her to a fitting-out pier at the nearby Portsmouth Naval Yard. The scene was not unlike that of December 14, 1940 when Mrs. Knox christened the first carrier *Hornet* (CV-8, Hull No. 385) on the same shipway. A green and gold signboard nearby showed a *Hornet* superimposed on the islands of Japan. Large block letters declared "Hull 385 started it, Hull 395 will finish it!". Coincidentally, August 30, 1943 was the thirtieth anniversary of the day when Admiral George Dewey and the General Board proposed the creation of the Department of Naval Aviation. Secretary Knox then made a speech covering the short but colorful history of

the previous carrier *Hornet* from her launching to her loss at the Battle of Santa Cruz less than a year before. In concluding his heart-stirring address, Knox proclaimed "The *Hornet* is Dead, Long Live the *Hornet*!".

At the pier, the process known as "fitting out" was begun. This process, which normally takes several months, sees the ship completed and ready for commissioning. Here, giant cranes moved heavy machinery into position in the ship. The island superstructure and masts were completed while guns, turrets, arresting gear, catapults, radar and other equipment were installed. Living quarters, galleys, messing compartments, storerooms, medical compartments, laundry facilities, machine shops and numerous other spaces were painted and fitted with furniture and other fixtures.

Shortly after launching, members of the assigned crew began arriving to assist with *Hornet*'s fitting out. The Supply Department was represented by the Supply Officer and two storekeepers at the launching of *Hornet*. Supply Department personnel commenced to report the following week and the task before them was daunting - place an aircraft carrier in commission in less than three months instead of the peacetime standard of six or more months.

Halfway through the fitting-out period, *Hornet* was moved across the bay to the piers of the Norfolk Navy Yard to complete fitting out and get ready for sea. Huge lists of allocated materials, including aviation supplies at the Norfolk Naval Air Station and general stores at the Norfolk Navy Yard, had to be assembled and tallied. Spare parts had to be inventoried, recorded and stowed away. Food provisions, ship's stores and ship's service supplies, clothing and small stores, and countless items not covered by allowance lists, had to be procured and stowed aboard. Tons of paperwork in the form of files, stock cards, invoices, ledgers, etc. required as many man-hours as loading so that *Hornet* could begin to operate logistically from the date of her commissioning. Over 1600 tons of materials disappeared into the innumerable spaces of the ship. *Hornet* literally became a floating city with material and equipment necessary to not only function as a vessel of war, but to support every facet of her crew's existence.

Three months later, the new warship was pronounced complete and ready for commissioning. On November 29th, the officers and crew in dress uniform assembled on the frigid flight deck in preparation for the traditional ceremony which would officially place *Hornet* in commission as a combat vessel of the United States Navy. Numerous dignitaries came aboard *Hornet* for the event, moored alongside Pier #2 at the Norfolk Navy Yard, including Secretary of the Navy and Mrs. Frank Knox and Captain and Mrs. Browning.

At 1:00 pm, as Mrs. Knox presented the battle flag from *Hornet* No. 7 (CV-8), Secretary Knox ordered this new *Hornet* placed in commission. Following the invocation by Chaplain Zaun, Captain Browning formally accepted the ship and read aloud his orders. Taking command of the great carrier, his first order was "Set the watch", at which point members of the crew took their stations in the new ship. After an address by Secretary Knox, the commissioning entourage left the ship and the crew turned their attention to the completion of work left undone by the shipyard, outfitting, loading of provisions, and getting the ship for her first shakedown cruise.

War in the Pacific

The day after her commissioning, *Hornet* was placed into Norfolk's Dry Dock #4 where her hull, rudder, underwater fittings and all outboard valves were inspected in preparation for shakedown. Three days later, *Hornet* was refloated and moored at Pier #2 where the extensive preparations for her maiden cruise continued. The ship's boilers and engine turbines were tested for safety, operation and control, while function of the rudder was verified from both the bridge and secondary conn locations. Last minute food provisions were brought aboard. Aviation oil and fuel were loaded as well as bunker oil for *Hornet*'s thirsty boilers. Ammunition for the ship's 5- inch gun and other gun batteries was loaded and secured. The ship signal flag and radio call sign (NBGC) was issued by the Navy and Air Group 15 was assigned to *Hornet*.

On December 19th, *Hornet* pulled out to go to sea for the first time to begin her rigorous sea trials in the naval operating area off Chesapeake Bay. The great vessel was tested for speed, endurance, fuel consumption, maneuvering ability and overall seaworthiness, while her equipment was calibrated and adjusted to suit operating conditions. These tests were utilized to set standards for the service operation of the ship. The crew continued training and became familiar with every aspect of their new ship and its use as a weapon of war and their response to General Quarters was perfected through countless drills. Radio, electronics and radar equipment was calibrated and all gun emplacements were fired for structural tests.

January 1, 1944 saw the first arrested landing on *Hornet*'s teakwood flight deck as a TBM from Air Group 15 came aboard. For the next two weeks, shipboard engineering tests continued while pilots of Air Group 15 conducted carrier qualifications on *Hornet* in preparation for shakedown as well as providing *Hornet*'s flight and hangar deck personnel with valuable experience and training. Pilots from Air Group 15 also provided aircraft for target tracking for the anti-aircraft gunners and towed target sleeves for live fire exercises. The remainder of the Air Group's F6F-3 Hellcats, TBM Avengers and SB2C Helldivers came aboard during maneuvers in Chesapeake Bay.

Hornet returned to Norfolk following her sea trials for post-trial inspection and various adjustments to her equipment. After loading aviation gasoline and bunker oil, the carrier departed for a hurried shakedown cruise in the Bermuda operating area, escorted by the destroyers *Forrest* (DD-461), *Corry* (DD-463), *Hobson* (DD-464) and *Carmick* (DD-493). For the next two weeks, the ship simulated a wartime tempo of operations, conducting exercises in gunnery, underway refueling, maneuvering, various calibration tests and intensive flight operations. The Engineering and Communications departments proceeded with rigorous tests and drills. *Hornet* towed a target sled for dive-bombing exercises and served as an "enemy" ship while her pilots perfected weapons delivery profiles and attack techniques as she maneuvered at general quarters to repel their "attacks". During the two weeks of fast-paced flight deck operations, the unforgiving nature of carrier aviation was brought home to everyone aboard as a Hellcat crashed into the sea on takeoff and five other aircraft were lost in landing accidents with the loss of three aircrewmen.

Hornet returned to Norfolk Navy Yard on February 1st for post-shakedown availability and evaluation. Her shakedown cruise had consisted of fourteen days instead of the usual four to five weeks. Although Captain Browning urgently requested time for additional training for his ship and air group, it was refused due to the critical need for carrier decks in the Pacific.

The new carrier departed Norfolk on February 14, 1944, passed through the Panama Canal five days later and arrived at San Diego on the 27th. While weathering a severe storm off Cape Hatteras while enroute, many of the green

sailors were actually that color and hanging over the rails! Before sailing for Pearl Harbor, *Hornet*'s crew learned that they would transport 2,000 Marines, their combat gear and equipment, including 263 jeeps and other vehicles and 87 dogs. It was said that a Marine was tucked into every conceivable space that was large enough to hold him.

The five-day trip provided an opportunity to make up some of the crew and air group training time lost by the curtailed shakedown cruise. Upon arrival at Pearl Harbor, the Marines were offloaded and one of the more controversial episodes aboard *Hornet* occurred when Captain Browning, evidently displeased with the performance of Air Group 15, requested that they be detached as "not combat ready". The request was approved by ComAirPac and Air Group 2 came aboard as the lethal sting of *Hornet*'s tail, under the command of CDR. Roy L. Johnson on March 8th. Air Group 2 had previously seen combat while assigned to *Enterprise* (CV-6). Following two short training cruises in the Pearl Harbor operating area, the new air group was declared combat ready.

ADM. J.J. "Jocko" Clark, ComCarDiv 13, came aboard on March 15th, making *Hornet* his flagship. Later that day *Hornet* left Pearl Harbor astern as she steamed toward the forward area for her combat debut. Arriving at Majuro in the Marshall Islands on the 20th, she met the 5th Fleet and became part of Task Force 58, assigned to the Task Group under RADM A.E. Montgomery (Task Force 58 was divided into four Task Groups). Five days later, after pulling out with TF-58, she crossed the equator for the first time. *Hornet* drew first blood on March 29th as her Combat Air Patrol (CAP) splashed a twin-engine Japanese "Betty" patrol bomber which had ventured too close.

Hornet began a series of Asiatic-Pacific raids on April 3rd as part of TG-58.2 with *Bunker Hill* (CV-17), *Monterey* (CVL-26), and *Cabot* (CVL-28). Her pilots conducted aerial mine-laying operations at Palau to block the main harbor entrance as well as strikes on Yap, Ulithi, Woleai, and the Caroline Islands. All enemy aircraft encountered were destroyed while various ground installations were heavily damaged. Other carriers of Task Force 58 included *Yorktown* (CV-10), *Wasp* (CV-18), *Enterprise* (CV-6), *Lexington* (CV-16), *Essex* (CV-9) and six other CVLs.

The Task Group retired to Majuro on April 6th for seven days of "rest and replenishment", during which time "Jocko" Clark took command of the Task Group. *Hornet* weighed anchor on April 13th and began operations eight days later in support of the landings and occupation of Hollandia on the northwest coast of New Guinea. The Task Group made softening up strikes against airfields and enemy installations on Wadke and Sawar, and then moved to destroy fuel dumps at Sarmi in northern New Guinea before heading northward to join Task Force 58 for preliminary strikes against Truk. Located in the Western Carolines, the island was Japan's largest staging area, supplying ships, aircraft, fuel and other war materials to the various outer rings of Japanese-occupied islands. As one of Japan's largest forward bases, Truk maintained a rather formidable force of land-based aircraft as part of an overlapping umbrella of protection for nearby islands. Concentrated attacks on Truk destroyed most of the defending planes and neutralized Truk as a military threat, allowing Admiral Nimitz to bypass its garrison of 50,000 Japanese soldiers and leap 1,000 miles across the Pacific to the Marianas.

On May 1st, following a "milk-run" strike on the Japanese airfield at Ponape, tragedy struck after an otherwise routine recovery. An SB2C, flown by LT. Jack Taylor, returned with a hung-up 100-pound bomb. After numerous attempts to jettison the weapon, he was instructed to come aboard after the other strike aircraft had landed. As the Helldiver touched down, the bomb broke loose and bounced forward down the deck, detonating upon its second contact with the deck, killing two men and wounding thirteen. In an unusual twist of fate, one of the men killed had been asleep under an airplane on the hangar deck far below when a piece of shrapnel passed through the flight deck, gallery deck spaces and the airplane with enough force to take his life. It was accidents such as this that continually reminded everyone involved of the perilous reality of flight deck operations. One never knew when things might go horribly wrong.

Hornet sailed for the anchorage at Kwajalein in the Marshall Islands on May 3rd for R & R, crossing the equator later that day to the dismay of all the "pollywogs" on board. When a naval vessel crosses the equator, those on board who have done so previously are called "shellbacks" and those who haven't are known

as "pollywogs". The two-day initiation by the Shellbacks is an experience one never forgets. The senior shellback on board is appointed the mythical King Neptune Rex, who presides over the ritual. During the trip from Ponape to Kwajalein, two days were devoted to the tremendous number of pollywogs aboard who, although having crossed the equator several times, had not been duly initiated. The initiation, not unlike the hazing in a college fraternity, consisted of any number of humiliating rituals which the shellbacks could conjure up. Heads were shaved and covered with axle grease, victims were forced to drink "special" concoctions normally considered unfit for human consumption, dunking tanks were set up, questionable meals were forced to be eaten while sitting on the deck, and two rows of shellbacks stood on almost the entire length of the flight deck the for the weary inductees to "run the gauntlet", complete with thrashing with specially-made canvas paddles (hopefully containing no wood). Since rank and rate are suspended during the time of the initiation, some of the pilots and other officers who were pollywogs could be seen standing lookout watch on the flight deck while standing in a barrel, wearing a diaper no less! Other unfortunate individuals were ordered to wear full dress uniforms with heavy jackets, made unbearable by the tropical heat and humidity. Although a number of fist fights resulted from the actions of overly enthusiastic shellbacks, the proceedings were all in fun and in the end each man was given a special card certifying him as a shellback. This card was a carefully guarded item since it was a shellback's only proof of his initiation in the event he would leave *Hornet* for assignment to another ship that later crossed the equator.

The first months of operation of a combat vessel are, at best, very trying and difficult times as the crew, assembled from tremendously varied backgrounds, struggles to learn new skills and responsibilities and bring their talents together as a team. On no warship is this effort more important than on an aircraft carrier where the crew must learn not only the workings of the ship and its multitude of combat systems, but must integrate those with a complete air group of combat aircraft and their support structure. While wise leadership can serve to transform the carrier and her crew into a precision instrument of war, a weak or unstable command can hinder the process. Such was the situation between the

crew of *Hornet* and CAPT. Miles Browning. Browning was described as a man with great intellect, but his short temper and vicious personal manner had made him quite unpopular with those who knew him in the Navy and things were no different aboard *Hornet*. The growing tension aboard *Hornet* would soon come to a head with a very bizarre incident. After seven days at Kwajalein, *Hornet* sailed the short distance to rejoin the Task Force anchored at Majuro. On the night of May 15th, while the carrier rode quietly at anchor in Majuro Lagoon, a movie was being shown on the hangar deck when a carbon dioxide bottle at frame 70 on the port side of the hangar deck accidentally discharged. Due to the hissing of escaping gas, confusion and panic resulted and when someone yelled something about a bomb about to explode, the crowd of over 1500 men surged forward and to starboard. In the ensuing crush, 31 men were injured and two were pushed overboard through the hangar deck opening, one of them drowning. Captain Browning's harsh actions following the incident resulted in his being found guilty of negligence by a court of inquiry and relieved of his command on May 29th. CAPT. William D. Sample took command of *Hornet* that day and his strong yet fatherly manner soon had the ship's company operating in a very professional and competent way.

In June 1944, the Navy adopted geometric designs to identify aircraft of the different air groups aboard the various carriers. At this time, *Hornet*'s Hellcats, Avengers and Helldivers sported a large white dot on the wing and vertical stabilizer for identification. That same month CDR. Jack Arnold of Torpedo Squadron Two relieved Roy Johnson as CAG Air Group Two.

On June 6, 1944, word was received that the Allied forces had landed on the Normandy Beaches in the European Theater. Spirits aboard *Hornet* soared as the Task Force sortied from Majuro enroute to the Marianas Islands. The Marianas, which included the strategic islands of Saipan, Guam and Tinian, would receive the attention of *Hornet*'s Air Group for the next seven weeks. During the Marianas operations, more than 3,000 sorties would be flown from *Hornet*'s flight deck during the attack and occupation of Saipan and VF-2 would distinguish itself by splashing 233 Japanese planes of all types.

Saipan was defended by a garrison of 32,000 Japanese under the command of the aged LT.GEN. Yoshitsugu Saito. An American armada of 535 ships, commanded by ADM. Raymond Spruance, carried 127,000 men, of whom two-thirds were Marines to assault the Japanese stronghold. On June 11th, prior to the invasion, softening-up strikes were begun on enemy installations on Rota, Saipan and Tinian and the Agana and Orate airfields on Guam. On the 13th, LT. Donald Brandt of VF-2 was shot down while attacking Tiyan airfield on Guam, parachuting into the waters of Agana Bay barely 500 yards from the beach and Japanese shore guns. In a daring rescue, the submarine USS *Stingray* (SS-186), braving coral shallows, sailed in submerged at periscope depth and allowed LT. Brandt to tie his life raft to her periscope as enemy shellfire splashed all around. After slowly towing the wounded aviator out to sea for more than an hour, *Stingray* surfaced and brought him aboard. While this was occurring, six of VF-2's Hellcats, led by LT. F.K. Blair, conducted the longest flight ever attempted by carrier-based fighters when they flew 350 miles to find and attack an enemy convoy. They returned safely to the ship after leaving three destroyers, a cruiser and a merchant ship burning.

On June 15th, as landings were begun on Saipan, *Hornet*'s Task Group was ordered north to conduct the first raids on the Bonins and Volcano Islands. *Hornet* penetrated to within 600 miles of Tokyo and her planes to within 400 miles. While flying cover for the bombers, Hellcat pilot LT. lloyd G. Barnard of VF-2 became *Hornet*'s first "Ace in a Day" by downing five enemy aircraft confirmed on his first combat mission. He became the first of ten pilots to eventually score five or more aerial victories in one day while flying from *Hornet*'s deck (all in F6Fs) - a record for all carriers.

Battle of the Philippine Sea

When Admiral Spruance received reports from his submarines of the approach of a Japanese fleet of nine CVs and five battleships, he postponed the planned invasion of Guam and assembled Mitscher's Task Force of fifteen carriers and seven battleships 200 miles west of Saipan to provide air cover for U.S. forces which had landed on the island three days earlier. Japanese VADM Jisaburo Ozawa had orders to engage and destroy the U.S. Pacific Fleet and intended to seize the opportunity while the Americans were invading Saipan. On the morning of June 19, 1944, Japanese carrier and land-based aircraft began the first of four concentrated air attacks on the American Task Force. *Hornet*'s pilots were airborne at 0720 to hit Orote Airfield on Guam, destroying aircraft on the ground, repair and ammunition facilities, fuel dumps, and dropping delayed-fuse bombs into the runways to hinder night operations by the Japanese. Although the Japanese fleet was the first to locate it's adversary, American radar gave sufficient warning for fighters to swarm up from the U.S. carrier decks to repel their assault in a hot, cloudless sky with perfect visibility. Although over 400 enemy aircraft attacked, the few that penetrated the Combat Air Patrol (CAP) screen fell victim to the fleet's antiaircraft guns. In what became known as "The Marianas Turkey Shoot",

Japan lost 328 carrier-based aircraft and 50 land-based aircraft while the U.S. lost 23 aircraft and six others destroyed operationally. Hellcat pilots from *Hornet* destroyed 52 enemy planes with no losses. This had been the greatest carrier battle of the war with fifteen carriers in the American fleet carrying nearly 950 aircraft to the Japanese' nine flattops with over 450 warplanes. U.S. submarines also got into the action during the Turkey Shoot, sinking two Japanese carriers. It is widely believed that the devastating losses incurred by Japan in the Battle of the Philippine Sea were instrumental in their resorting to the desperate kamikaze tactics used so effectively in the final ten months of the war.

During the many aerial engagements, ENS. Wilbur "Spider" Webb and LT. Russell Reiserer from *Hornet* splashed six and five enemy planes respectively. June 19th also saw four pilots from other carriers also achieve "Ace in a Day" status (David McCampbell, George Carr, and Charles Brewer from *Essex* and Alex Vraciu from *Lexington*). Shortly before his action, for which he was awarded the Congressional Medal of Honor, Webb made one of the most famous radio transmissions of the Pacific war: "Any American fighter near Orote Peninsula, I have forty Jap planes surrounded and need a little help."

Around 1530 the next afternoon, a TBF Avenger from *Wasp* (CV-18) spotted the main Japanese carrier fleet bearing 290 degrees at 275 miles from the Task Group. VADM. Marc Mitscher, making one of the most difficult decisions of his career, ordered "Launch first deckloads as soon as possible. Get the carriers!". Task Group 58.1, which included *Hornet*, *Yorktown* (CV-10), *Belleau Wood* (CVL-24) and *Bataan* (CVL-29) launched a total of 75 airplanes beginning at 1624, commanded by *Hornet*'s CAG, CDR. Jackson A. Arnold. In all, eleven of the Task Force's carriers launched a total of 240 aircraft into the sunset and beyond normal fuel range to find the retiring Japanese armada. Arriving at dusk over the two enemy carrier divisions, Arnold selected the Shokaku-class carrier *Zuikaku*, Ozawa's Division One flagship, as their primary target. LT. H.L. Buell of VB-2 pushed over first with his division of six Helldivers and scored several lethal hits on the massive flight deck. Helldivers from *Yorktown* followed, inflicting several more hits until the warship was all but obscured by smoke and flame. *Zuikaku* was believed to have gone down and *Hornet*'s VB-2

was officially credited with the sinking, however the carrier survived due to the skill and training of her crew only to be sent to the bottom during the Battle of Leyte Gulf four months later.

It was long after dark when the returning aircraft arrived over the Task Force, all of them critically low on fuel, many badly shot up and their pilots wounded. The men on *Hornet* could hear the planes circling in the darkness, the engines coughing and failing to catch again, and the heavy splashes as they ditched in the sea. In the *Lexington*'s flag plot, Admiral Mitscher, after much deliberation, finally gave the order "turn on the lights" in defiance of the enemy submarine threat. This order undoubtedly save the lives of many airmen who would have otherwise been lost at sea. Of the 240 aircraft launched that afternoon, 14 aborted for various reasons, 20 were lost in combat over the enemy fleet, and 80 were lost in deck crashes and water landings.

June 23rd found *Hornet*'s aircraft pounding installations on the island of Pagan in the Marianas, followed the next day by her second Bonins raid with strikes on Iwo Jima and Chichi Jima. VF-2 set a record on that day by sending 67 enemy planes crashing into the sea. Following four days of R & R at Eniwetok, *Hornet* passed her 50,000-mile mark while conducting her third raid on the Bonins including strikes on the nearby Volcano Islands. On July 6th, Air Group 2 began two weeks of daily strikes on Guam and Rota in preparation for the upcoming Marine landings. After the Marine landings of July 21st, *Hornet* aircraft continued to conduct operations in support of the capture and occupation of Guam. During this period, three days of strikes and photo reconnaissance sorties were flown against Palau, Yap, Woleai and Ulithi.

CAPT. Austin K. Doyle reported aboard on August 2nd as relief for Captain Sample while *Hornet* was anchored at Tanapag Harbor, Saipan. Soon *Hornet* was underway for the Bonins to strike aircraft, shipping and ground installations on Chichi Jima and Iwo Jima. A nine ship enemy convoy, discovered speeding northward from Chichi Jima to Japan, was pounced on and decimated by *Hornet* aircraft. During the attack on the convoy, *Hornet* sent search planes within 175 miles of Honshu, and the ship herself steamed to within 400 miles of the same coast. At that time, it was the closest approach to the Japanese mainland of any U.S. Naval aircraft or surface ship.

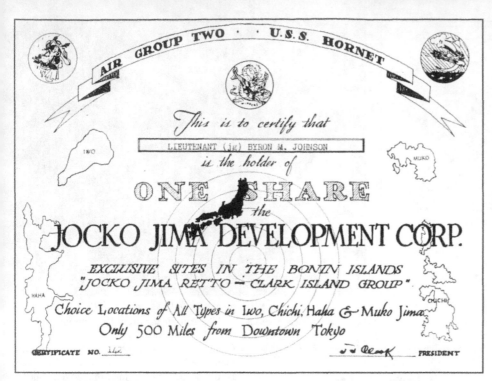

Hornet began her fourth series of raids on the Bonin Islands on the morning of August 3rd. RADM "Jocko" Clark's attacks on the Bonins were so frequent that the Volcanos and Bonins became known among *Hornet* and air group personnel as "Jocko Jima Retto -Clark Island Group" and a "Jocko Jima Development Corporation" was formed aboard *Hornet* for the purpose of "developing and selling shares of real estate advertised to be within 500 miles of downtown Tokyo". Share holders were given printed certificates which indicated choice property locations on Iwo, Chichi, Haha, and Muko Jima and each was signed by RADM Clark as president of the mock corporation. Admiral Mitscher was issued share No. 1 and Clark share No. 2. "Jocko", who enjoyed a special rapport with his officers and sailors, had earned their respect and trust as a commander.

CAPT. Austin K. Doyle officially relieved Captain Sample as *Hornet*'s skipper on August 8th as the carrier steamed for Eniwetok in the Marshall Islands for rest and replenishment. Anchoring in berth 526, Eniwetok harbor, Eniwetok Atoll in the Marshall Islands, *Hornet* remained for almost three weeks in preparation for the upcoming operations in the Western Caroline Islands. On August 26th, VADM Marc Mitscher, Commander of Task Force 58, came aboard for the first time to honor the ship and crew for the vital part they played in the conquest of the Marianas. During the most impressive ceremony the ship had witnessed since her commissioning, Admiral Mitscher conferred over 200 awards for gallantry in action to 124 of *Hornet*'s airmen and crew members, including thirteen Purple Heart Medals. Mitscher, who had been the first captain of the first aircraft carrier to bear the name *Hornet* (CV-8), told the assembled crew of the new *Hornet*: "When I was aboard the *Hornet* the last time, I thought she was the greatest ship in the Navy; but now that I am back I find that she is even better".

Hornet weighed anchor on August 29th to begin a series of operations that would keep her busy for the next five months. Along with *Hornet*, seven other CVs and eight CVLs sortied from Eniwetok carrying over 1,000 planes. The upcoming Western Caroline Islands Operations would involve the capture and occupation of the Southern Palau Islands. Beginning on September 6th, *Hornet*'s air group bombed, rocketed and strafed Japanese positions on Anguar and Peleliu for three days to open the offensive in support of the invasions in the stepping-stone operation. 45,000 Marines and soldiers stormed Peleliu under stiff resistance. The brutal battle lasted nearly a month and left 1800 Marines dead and over 8,000 wounded. More than 11,000 Japanese were killed. Following the Palau operations, *Hornet* sailed west and began five days of air strikes aimed at airfields and installations on Cebu, Davao, Mindanao and the Negros Islands in the Southern and Central Philippines.

By September 1944, VF-2 had the distinction of being the top fighter squadron in the Pacific with more total victories and more "ace" pilots than any other fighter squadron had amassed in the war up to that time. Out of VF-2's fifty pilots, 28 were confirmed aces, having scored five or more victories in aerial combat. *Hornet*'s VB-2 also had a claim to fame during the month when a change in the squadron's complement was made in order to answer a need for more fighter aircraft for the upcoming Philippine operations, during which *Hornet* would be hitting large Japanese bases in that area for the first time. Twelve of VB-2's 36 Helldivers were replaced with F6F Hellcats to be used as fighter-bombers - the first actual assignment of fighter-bombers on a carrier.

Steaming southwest to the Moluccas (northwest of New Guinea), *Hornet* began the Western New Guinea Operations on September 15th by supporting the amphibious landing operations on Morotai Island. On September 21st, *Hornet* turned her attention toward the Philippines, conducting repeated strikes on airfields, installations and shipping in and around Manila. The continuous pounding of the airfields had all but

eliminated enemy air opposition in the area and the men aboard *Hornet* and the other ships of the task force slept easier that night. At dawn on the 22nd, the defensive CAP was launched to relieve the night fighters and a low, thin overcast obscured the morning sun. The ship had turned into the wind and was preparing to launch a deckload of aircraft loaded with bombs, rockets, ammunition and fuel when a lone bogey was spotted on radar approaching *Hornet* from the stern. The CAP aircraft were patrolling above the clouds and couldn't see the enemy plane as the Japanese pilot made his run on *Hornet*, flying up the ship's wake. The Zero, carrying a 500-lb bomb on a belly rack, dove toward *Hornet*'s stern and flew up the centerline of the carrier at 50 feet above the flight deck, rocking his wings wildly in an apparent effort to release the deadly cargo on his vulnerable foe. Passing the bow, the enemy pilot made a hard turn to port and the hung-up bomb fell harmlessly into the sea. He then made two more runs on *Hornet*, strafing the loaded deck with machine gun fire, holing airplanes and wounding several men as every gun on *Hornet* and nearby ships blasted away at the intruder. Miraculously, there was no explosion or fires, which could have doomed the ship.

He was preparing for a third run when a Hellcat of the CAP came screaming in to engage the attacker. As he began firing at the Zero, the enemy pilot pulled hard on his control stick and zoomed vertically into the low cloud deck with the F6F pilot hot on his tail. Moments later, an airplane fell out of the clouds and crashed into the ocean. Assuming the Zero had crashed, a big cheer rang across *Hornet*'s deck, but unfortunately it was the F6F and not the Zero falling out of control. The Japanese pilot then descended out of the clouds and flew by the ship while performing a slow roll, with all AA guns still blazing as he flew out of sight. To many aboard who witnessed this unusual event, the enemy pilot's bravery and flying skill were nothing short of spectacular.

Hornet's air group pounded enemy airfields and defense installations on Cebu and Negros in the Central Philippines on September 24th before returning to the fleet base at Manus in the Admiralty Islands four days later. In late September, Admiral Clark, having received orders for other duty, lowered his flag, packed his gear, and herded his omnipresent staff down the gangplank of *Hornet* to the tune of "Auld Lang Syne". To the crew, "Jocko" had become an integral part of *Hornet*. With his promotion to Rear Admiral, he had left his post as Commanding Officer of *Yorktown* (CV-10) to take up his new duties as the Commander of Carrier Division 13 aboard the new *Hornet*. He arrived aboard a green, untried and untested ship six months earlier and left a carrier which was now a proud, battle-hardened veteran.

September 29, 1944 brought another major change to *Hornet* with the detachment of Air Group Two (CVG-2) for a well-earned rest. After arriving from Pearl Harbor on the troop ship *General Ernst*, Air Group 11 (CVG-11) boarded *Hornet* under the leadership of CDR. Frederick R. Schrader, and would remain on board as her "long guns" until January 1945. Commander Schrader would be lost in action a few weeks later and the air group would have two acting

1943   *Fighting Squadron Two*   **1944**
"Makin to Manila"

1943	U. S. S. Enterprise
Nov. 19	Invasion Gilbert Islands
	Makin, Tarawa
Dec. 4	Raid, Marshall Islands
	Kwajalein, Ebeye, Roi
1944	**U. S. S. Hornet**
Mar. 30	Raid, Palau Islands
Mar. 31	Peleliu, Eil Malk, Koror
	Anguar, Uruhthapel
	Babelthuap, Malakal
Apr. 1	Raid, Woleai Islands
Apr. 21	Invasion, Hollandia, New Guinea
Apr. 24	Wakde, Sawar, Sarmi Point
Apr. 28	Raid, Truk Islands
Apr. 30	Dublon, Param, Fateu,
	Fefan, Eten, Uman
May 1	Raid, Ponape
June 11	Invasion, Mariana Islands
Aug. 6	
June 11	Raid, Mariana Islands
June 13	Guam, Rota
June 13	Raid, Jap Convoy (350 miles)
June 15	Raid, Bonin-Kazan Islands
June 16	Iwo, Chichi, Haha Islands
June 19	Battle, Philippine Sea. (Air bat-
June 20	tle west of Guam. Air attack
	on Jap Carrier Force.)

June 23	Raid, Marianas, Pagan Island
June 24	Raid, Bonin-Kazan Islands
	Iwo Jima
July 3	Raid, Bonin-Kazan Islands
July 4	Iwo, Chichi Jima
July 6	Raids, Invasion Mariana Islands
July 21	Guam, Rota
July 25	Raid, Yap Islands, Lesser Caro-
July 28	lines, Yap, Sorol, Fais,
	Ulithi
Aug. 4	Raid, Bonin-Kazan Islands
Aug. 5	Iwo, Chichi, Haha, Muko
	Jima
Sept. 7	Raid, Palau Islands
Sept. 8	Anguar, Ngesibus
Sept. 9	Raid, Mindanao, Philippine
Sept. 10	Islands
Sept. 12	Raid, Visayan Group, Philippine
Sept. 13	Islands, Cebu, Negros
Sept. 14	Raid, Mindanao, Davao Gulf,
	Philippine Islands
Sept. 16	Invasion, Moratai, Dutch East
	Indies
Sept. 21	Raids, Manila, Philippine
Sept. 22	Islands
Sept. 24	Raid, Visayan Group, Philippine
	Islands

Comdr. Wm. A. Dean, U.S.N.
Commanding Officer

Score

Enemy planes shot down	261
Destroyed on ground	245
Total destroyed	506
Ships destroyed	50,000 tons
Strikes	184
Sorties	2050
Combat Hours	14,090
Own combat losses:	
In aerial combat	3
To enemy A.A.	4

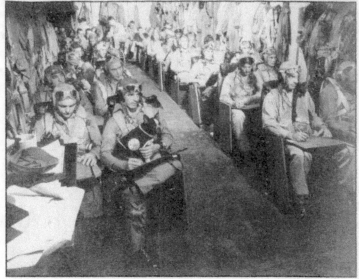

VF-11 in Ready Room One on USS Hornet, late 1944.

CAGs before CDR. R.E. Riera took over as skipper of the group. Two years earlier, Air Group 11 was to have been assigned to the old *Hornet* (CV-8), however she was sunk before that meeting occurred.

On October 4th, the 10,000th arrested landing was recorded on *Hornet's* flight deck as the pilots of AG-11 renewed their carrier qualifications in preparation for the upcoming combat cruise. As Task Force 38 prepared to sail with the Halsey's Third Fleet, the weather degraded into a severe typhoon which lashed the ships for four days. Due to the heavy weather, the group had averaged only 1.5 landings per pilot. It is doubtful that any carrier air group has ever been thrown so abruptly into such violent operations. In Task Force 38, *Hornet* was joined by the carriers *Essex* (CV-9), *Enterprise* (CV-6), *Intrepid* (CV-11), *Franklin* (CV-13), *Lexington* (CV-16), *Bunker Hill* (CV-17), *Wasp* (CV-18), *Hancock* (CV-19) and eight CVLs. On October 10th, a series of strikes were begun which led up to what would be the last great naval battle in the war against Japan. *Hornet* penetrated the inner ring of Japanese homeland defenses with strikes on Nansei Shoto and Okinawa in the Ryukyu Island chain. The next day she turned south to strike installations on Aparri on northern Luzon. On the 12th, *Hornet's* task group moved north and hit airfields and related facilities at Formosa in preparation for the assault on Leyte. Over 500 Japanese planes were destroyed at a cost of 79 American planes. Formosa proved to be a particularly formidable target as the Japanese were well-prepared and waiting for the American onslaught. For four days and nights the men of *Hornet* knew what it was like to be the hunted as well as the hunter as they remained at general quarters almost continuously to ward off attacks by Japanese land-based planes. October 13th was a red-letter date for *Hornet's* gunners as they splashed a Japanese "Emily" bomber which had penetrated the CAP and task force perimeter - the first enemy plane downed by the ship's guns!

On October 15th, *Hornet's* planes launched to pound enemy airfields and other installations on Luzon. These strikes continued through the 18th when the air group's wrath was turned toward Leyte in softening-up strikes against the Visayas in tactical support of landing operations by U.S. Southwest Pacific Amphibious Forces on Leyte, which began on October 20th.

Battle for Leyte Gulf (Second Battle for the Philippine Sea)

Japanese strategists had correctly calculated that the Americans would assault Leyte in their attempt to recapture the Philippines and formulated a plan, called "Sho-Go" ("Victory Operation"), for a general decisive battle intended to crush any American offensive along the vast island chain. The plan called for the Japanese fleet to be split into three separate forces. A small Northern Force under VADM Jisaburo Ozawa, which included four carriers with few planes (the Battle of the Philippine Sea had destroyed most of his aircraft), would sail in from the north and attempt to decoy Halsey's 3rd fleet (including *Hornet*) northward and away from the Leyte beachhead and VADM Thomas Kinkaid's supporting Seventh Fleet. VADM Takeo Kurita, whose fleet constituted sixty percent of Tokyo's major naval units, was to take his Central Force through the San Bernardino Strait between Luzon and Samar and drive into Leyte Gulf from the north. The smaller Southern Force, under VADM Shoji Nishimura, was to come through Surigao Strait and enter Leyte Gulf from the south. The American beachhead, with its unloading ships, would be caught between the Central and Southern forces and wiped out, along with Kinkaid's supporting Seventh Fleet. Then when Halsey returned, his force would be engaged and destroyed in one great battle.

The Americans drew first blood on October 23rd. Kurita, steaming in from the west, was detected and attacked by two U.S. submarines which sank two cruisers and disabled a third. The next day in the Battle of the Sibuyan Sea, one of the Japanese Navy's great battleships, the *Musashi*, absorbed nineteen torpedoes and seventeen bomb hits from U.S. carrier planes before going down. During the battle, Japanese land-based planes hit the light carrier *Princeton* (CVL-23) with a single bomb which caused secondary explosions of armed aircraft on her hangar deck, resulting in her loss. She was the only CV or CVL lost after the first *Hornet* (CV-8) two years earlier in the Battle of Santa Cruz. Later that day, Halsey fell for Ozawa's decoy trick and, in a move that would be severely questioned later, steamed north in hot pursuit, unaware that the enemy flattops were almost devoid of planes. The next day, in the Battle off Cape Engano, three task groups of Halsey's task force intercepted Ozawa's retreating Northern Force, sinking four carriers, a cruiser and two destroyers. At the same time, Admiral Kinkaid, guessing correctly that another enemy force might approach from the south, steamed to Surigao Strait, where his battleships and cruis-

"Admiral Halsey Adds to Navy's Treasury of Historic Words" cartoon by Berryman, 1944.

ers "capped the T" of Nishimura's Southern Force, literally blowing it to bits as it came into range.

The next day, Kurita's still strong Central Force entered Leyte Gulf and charged almost into the middle of Kinkaid's force of sixteen escort carriers. Although the force of CVEs were completely out-gunned, they were able to sink three enemy cruisers and so confused the Japanese that the enemy force withdrew without shelling the invasion beaches. Four ships in Kinkaid's fleet were sunk, including the escort carrier *Gambier Bay* (CVE-73). *Hornet* and Task Group 58.1 had been refueling at sea when a frantic call for help was received from Kinkaid's escort carriers. Refueling was immediately discontinued and *Hornet* steamed at flank speed to contact units of the rapidly retiring enemy fleet. Flying two long-range strikes against the powerful enemy force, *Hornet* pilots scored hits on several capital ships before their escape through the San Bernardino Strait.

The Battle for Leyte Gulf actually consisted of four separate naval actions and, in terms of the numbers of men, planes, ships and distances covered, stands as the greatest naval battle in history. A total of 321 ships and 1,996 aircraft participated in the events which put an end to the Japanese fleet as an offensive force. Leyte is believed to be the first deliberate use of organized kamikaze attacks. By the war's end, kamikazes had sunk or damaged over 300 U.S. ships and caused 15,000 casualties. When the bitter struggle for Leyte had ended, the Japanese had lost 56,263 dead against American deaths of 2,888. Only 389 Japanese soldiers had surrendered.

On October 26th, *Hornet's* air group flew wide-ranging combat air patrols and fighter sweeps against airfields and harbor facilities in the Visayas. Morale on *Hornet* was high and the ship's "Plan of the Day" for that day read:

Today will be a field day! Air Department dust off all overheads, removing any snoopers which may be adrift and sweep all corners of the Philippines, sending to the incinerator or throwing over the side (first punching hole in bottom) any Nip cans, AP's or AK's still on topside. Gunnery Department will assist as necessary. Engineering, continue to pour on the coal. Medicos stand by with heat rash lotion. Damage Control observe holiday routine.

Hornet set sail for the fleet anchorage at Ulithi, arriving on October 29th when recreation parties went ashore for a well-earned rest while the ship underwent replenishment and reprovisioning. The Task Group left Ulithi astern on November 2nd to resume offensive operations in the Philippines. While conducting raids on Clark field on Luzon on November 5th and 6th, *Hornet* splashed 29 enemy aircraft and destroyed over 70 on the ground. Five days later, *Hornet's* aircraft and those of the other three carriers in her task group pounded a Japanese convoy in Ormoc Bay on the west coast of Leyte Island, sinking six troop transports and two destroyers and leaving a number of ships burning. Air Group 11's pilots celebrated Armistice Day by sinking one enemy destroyer and damaging two others.

Air Group 11 dashed in to Manila Bay on November 13th to hit two large and seven medium transports. In addition to flaming ten enemy planes, an ammunition train was turned into an inferno. The next day four more transports were hit and two more Japanese planes were splashed by Hellcats. As the task force withdrew under the cover of darkness, smoking oil slicks marked the last resting place of fifteen freighters and transports and a light cruiser, while the harbor was illuminated by the burning hulks of 43 other damaged vessels. On the 19th, strikes were conducted on Clark field on Central Luzon and shipping at Subic Bay and the Lingayen Gulf. A large freighter was left burning at Subic and several aircraft were destroyed on the ground at Clark field, including two in the air. *Hornet* conducted a strike on the island of Yap on her way to the peace and quiet of Ulithi, where she would remain at anchor until December 10th. Beer parties and sporting events on the isle of Maug Maug helped the men of *Hornet* forget the rigors of combat.

VADM. "Jocko" Clark returned to *Hornet* on November 24th. Everyone came to attention as he made his way up the gangplank and, as he stepped onto the hangar deck, the crowd of men exploded in wild cheering for their former leader. Upon hearing the applause, Clark laughed and threw up his hands saying "Glad to be back boys, glad to be back".

Hornet passed the 100,000-mile mark on December 13th as she steamed back toward Luzon. A day later she began three days of strikes against the airfields on Central Luzon, the Bataan Peninsula and the Philippine Islands to suppress enemy air opposition in support of the amphibious landings on Mindoro Island on December 15th. During the Philippine Liberation operations, *Hornet* was part of Task Group 38.2 with *Lexington* (CV-16), *Hancock* (CV-19), *Independence* (CVL-22) and *Cabot* (CVL-28). In all, Task Force 38's four task groups consisted of eight CVs and eight CVLs. During the operation, *Hornet's* planes clobbered an 8,000-ton transport in Subic Bay and splashed six bogeys.

On December 18th and 19th, all strikes were canceled as the task force weathered one of the worst typhoons ever encountered. Three destroyers capsized and many of the ships incurred varying degrees of structural damage. Following the storm, the task groups returned to Ulithi on December 24th and remained there until the end of the year. On Christmas day, 1944, the hangar deck was piled high with gifts and even Santa Claus made an appearance.

Hornet sailed from Ulithi on December 30th for a war cruise that was to last three weeks and take her for the first time into the South China Sea, where she would launch almost daily strikes against Formosa and the Ryukyu Island chain with shipping and aircraft on the ground as primary targets. The new year opened on January 3, 1945 with two days of sorties against Formosa and the Pescadores Islands before foul weather canceled all flight operations. The 6th and 7th found *Hornet* planes pounding Pork and Neilson airfields on Luzon. Two days later, the task force steamed north to hit Heito, Kato, Koshun and Giran airfields on Formosa. *Hornet* passed through the Bashi Channel into the South China Sea on January 10th and began long-range search operations the following day.

On the 12th of January, strikes were made on Saigon and Cam Ranh Bay in French Indo-China. *Hornet's* pilots sank a Katori-class cruiser, a destroyer escort, a large oiler and two medium freighters, in addition to seven DEs and nine freighters which were damaged, beached or set afire. Three days later, the task group blasted shipping yards and docks at Hong Kong and Kowloon on the China coast. During shipping strikes on Formosa, two destroyers were severely damaged, one of which had just come out of dry dock. *Hornet* recorded her 15,000th arrested landing during return strikes on Formosa and the Pescadores. On the 22nd, Air Group 11 pilots flew extensive photo-recon missions over Okinawa to obtain comprehensive photographic coverage for use in the future invasion of that tropic, but well-defended island. Returning to Ulithi on January 26th, *Hornet* dropped anchor for a two-week period of rest and replenishment. During this time, on February 1st, Air Group 11 detached from *Hornet*. Admiral Clark presented awards to 73 members of the air group, including: 10 Navy Crosses, 1 Legion of Merit, 1 Silver Star, 13 Distinguished Flying Crosses (DFC), 41 Air Medals and 7 Purple Hearts. The mem-

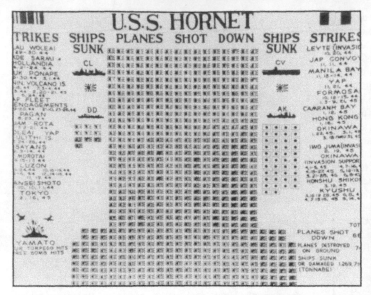

bers of the air group then departed for Pearl Harbor aboard the USS *Kassan Bay* (CVE-69), and then to NAS Alameda aboard the USS *Curtis* (AV-4).

Air Group 17 (CVG-17) came aboard CV-12 the next day, transferring their gear to *Hornet* by cargo net and landing craft while the ship's band gave them an exuberant welcome. After a month on Guam, it was good to finally be aboard ship with great food, clean sheets and soft bunks. After getting squared away and checking over the Hellcats, Avengers and Helldivers left for them by Air Group 11, the carrier and its new group underwent a short shakedown cruise during which the usual group training exercises were carried out. Air Group 17, reformed only ten months earlier, was finally declared ready for the combat debut they had so eagerly awaited.

The coral, palm-covered islands surrounding Ulithi were left behind on February 10, 1945 as *Hornet* sailed with Task Force 58. *Hornet* was assigned to Task Group 58.1 with the carriers *Wasp* (CV-18), *Bennington* (CV-20), *Belleau Wood* (CVL-24) and *San Jacinto* (CVL-30). The other three task groups of Task Force 58 included the carriers *Enterprise* (CV-6), *Franklin* (CV-13), *Randolph* (CV-15), *Essex* (CV-9), *Bunker Hill* (CV-17), *Hancock* (CV-19), *Yorktown* (CV-10), *Intrepid* (CV-11) and the light carriers *Cabot* (CVL-28), *Bataan* (CVL-29), *Langley* (CVL-27) and *Independence* (CVL-22).

On the morning of February 16th, *Hornet* kept a date her predecessor had made some 34 months before by making the first carrier strikes on Tokyo since (since Army B-25s from CV-8 had flown the Doolittle Raid). The first strike set out to neutralize the airfield at Hachijo Jima, a major island outpost 150 miles south of Tokyo. Meanwhile, *Hornet*'s fighters were working over the airfields at Hammamatsu, Yokosuka and Tateyama and patrolling the area off Tokyo Bay, searching for targets of opportunity and strafing planes on the ground, while knocking down the few enemy planes found airborne. Air Group 17 fought foul weather to rain fire and destruction on airfields and aircraft facilities. The following day's operations were much the same with the strike group this time visiting Toyohashi and the fighters strafing aircraft and installations on Tateyama, Atsugi, Otawa and Yokohama. Massive sweeps were conducted on coastal ar-

eas, sinking and damaging many vessels including an escort carrier in Tokyo Bay. Due to continued bad weather the entire operation was broken off and the task force headed south.

Strikes were begun on Chichi Jima on February 18th in preparation for the invasion of nearby Iwo Jima. Iwo was used by the Japanese as a radar warning station and fighter interceptor base and could not be passed by in the "island hopping" used elsewhere. Enemy fighters attacked B-29s from its airfields and it was much needed as an emergency field for Superfortresses in trouble and as a base from which U.S. fighters could fly escort to Japan for the massive bombers. Although Iwo is only five miles long and two and one half miles across at its widest point, 60,000 Marines were engaged to secure the volcanic island, after it had been shelled almost daily for six months prior to the invasion. Beginning on February 19th, *Hornet* pilots rocketed, bombed and strafed positions on Iwo for six straight days in direct support of Marine operations there. When the fighting was over, the battle for the eleven square mile island had cost the Marines 20,965 casualties, including 5,900 dead, while over 23,000 Japanese were killed. By war's end, numerous B-29 crews had used Iwo as an emergency landing strip. Once Iwo's beachheads were secure, *Hornet* sailed north of Tokyo where her aircrews pulverized airfields in the metropolitan area. On March 1st, *Hornet* conducted one support strike on Okinawa while retiring to Ulithi for reprovisioning.

Dropping on March 4th, *Hornet*'s weary crew enjoyed ten days of R & R on Ulithi and the nearby island of Maug Maug. On the 10th, while *Hornet* was at the anchorage, B-29s from Guam, Tinian and Saipan attacked Tokyo in what would become the single most destructive bombing mission ever recorded - 97,000 killed, 125,000 wounded and 1,200,000 homeless. On the evening of March 11th, while much of the crew watched a movie on the blacked-out hangar deck, the tranquility of the tropical evening was shattered when a lone Japanese plane circled low and dove into the lighted fantail of *Randolph* (CV-15), anchored just off *Hornet*'s bow, killing or wounding many of her crew.

The task force departed Ulithi on the 14th to begin the Okinawa-Gunto operations. Okinawa, a 700 square mile island only 350

miles from Japan proper, possessed good harbor facilities and ample room to stage troops and equipment for the invasion of Japan. During the extended campaign, *Hornet* would be at sea for forty straight days and would launch strikes on 32 of those days. Her pilots would fly over 4,000 combat sorties and the ship would be attacked on 105 separate occasions. The carrier would be at sea longer without dropping her anchor than at any time in her history and her ship's gunners would fire more rounds in earnest than they had during the entire previous year. During the Okinawa campaign, over three thousand Japanese suicide pilots, in attack clusters called "kikusuis" (floating chrysanthemums), threw themselves at the U.S. fleet, sinking 21 ships.

The operations commenced early on the morning of March 18th as *Hornet*'s air group moved out to conduct strikes on various airfields in the Kyushu area, destroying many aircraft on the ground as well as in the air. LCDR. Marshall "Marsh" Beebe, CO of VF-17, and LT. Robert C. Coats each downed five enemy planes on this day near Kanoya airfield. The following day, *Hornet* and other carriers of the task force moved in and launched aircraft which then sped over the island to attack Japanese ships anchored at the Kure and Kobe naval bases in the Inland Sea. As the pilots nosed over and made their daring bomb runs, CV-12 steamed only 40 miles off the coast of Shikoku. The task force was under almost constant attack by kamikazes during these strikes. It was during this period that *Hornet*'s sister ship *Franklin* (CV-13) was hit hard. A lone enemy dive bomber sped in low and fast and dropped two 500-pound bombs onto the aft flight deck, which was loaded with fueled and bombed planes awaiting the order for takeoff. The ship was set afire and racked by explosions that turned the valiant carrier into a fiery hell. Suffering 724 killed and 265 wounded, the doomed ship somehow was saved by the miraculous efforts of her courageous crew and in the end was able to sail home under her own power for repairs. Although "Big Ben" would be completely rebuilt from the hangar deck up, she would never see action again.

March 23rd began a week of intensive fighter sweeps over Okinawa to destroy as much of the Japanese air force as possible in preparation for the invasion. On the 24th, a convoy of seven enemy ships was sighted well out in the East China Sea. A strike group was immediately launched and, after two hours of flying, located their quarry and bored in for the kill, wiping out the entire convoy of merchantmen and their escorts. One cargo ship, evidently carrying munitions, exploded in a tremendous mushroom-shaped fireball sending debris 3000 feet skyward. For the next several days, strikes were flown against installations on Kerama Retto, Amami, Okinawa and Kyushu. Four days after the first convoy attack, a strike group was launched on what would come to be called the "badger hunt", searching for a Japanese task force which, as it turned out, did not exist. After covering a major part of the Pacific Ocean before calling it quits, the pilots made a fighter sweep pass at southern Kyushu, destroying two bogeys in the air and twelve on the ground. An exhausted group of men landed aboard *Hornet* well after dark.

Softening-up strikes on Okinawa were begun on March 31st. U.S. Marines hit the beaches of Okinawa on April 1st (Easter Sunday). During the landings, *Hornet*'s air group flew in advance of the Marines, strafing and rocketing forward positions and forcing the Japanese defenders to keep their heads buried. So massed were the carrier planes over the beaches, that a target coordinator, acting as an aerial traffic cop, directed one group down at a time to strike their assigned targets. Strikes on Kyushu and the Ryukyu Island chain continued while the threat of suicide pilots remained high. By the evening of April 6th, the task force had accounted for the destruction of over 85 kamikazes. The Okinawa campaign, which had cost the Navy 34 ships sunk and 368 damaged, also claimed the lives of 4,900 American sailors killed or reported missing and over 4,800 wounded. After the conquest of Okinawa, *Hornet* and her sister ships roamed at will in Japanese waters, pounding airfields, railyards and other military targets and facilities beyond the reach of the B-29s.

On the morning of April 7th, search planes spotted a large Japanese surface force proceeding south from Kyushu supposedly to threaten U.S. support units off Okinawa. The carriers of the task force immediately shifted north and launched a total of over 350 planes to intercept the enemy fleet, consisting of the super battleship *Yamato*, two light cruisers and ten destroyers. *Yamato*, at 72,000 tons, was the largest battleship ever built (along with her sister ship *Musashi*). The Japanese believed her unsinkable

and sent her, along with remnants of their surface fleet to be used as kamikazes. Carrying only enough fuel for a one-way trip, it is believed the Japanese intended to beach the behemoth and annihilate the U.S. fleet with her 18-inch guns, however she was caught in the East China Sea 90 miles southwest of Kyushu by Mitscher's planes. Pilots from *Hornet* attacked *Yamato* first, delivering four torpedoes and three bombs into the armored giant. After over two hours of continuous attack by dive bombers, torpedo planes and fighters, the great battleship rolled over and sank after taking eight torpedoes and numerous armored-piercing bombs, becoming Davy Jones' main exhibit. When the enormous hulk of *Yamato* finally went under, she took 2,488 of her crew with her, leaving only 269 to survive. During the onslaught, an AGANO-class light cruiser and four destroyers also were sunk and several others damaged.

In the days that followed, large numbers of Japanese planes roared down on the task force from their bases on Kyushu. On April 12th, *Hornet* saw the 20,000th landing on her flight deck as her combat air patrol pilots bagged 33 Japanese planes. When word came that afternoon of President Roosevelt's death, the men on *Hornet*, though saddened, had little time to pause and reflect on the loss of the leader who had brought them so far. The President's son, John Roosevelt, was an officer aboard the ship at the time of his father's death. The next day, VF-17 splashed nineteen enemy planes including two twin-engine planes carrying a new form of kamikaze - BAKA rocket bombs and their suicide pilots. In the early hours of the 15th, Japanese planes were in the air over the ship dropping parachute flares which lit up the sky for miles around. Later that day, fighter patrols around the ship and in the vicinity of Okinawa knocked down 32 enemy planes while a fighter sweep over Kanoya accounted for 13 more for a grand total of 45 enemy planes shot down during the day's operations.

Beginning on April 16th, strikes were flown almost daily against Japanese ground forces on Okinawa and the airfields on Kikai with little or no air opposition. On the 27th, after almost seven weeks of continuous operations, the ship turned toward her advanced base at Ulithi. During this second cruise, 4,205 sorties had been flown by planes of the air group, 265 enemy planes were shot down and 109 destroyed on the ground. Twenty ships had been sunk and 129 listed as probably sunk or damaged.

Arriving at the anchorage on the last day of April 1945, the weary men of *Hornet* and Air Group 17 enjoyed shore parties, group baseball games, fishing, swimming and relaxation while *Hornet* was reprovisioned. The loading of supplies and ammunition went on from early in the morning until late at night. After nine days the ship was again ready for sea. Weighing anchor on May 9th (the day after "VE day"), *Hornet* began what would be her last combat sortie of World War Two with air support strikes against Okinawa two days later. *Bunker Hill* (CV-17), another of *Hornet*'s sister ships, met with a fate similar to that of *Franklin* when she suffered hits by a 500- pound bomb and a kamikaze on her flight deck, killing 396 of her crew and wounding another 264. On May 13th, Mother's Day, President Truman declared a national day of prayer in memory of the boys who made victory in Europe possible. For the next two days, strikes were launched against airfields and installations at Kyushu, Shikoku, Kanoya and Izumi. The highlight of this two-day stand was the bombing of the Kumamoto aircraft assembly plant in north central Kyushu. This was the heaviest carrier strike against the Japanese homeland since the Inland Sea strike of March 19th. The recently completed plant itself, covering an area equal to five city blocks, was almost entirely leveled, and had not even completed an airplane yet! A day later, massive fighter sweeps ripped apart airfields at Tochiarai, Tomitaka, Kushira, Kanoya, Kochi and Matsuzama, netting another eleven planes shot down, twenty destroyed on the ground and numerous small craft sunk or damaged.

Hornet surpassed the 150,000-mile mark on May 17th as she began three days of strikes on Okinawa. The air group stood down on the 20th as *Hornet* took on bombs and ammunition at sea before continuing their raids on Japanese positions on and around Okinawa. The remainder of May was rather uneventful as Japanese air opposition was almost negligible, although *Hornet*'s fighters continued their daily patrols over Okinawa and the surrounding islands. Close air support operations were flown over Okinawa and on several occasions the Avengers dropped supplies to Marines in forward positions. The airfields at Kikai and Tokuno were kept under constant attack and on May 22nd *Hornet*'s fighters and "torps" helped wipe out a small convoy of ships north of Amami O Shima. When Admiral Halsey relieved Admiral Spruance on May 27th, *Hornet* once again became part of Task Force 38.

CV-12's flight deck cut off to repair bow damage caused by a typhoon.

CV-12 with its repaired bow at Hunter's Point.

Hornet retired east of Okinawa on June 3rd to begin at-sea refueling. When word was received of an approaching typhoon, refueling operations were discontinued and completed the next day from the USS *Sebec* (AO-87). Early on June 5th, entering the edge of the typhoon, the ship began to encounter mountainous pyramidal seas with waves 50-60 feet from crest to trough. Shortly after 0500, the barometer dropped to a low of 28.30 inches and the winds reached 110 knots with gusts to 120 knots. Lookouts reported the vessel taking green seas over the flight deck. Due to the mountain-like waves, *Hornet*'s bow was lifted completely out of the water and then plunged swiftly downward into the abyss as the ship gave a mighty shudder in her attempts to recover. The force was too much for even the steel-reinforced structure to endure and the forward edge of the flight deck back to frame #4 collapsed, a distance of twenty-four feet.

As the ship continued to pass through the edge of the eye of the mighty storm, other relentless waves further weakened additional sections of the flight deck.

The next day, after receiving fuel from the USS *Marias* (AO-57), flight operations were resumed. After pushing two storm-damaged aircraft (a TBF and an F6F) over the side, thirteen "flyable duds" were flown to the USS *Attu* (CVE-102) and the USS *Salamaua* (CVE-96) and seven planes were flown to other carriers in the task group as replacements. *Hornet* then received fifteen fighters as replacements. That afternoon, as fighters were launching over the damaged bow, an F4U Corsair from *Shangri-La* (CV-38) spun in on takeoff due to the turbulence over the bow caused by the overhanging portion of the collapsed flight deck. The pilot was rescued by the destroyer *Dehaven* (DD-727). Upon seeing this, Admiral Clark charged down from the island and marched up the flight

deck to view the damage for himself. After taking a long look, "Jocko" began waving his arms and immediately ordered the fighters turned around 180 degrees. The ship's engines were reversed and, while *Hornet* backed down at 18.5 knots, 24 Hellcats were launched over the stern to search for various vessels of the task group which were unaccounted for as a result of the typhoon. This was the first time aircraft had been launched over the stern of a carrier in wartime. Word of the unusual operation spread throughout the ship and it seemed that anyone who could was in the catwalks or on the island to view the event.

On the 7th, launching over the bow was resumed as the task group returned to continue operations in support of TF-51 in the Okinawa area. The following day *Hornet* launched forty Hellcats against Kanoya airfield on Kyushu, 279 miles distant. The fighters dropped 260-pound fragmentation bombs and took damage assessment photos after the strike. A strike against Daito Jima was conducted on the 9th as Helldivers delivered bombs and Hellcats dropped napalm tanks on a radio station and barracks. Other F6Fs escorted two rescue seaplanes from the USS *Oklahoma City* (CL-91) which accompanied the mission. A day later *Hornet* aircraft covered the bombardment of Minami Daito Jima by task force battleships and destroyers before departing for San Pedro Bay at Leyte Gulf. During the brief period of R & R, the crew went ashore, bought souvenirs from the Filipinos, enjoyed beer parties and went swimming.

June 15, 1945 was a red-letter day for the men of *Hornet* as the scuttlebutt about them going home soon was confirmed when Captain Doyle announced that *Hornet* would return to San Francisco for repairs. On this day "Jocko" lowered his flag and left the "Gray Ghost" to report to Guam for temporary duty.

The ship weighed anchor on June 19th, leaving San Pedro Bay behind enroute to Pearl Harbor. During the trip the crew sunned themselves on the flight deck, played catch and volleyball, caught up on their sleep and wondered why their fast carrier seemed to move so slowly. *Hornet* moored at Ford Island in Pearl Harbor on the 29th and departed three days later, arriving at Pier #2, Alameda Naval Air Station in San Francisco Bay on July 8th after passing under the Golden Gate bridge. It was said that although the Golden Gate was alleged to have been constructed of steel, to the crew of *Hornet* it was made of solid gold, gleaming in the warm California sunshine, welcoming them home.

After unloading aircraft and unspent ammunition, *Hornet* moved across the bay two days later and put into Dry Dock #4 at the Hunter's Point Navy Yard to begin typhoon repair and a much-needed overhaul. CAPT. C.R. Brown relieved Captain Doyle on August 1st as CV-12's Commanding Officer. When her hurried repairs were completed, a ship's open house was held at Hunter's Point for the public on August 12th. *Hornet* looked awesome with her new paint and armament as over 100,000 visitors came aboard in one day to view the veteran of the Pacific battles. Stories in newspapers across the country praising her exploits hit the press the same day as the story of the atomic bomb, stealing

Hornet's thunder in the eyes of many former *Hornet* men. The public realized that this new *Hornet* had indeed avenged the loss of her predecessor, lost nearly three years before. The war was now officially over and as the Japanese surrender was signed aboard the battleship *Missouri* (BB-63) in Tokyo Bay, *Hornet* was tied up at Hunter's Point undergoing tests. The indomitable carrier departed the Navy yard on September 12th for post-repair sea trials, returning the next day to Alameda's Pier #3.

Following completion of repairs at San Francisco's Hunters Point Shipyard, *Hornet's* hangar bay was reconfigured as a giant bunkroom and she participated in five cruises as a part of Operation "Magic Carpet", returning veterans from Pearl Harbor and Guam until the spring of 1946. *Hornet* was decommissioned on January 15, 1947 and joined her sister ships *Intrepid* (CV- 11), *Antietam* (CV-36) and *Shangri-La* (CV-38 in the reserve fleet at Hunters Point. She would remain there in idle silence for the next four years

The Post-war Years

After four and a half years in reserve storage at San Francisco, *Hornet* was recommissioned in March 1951 and sailed with a limited crew through the Panama Canal to the Brooklyn Navy Yard in New York. There she was decommissioned and her first modernization program was begun. This modernization, known as SCB-27A, gave her more powerful catapults and arresting gear, a strengthened flight deck, a new streamlined island, new ammunition lifts and numerous other improvements to facilitate the new jets and heavy attack bombers.

In May 1954, after sea trials and shakedown, *Hornet* departed for an eight-month global cruise. Mediterranean operations included stops at Portugal, Italy, Egypt, and other exotic ports of call. After transiting the Suez Canal, *Hornet* made stops for R & R at Singapore and the Philippines before joining the Seventh Fleet in the South China Sea in late June. A few days later in the "Hainan Incident", aircraft from *Hornet* and *Philippine Sea* (CVA-47), operating as part of *Hornet's* task group, shot down two Chinese Communist LA-7 fighters which attacked while the

American aircraft were searching for survivors of a British airliner shot down earlier by Chinese fighters. *Hornet* departed for her second WestPac cruise in May 1955 for what would be an eventful seven months. In addition to the scheduled Operational Readiness Inspection (ORI), the ship and crew weathered no less than thirteen typhoons before losing the number three propeller near the end of the cruise. Upon returning to San Diego, *Hornet* sailed a short time later to the Puget Sound Naval Shipyard to begin SCB-125, her second modernization. Included in the SCB-125 program was the installation of an angled landing deck, a fully-enclosed "hurricane" bow, an improved dual arrestor wire system, a redesigned Primary flight Control, a new starboard deck-edge elevator and a myriad of other improvements to keep *Hornet* on the leading edge of carrier technology. The "hurricane" bow which is standard on modern carriers was developed because of typhoon damage received by *Hornet* and *Bennington* in 1945.

Following This extended yard period, *Hornet* conducted extensive sea trials and shakedown to try out her new features and prepare Air Group 14 for the upcoming 1957 WestPac cruise. During the cruise, *Hornet* lost another propeller and an AD Skyraider was damaged by Chinese ground fire while patrolling near the Swatow Peninsula before the ship returned to San Diego. *Hornet's* fourth WestPac cruise was completed in June 1958 and shortly thereafter, she was designated CVS-12 (anti-submarine warfare carrier). In August, the carrier entered the yards at Bremerton for overhaul and conversion to CVS. Upon completion, *Hornet* became a reliable, efficient and highly specialized base for aircraft whose purpose it was to detect and destroy enemy submarines.

Hornet completed two WestPac cruises in 1959 and 1960 before returning to Puget Sound for a major overhaul in February 1961. In June, *Hornet* was boarded by over 25,000 visitors during a three-day open house in Tacoma. During that time, over one million people in the Seattle-Tacoma area watched a 12-hour telecast from *Hornet* in honor of the 50th Anniversary of Naval Aviation. In November, units of *Hornet's* deck and damage control divisions rendered aid in combating devastating fires

which roared through the Hollywood Hills in suburban Los Angeles. *Hornet's* 1962 WestPac deployment included operations with the Seventh Fleet in crisis-ridden Southeast Asia and patrols off the troubled Chinese islands of Quemoy and Matsu.

CV-12 demonstrated her fitness and readiness during 'Operation Gold Ball" with Task Force 10 which was observed by President John F. Kennedy from the deck of *Kitty Hawk* (CVA-63) during June 1963. CVSG-57 came aboard *Hornet* in October for her eighth WestPac cruise and, during "Operation Blackjack", the carrier participated in coordinated U.S./Nationalist Chinese amphibious exercises off the coast of Taiwan. Upon returning, *Hornet* entered the yards at San Francisco for FRAM II, her fourth major conversion since World War II. This $10 million modernization upgraded *Hornet's* ASW capabilities, including new sonar and electronic equipment. In addition to a new closed-circuit television system and Gemini Space recovery communication facilities, an aluminum surface was installed over the flight deck landing area and the boilers and main propulsion gear were completely overhauled. During refresher training off the coast of California, an SH-3A Sea King helicopter launched from *Hornet's* flight deck on a proposed endurance flight. Landing 16 hours and 2,075 miles later aboard *Franklin D. Roosevelt* (CVA-42) in the Atlantic, the chopper had established a new non-stop distance record.

Six months later, *Hornet* departed the west coast for her ninth WestPac cruise and first Vietnam war deployment. She provided the Seventh Fleet with ASW service, surface surveillance and war zone search and rescue, while her detachment of four Marine A-4 Skyhawks flew 109 combat sorties from *Midway's* (CVA-41) flight deck. Between two periods on Yankee Station, CV- 12 conducted joint exercises in the Sea of Japan with Squadron 11 of the Republic of Korea Navy.

Hornet set course for Pearl Harbor in August as the Prime Recovery Ship for the unmanned Apollo 3 (AS-202) space capsule. After practicing recovery operations with a training capsule, *Hornet's* recovery team successfully plucked the capsule from the Pacific on August 25th after it rocketed three quarters of the way around the world in 93 minutes.

Hornet's Recommissioning Ceremony under the towers and bridges of Manhattan.

January 1967 found *Hornet* undergoing her annual Operational Readiness Inspection and participating in Exercise "Snatch Block" in preparation for her upcoming second Vietnam war cruise. Operations supporting the Seventh Fleet in the Gulf of Tonkin continued through the remainder of spring and much of summer. *Hornet* returned to Long Beach in October and began an extensive overhaul period which lasted until May 1968.

In September 1968, *Hornet* set sail from Long Beach for her eleventh and last WestPac deployment, relieving *Bennington* (CVS-20) at Yokosuka, Japan before continuing on to duty on Yankee Station. *Hornet* spent Christmas and New Years at Sasebo, Japan and returned to the Tonkin Gulf before deploying to the Sea of Japan after a Navy EC-121 reconnaissance aircraft was shot down by North Korea. *Hornet* and her six destroyers arrived first, leading the attack carriers *Enterprise*, *Ranger* and *Ticonderoga*. Combined with support ships and many destroyers, this was the largest task force assembled for possible combat since the Korean war. While in the Sea of Japan, a *Hornet* S-2E Tracker detected and tracked a Soviet Whiskey-class submarine for 12 hours until it was clear of the area.

Apollo Recovery Operations

The historic carrier returned to Long Beach in May, 1969 for maintenance and repairs. At that time, *Hornet's* Commanding Officer, Capt. Carl J. Seiberlich, confirmed rampant rumors when he announced that *Hornet* had been chosen as the Prime Recovery Ship for the upcoming Apollo 11 manned lunar landing mission. At Pearl Harbor, *Hornet* loaded 120 personnel from NASA, GE, and ABC, along with several large broadcasting vans, a large bubble-covered satellite communications antenna, the training capsule known as "boilerplate", and the Mobile Quarantine Facility (MQF). As the enormous Saturn V rocket hurtled Neil Armstrong, Michael Collins and Edwin "Buzz" Aldrin into space, the crew of *Hornet* waited patiently on station in the Primary Abort Area some 1,650 miles southwest of Hawaii. Here they would be ready and in position in the event the flight was terminated during the first orbit.

Once the astronauts were on their way to the moon, *Hornet* sailed north to the Prime Recovery Area. Four days later, as Armstrong and

Aldrin began their descent to the moon, *Hornet's* highly-trained recovery teams continued to sharpen retrieval procedures. Two complete teams were also trained in the event of sickness or casualty. Simulated exercises (sixteen in all) were practiced under every possible sea condition and any conceivable hour of the day or night. In addition, for two days, dress rehearsals were practiced on board to perfect the ceremonies, television camera angles and lighting, etc. After all, the whole world would be watching the veteran carrier make history yet again.

By 04:00 on July 24, 1969, the ship was bustling with activity as the crew anxiously awaited the arrival of President Nixon. The President arrived aboard "Marine One" at 05:00 and, after receiving a briefing and touring the Mobile Quarantine Facility, was escorted to *Hornet's* Flag Bridge, from which he would observe the splashdown and recovery. A host of dignitaries were also present, including Secretary of State Henry Kissinger, Dr. Paine (NASA's administrator), Admiral McCain (CinCPac), and several other flag officers.

Hornet deployed four SH-3D Sea King helicopters from ASW Squadron 4 and three E-1B Tracer aircraft from VAW-11 (Early Warning Squadron). Underwater Demolition Team 11 handled the actual recovery from the sea. Two of the helicopters carried swimmers and recovery gear, the third served as a photo aircraft, and the fourth carried the decontamination swimmers, a flight surgeon, and served as the crew retrieval aircraft. Two of the E-1Bs provided "Air Boss" duty and standby, while the third served as a Communications Relay aircraft.

Radar and then radio contact was established with the command module (capsule) prior to parachute opening. The astronauts later confided in a debriefing session that they were able to relax after the parachutes deployed, knowing the Navy would find, retrieve and bring them home safely.

The swimmers were in the water almost immediately after the 05:52 splashdown and attached the floatation collar to the capsule. The capsule's hatch was decontaminated thoroughly with betadine before opening. Special biological isolation suits were tossed into the capsule and the hatch closed until the crew was ready for egress. Upon leaving the capsule, the crew was decontaminated by the swimmers who were

then, in turn, decontaminated by the astronauts. The astronauts and decontamination swimmer were hoisted aboard the helicopter by nets and transported to *Hornet*. The crew remained aboard the helicopter until it was lowered to the hangar deck, where they walked a few feet directly into the Mobile Quarantine Facility five minutes after coming aboard. An exuberant President Nixon congratulated the astronauts at the window of the MQF and invited them to a state dinner at the White House before boarding Marine One to begin his around-the-world good will tour.

A short time later, after Capt. Seiberlich skillfully maneuvered the carrier alongside the bobbing capsule, lines were attached, and the golden moon ship was gently hoisted aboard by *Hornet's* huge starboard boat and aircraft crane. A special trailer cradle received the capsule. After the command module was attached to the MQF by a sterile plastic tunnel, the precious film and lunar samples were removed, packaged for shipment and launched from *Hornet* aboard two aircraft for Hawaii and Johnston Island, and then on the Lunar Receiving Laboratory in Houston, Texas.

After the astronauts had a pleasant night's sleep, several ceremonies were held the next day in *Hornet's* hangar bay during the cruise back to Hawaii. At Pearl Harbor, the command module and Mobile Quarantine Facility were offloaded and then flown aboard Air Force transports from Hickam Air Force Base to Houston. *Hornet* then returned to Long Beach with a broom affixed to her masthead denoting a "clean sweep" and a large banner proclaiming "HORNET PLUS THREE".

Hornet returned to her normal ASW training and workups in the southern California operating area for the next two months. In September, Capt. Seiberlich announced to the crew that *Hornet* had been selected for her second Apollo recovery as the Prime Recovery Ship for the upcoming flight of Apollo 12 and its all-Navy crew in November, 1969.

Again in position in the Primary Abort Area for the launch of Apollo 12, *Hornet* was very nearly required to recover the spacecraft after it was twice struck by lightning during launch. After a thorough check aboard the spacecraft, all systems were declared operational and Commanders Pete Conrad, Allen Bean and Richard Gordon were on their way to the moon. *Hornet's* experienced recovery forces polished their techniques and executed another flawless recovery on November 24th.

Hornet's motto for the Apollo 12 recovery was "*Three More Like Before*". Days later, the historic carrier proudly steamed into Pearl Harbor with the Apollo 12 command module confidently displayed on the flight deck. Arriving at Long Beach on December 4th, the carrier's masthead again prominently display a broom.

Thirty years after those now-famous missions, *Hornet* is the one recovery aircraft carrier most remembered by those who tuned in to watch history unfold on live television. Literally hundreds of millions of people around the world watched as *Hornet* once again made us proud to be Americans.

The Great "Mothball" Fleet

On January 15, 1970, the Navy announced that the USS *Hornet* (CVS-12) would be deactivated by June 30th of that year. Several months earlier, the Board of Inspection and Survey had determined that the ship was in excellent material condition and it was decided that *Hornet* would be retained in the inactive reserve fleet after her decommissioning, preserved for potential future reactivation.

In *Hornet's* last ten-day ASW exercise in the first weeks of 1970, she opposed two nuclear submarines in a sophisticated game of cat and mouse. In February, during her last operational at-sea period, *Hornet* conducted carrier qualifications for five west coast squadrons. During the five-day CARQUAL period, *Hornet* recorded 1,310 arrested landings - more than one percent of all the landings made on her flight deck in her twenty-six years in the fleet. On February 20, 1970, those aboard *Hornet* witnessed the passing of an era as an S-2E Tracker, piloted by Cdr Gerald Canaan (CVSG-59) and co-piloted by

RADM Norman C. Gillette, made the last fixed-wing landing aboard *Hornet*, her 115,445th. Later that month, *Hornet* learned that she had been awarded six major fleet awards for her final months of active duty.

In March, *Hornet* began deactivation at the Long Beach Naval Shipyard, connected to the pier for life-sustaining electricity, water, steam and air pressure. Like umbilical cords, the sagging hoses and lines kept the carrier alive while the work of deactivation went on inside her hull. In place of the familiar sounds of aircraft turning up on her flight deck, the sounds of pneumatic hammers, deck crawlers, grinders and sanders made the air reverberate.

After the month-long yard period, *Hornet* sailed from her homeport of Long Beach for Bremerton, Washington to continue deactivation and preservation work. There her boilers and piping systems were drained and machinery and equipment was coated with preservative compounds. In dry dock, her hull was corrosion-proofed and painted while hull penetrations below the waterline were blanked with steel plates. Tanks and bilges were cleaned and preserved while external doors, hatches, scuttles, vent duct openings and stacks were sealed from the elements. The entire wooden flight deck was covered with a layer of protective foam. In addition to fire and flooding alarms, dehumidification machines and cathodic protection equipment was installed.

Hornet was decommissioned at 10:40 am on Friday, June 26, 1970 in official ceremonies conducted aboard the ship. Captain Carl J. Seiberlich, her last Commanding Officer, ordered the watch secured and was the last man to leave the great carrier, honoring her with one final salute before his departure. In the final moments of the ceremony, *Hornet's* records were officially delivered to the Commanding Officer of the Inactive Ships Maintenance Facility, Puget Sound Naval Shipyard, Bremerton, Washington.

For the next twenty-four years, while *Hornet* rode quietly at anchor in the still, clear water of Puget Sound, six new nuclear carriers would join the fleet and the remaining nine active Essex-class carriers would be retired. During that time, fourteen of *Hornet's* twenty remaining sister ships would meet their end with the shipbreaker's torch as she sat motionless in erie silence, broken only by the shrill cries of sea gulls and the sound of cars on a nearby highway.

Efforts to Save *Hornet*

In 1981, a study was performed to examine the feasibility and requirements of reactivating the remaining Essex-class carriers with a limited modernization plan to support A-4 Skyhawk operations. A determination was made indicating that *Hornet* would not be suitable for the planned modernization and mission, but that her excellent material condition might warrant her reactivation in some other capacity to support then-President Ronald Reagan's build-up to a 600-ship Navy. However, no such program was implemented and, while Naval shipyards around the country buzzed with activity, *Hornet* and her sisters remained in the tranquil waters of Puget Sound.

In October 1987, a detailed material inspection by the Board of Inspection and Survey found *Hornet* unfit for further service since all of her installed systems were obsolete and the ship did not meet current habitability, safety and pollution abatement requirements. Found obsolete were *Hornet*'s electrical distribution system, internal communications systems, combat communications systems, magazine sprinkler systems, CIC equipment, special weapons storage systems, fire protection systems, berthing and sanitary facilities, medical and dental compartments, food service equipment and furnishings, all aviation facilities, her "M"-type boilers, etc. Although *Hornet* was in relatively good condition, technology and the radical advances in every facet of carrier and naval operations in the last eighteen years had simply passed her by. In December 1988, the Carrier Programs Division of the Chief of Naval Operations agreed that obsolescence had made *Hornet* and the other remaining Essex-class carriers (*Bennington*, *Oriskany* and *Bon Homme Richard*) unfit for modernization or reactivation and recommended their disposal. In addition to occupying valuable moorage space at Puget Sound, the cost of maintaining *Hornet*'s dehumidification, cathodic protection and inspection systems was approximately $82,000 annually.

Hornet was stricken from the Naval Vessel Register on August 19, 1989 by the Secretary of the Navy. This legal preliminary to disposal removed all maintenance funding from *Hornet*. On March 14th of that year, when it was known that *Hornet* would be stricken, the USS *Hornet* Historical Museum Association, Inc. was formed to promote saving her from the shipbreaker's torch and develop the carrier into an air, sea and space museum in the Puget Sound area.

In August, the Navy offered CVS-12 for donation as a naval museum under Title 10, U.S. Code, section 7308, which permits transfer of title of Navy vessels for such purposes to communities and organizations who can demonstrate an ability to maintain the vessel at no additional cost to the Federal government. Interest was expressed by the Disney Corporation but the only application received was from the USS *Hornet* Historical Museum Association.

In response to the application, the Navy requested "evidence of firm financial commitments and cash on hand to offset all towing costs, refurbishment costs, mooring preparation, insurance, continuing maintenance, employee salaries,...etc." and "confirmation of the availability of a long-term, acceptable mooring site". The *Hornet* Association estimated the cost of these requirements to be $6-7 million. *Hornet*'s official status was changed to "donation hold", which prevented disposal actions such as stripping of equipment and demilitarization work from being performed.

In order to generate public awareness of the *Hornet* Association's efforts, two high- visibility events were held aboard *Hornet* that year. The first, in April 1989, brought more than 750 guests together on *Hornet*'s flight deck for the 47th Anniversary Reunion of the Doolittle Raiders' attack on Tokyo. This group is famous for having flown sixteen B-25 Mitchell bombers from the flight deck of the first carrier *Hornet* (CV-8), from which CV-12 was named. The ceremony

began with a division of Navy A-6 Intruders in tight formation making a fly-by "on the deck" precisely on the last note of the National Anthem as planned. Later during the ceremony, four Army National Guard AH-1 Cobra gunships escorted a lone Navy Sea King helicopter into view. There, upon Sinclair Inlet, in honor of the Raiders who didn't return, was dropped a commemorative wreath. As the wreath hit the water, four USAF F-15 Eagle jet fighters thundered over the Navy helicopter in fingertip formation. The emotional ceremony concluded with the A-6s returning low and fast, passing on the final note of "Anchors Away" in a missing man formation. Three months later on July 24th, the twentieth anniversary of *Hornet*'s historic recovery of the Apollo 11 capsule and crew was celebrated on the hangar deck of *Hornet*. Apollo 11 astronaut "Buzz" Aldrin and Apollo 12 astronaut Richard Gordon met with 300 guests to reminisce one of the most significant events in scientific history - man's first walk on the moon.

In December 1990, a year-long study suggested Commencement Bay, across Puget Sound near Tacoma, as an optimum location for the

Hornet museum. Following an application to the Department of the Interior by the *Hornet* Association, citing the carrier's historical significance, *Hornet* was designated a National Historic Landmark a year later on December 4 1991. As a result, *Hornet* was photographed in detail inside and out as part of the Historic American Engineering Record (HAER) recordization program.

The *Hornet* Association had assembled a great deal of expertise to handle the promotion, management and conversion of the ship into a truly outstanding museum. Despite having the support of local mayors and politicians, Washington's governor, former-President Nixon, and numerous senators, congressmen and admirals, funding commitments were slow in coming. Extensions to the Navy's "donation hold" on *Hornet* were granted several times at the request of the *Hornet* Association. The final extension expired on January 31, 1992, two years beyond the original expiration date.

Mr. Gene Nelson, former Bremerton mayor and past president and member of the Board of the *Hornet* Association put forth a unique offer to the Navy. He proposed that the Navy permit

The flight deck crash and salvage crane on the bow of the USS Hornet (CVS-12) raises a SH3A helecopter from the fantail of the USS Long Beach (CG[N]-9) where it had an emergency landing.

27

Hornet (XCVS-12) in mothballs at Bremerton, Washington, 1990.

the Association to tow CVS-12 to Tacoma, Washington where it had a commitment of suitable moorage. The Association would pay all costs involved in towing the vessel, and subsequently, all costs required to maintain it, including insurance for a period of five years. During that period the Navy would retain title to the ship. If at the end of that period of time, the *Hornet* Association had not been able to obtain the funds required to establish and operate the proposed naval museum, the Navy could then scrap the vessel.

After a lengthy review of the proposal, the Navy declined the offer citing various legal constraints and concerns. The disappointment among *Hornet* supporters, who believed the proposal to be entirely reasonable and proper, was almost overwhelming. Many began to realize that *Hornet* may be destroyed just as *Enterprise* (CV-6) in 1958. In an official proclamation in support of *Enterprise's* preservation, Congress had designated her as "the one ship which most symbolizes the U.S. Navy in World War II". An elaborate plan had been conceived to berth her in the Potomac River near the Washington Monument as a permanent memorial. However, supporters were given a very short amount of time to raise the necessary funds and in the end *Enterprise* was torched apart in 1958 - an act considered nothing short of criminal by many historians.

The Navy appraised *Hornet* at $200,000 and sale bids were put out to scrap companies. Meanwhile, the *Hornet* Club held its final emotional reunion aboard *Hornet* on December 15, 1992 in her berth at Puget Sound. A bid on *Hornet* was awarded to Astoria Metals on April 14, 1993. Due to environmental concerns however, in the form of possible asbestos and PCB contamination from the ship, *Hornet's* move to Astoria was blocked by the EPA. After months of negotiations over who would be responsible for the proper disposal of these perceived dangers, the matter was settled and Astoria was cleared to move the ship, only to find that the Port of Astoria had withdrawn approval for dismantling there.

The Navy desperately needed the pier space at the Naval Inactive Ships Maintenance Facility for the *USS Ranger* (CV-61) which was undergoing preservation at Long Beach. *Hornet* was towed out of Bremerton on September 10th 1994, arriving at the Long Beach Shipyard fourteen days later for temporary storage. Astoria

Metals finally secured a berth at the old Hunter's Point Naval Shipyard and towed the great carrier from Long Beach, arriving at Hunter's Point on October 23rd.

At the time of *Hornet's* arrival at Hunters Point, Astoria Metals was heavily engaged in a project converting several stricken destroyers into floating powerplant barges. This, coupled with new and toughened EPA requirements for disposal of ship wastes, resulted in a delay in the beginning of the salvage and scrapping of the noble carrier.

A temporary reprieve from the cutter's torches came for *Hornet* when Captain Jim Dodge, Commanding Officer NAS Alameda, approached Astoria Metals about "loaning" the ship to NAS Alameda for a period of six months for display to help celebrate the "Preserving the Heritage" festivities at NAS Alameda. After several months, an agreement was made between the Navy and Astoria Metals. Captain Dodge would have overall responsibility for the safe and successful execution of *Hornet's* relocation plan and, as such, would assume much of the risk and liability for the venture.

Early on the crisp morning of May 11, 1995, numerous dignitaries and former *Hornet* crewmembers, including Albert Massé (CV-12 and USS HORNET Club board of directors) and daughter Roni Massé (present secretary/treasurer of the USS HORNET Club, Inc.), boarded Marine CH-53 helicopters and were flown from NAS Alameda's air terminal to land on *Hornet's* forward flight deck to ride the historic ship during the four-mile, three-hour move across the bay to Alameda's Carrier Pier #2. During the transit, Captain Dodge assembled the hundred or so guests and Navy handlers on the flight deck near the number two elevator. He then made a very stirring and knowledgeable presentation on *Hornet's* history and legacy and the plans for the ship during the next five months. It was at this time during the bay transit that the intention was voiced by those aboard to renew efforts to save the vintage ship from the scrapper's torches.

Hornet at NAS Alameda

Within days of *Hornet's* arrival at Alameda, Ray Vyeda, a past president of the Hornet Club, began to organize the many volunteers that were

coming forward to assist with the clean-up of the ship. The flight deck was cleared of debris and the ship's number "12" was repainted on both sides of the island superstructure. On May 18, 1995, Captain Dodge opened the flight deck for tours for former crewmembers and their families.

A base Open House was held on May 20th to kick off the five-month "Preserving the Legacy" celebration. This program was intended to showcase the tremendous history and significance of the naval air station since its development in 1941during the first dark days of World War II. The culmination of the effort would be the annual Fleet Week Celebration which would coincide with the naval air station's yearly Open House in October. *Hornet* became the star attraction for many of the events and festivities that would take place in the weeks and months to come. Throughout the period, the veteran carrier continued to receive the care and attention of the many dedicated volunteers who worked tirelessly on the historic warship. *Hornet's* 120,000-square-foot flight deck received two coats of haze gray paint and hangar bays 1 and 2 were thoroughly cleaned. Also cleaned and painted were the Flag and Navigation bridges, the pilot house, Primary Flight Control, the escalator, and the interior of the island at the flight deck level. In addition to having the number "12" repainted on the island, the enormous superstructure now sported *Hornet's* ribbons, radio codes and "Beware of Propellers" warning on the island's port side. The mounds of protective foam covering many of the hatches on the island were chipped away and the hatches opened and repainted. Through the determined efforts of the devoted laborers, *Hornet* began to shine to her former glory. During the weekly restoration/work periods, visitors were permitted to come aboard two days a week for impromptu guided tours of selected areas. In July, the non-profit Aircraft Carrier Hornet Foundation (ACHF) was formed to undertake the daunting task of rescuing the ship from the upcoming cutter's torches and preserving her for future generations of Americans to see and experience.

Fleet Week '95 saw *Hornet* once again in the spotlight to which she had become so accustomed a generation before. She was resplendent in her new paint and markings, with four vintage aircraft temporarily displayed on her flight deck and a string of flags strung from her bow to the top of her island and back to her stern. A large American flag waved proudly from her mast and smaller "*Don't Give Up The Ship*" flags flew from the forward flight deck and island as reminders of the mission of the ACHF volunteers. Over 25,000 visitors came aboard during the open house to tour *Hornet's* hangar bay, flight deck and island spaces. During that period, the ACHF sold hats, T-shirts, artwork, books and other memorabilia to support their efforts to preserve the gallant carrier.

Hornet also saw many of her former crewmen come aboard to see "their" ship one last time before she was to meet her end with the scrapper's torches. Throughout the ship, men could be seen enthusiastically showing off their ship to now-grown sons and daughters, while others renewed old friendships and laughed about "the old days". Still others quietly walked the hauntingly familiar decks alone in quiet reflection, perhaps reminiscing about long-ago experiences or events.

At one point, industrious volunteers rigged an operational signal light on *Hornet's* island and began to attempt to exchange communications with signalmen aboard the nuclear carrier *Carl Vinson* (CVN-70), tied up at a nearby pier. In 1945, semaphore and Morse code were one of the primary methods of discrete communications between ships and signalmen became experts at sending and receiving coded messages. During Fleet Week, a former *Hornet* signalman came aboard and was informed about the light. He evidently hadn't lost his touch after fifty years, for when he began sending Morse to the signalmen aboard the *Carl Vinson*, their first reply was "S-L- O-W D-O-W-N"!

Hornet was scheduled to be towed back to the old Hunters Point shipyard in mid-October following the conclusion of Fleet Week, when her scrapping was to begin. Negotiations regarding the ship's future had been ongoing between the ACHF and Astoria Metals for several weeks at this point. The groundswell of public support for *Hornet* had grown considerably. This, possibly combined with the growing uncertainty of profitability in scrapping the aged warship, prompted Astoria Metals to make and unusual request of the Navy. Astoria proposed that the ACHF be granted an extension of the time *Hornet* was to remain at NAS Alameda in order that fund-raising efforts could proceed. The Navy refused the request and ordered the execution of the carrier's salvage contract with the scrapping firm.

Hornet supporters were devastated, believing this to be ship's death knell. The ACHF filed suit against the Navy, seeking to prevent the ship's return to Hunters Point. However, the Navy agreed not to begin the scrapping operation until the matter was resolved in court. The Navy desired additional time to gain information regarding the ACHF's ability to develop a successful donation application package and long-term proposal/plan for the ship. *Hornet* had been designated a National Historic Landmark (NHL) in 1991. It was discovered that the Defense Marketing and Reutilization Service, during *Hornet's* sale for salvage, had not complied with the detailed regulations concerning the disposal of National Historic Landmarks such as *Hornet*. This meant that *Hornet's* sale had not been conducted properly, prompting Navy officials to cancel the sale contract with the scrapping firm. A few weeks later, the ACHF team was permitted to present an extensive brief to Navy officials on their master plan, which included business, financial, towing, mooring, environmental and maintenance concerns for the ship. As a result, the Navy agreed to place the historic carrier into the Navy's "Ship Donation Program" and gave the ACHF twelve months to generate the necessary funding to qualify to be given the opportunity to convert the ship into a museum.

Hornet would sit idly at the NAS Alameda pier for the next year while the ACHF went through the huge task of raising money and getting the word out about the project. The ACHF submitted their completed application package to the Navy in November, 1996 but funding remained the major problem. Efforts continued into 1997 and the ship remained at Alameda. In September, the ACHF received corporate pledges that put them over the top of the fund-raising goal. Word came down from the Navy that the ship would be awarded to the ACHF once logistics and administrative details were worked out. In October 1998, *Hornet* became the first major naval museum on the west coast, permanently moored at the piers of the now-decommissioned NAS Alameda.

A debt of extreme gratitude is owed to Captain Jim Dodge by the members of the Hornet Club and all who wish to see this National Historic Landmark saved for future generations of Americans to see and experience. Thanks to his bold initiative, *Hornet* will once again gleam in the spotlight of which she has become very accustomed during the last half century.

Chuck Self
USS Hornet Historian and author

Note: For a more detailed account of the complete history of the USS Hornet, see Mr. Self's book entitled: **_The USS HORNET, A Pictorial History of CV-12, CVA-12 and CVS-12_** , published by Turner Publishing Company.
    Copyright 1998 by Chuck Self
    All rights reserved.

This document is intended to be printed in the USS Hornet book being prepared by Turner Publishing Company for the USS Hornet Club, Inc. No other use is authorized. Photos provided by USS HORNET Club, Inc.'s Ships' Store – Attn.: Al Massé.

HISTORY OF CARRIER AIR GROUP 11 (CAG-11)

The histories of the Carrier Air Group Eleven (CAG-11) and the USS Hornet are tightly intertwined; it is therefore important to give at least a brief outline of the significant impact CAG-11 made. CAG-11 was formed at NAS San Diego in August of 1942; the formation included a Fighter Squadron (VF-11), a Bombing Squadron (VB-11), a Scouting Squadron (VS-11), and a Torpedo Squadron (VT-11).

On October 23, 1942, CAG-11 departed San Diego to relieve the air group that was then aboard the Hornet (CV-8). Unfortunately, the Hornet was sunk three days later, on October 26. With no carrier, the Air Group went to Hawaii and Fiji Island to undergo extended training, and then pursued land-based operations from Guadalcanal. VF-11 accounted for 55 air to air enemy kills. When this mission was completed, the Air Group returned to the United States, reformed, and on September 29, 1944 was transported to Manus in the Admiralties to board the Hornet (CV-12).

The most prolific squadron of the CAG-11 was the VF-11, a small group of which was more enduringly—and endearingly—known as the Sun Downers. Under Commanding Officer LDCDR Eugene Fairfax, the Sun Downers helped in scoring 103 total victories, which established them as the seventeenth-ranked Hellcat squadron of over eighty that flew F6F's in combat (Tillman).

The majority of the Sun Downers' strikes took place from October, 1944 to January, 1945 in the Philippines area. In October, they launched attacks against Nansei Shoto, Formosa, Luzon, Visayas, and other Japanese fleets, in offensive and defensive maneuvers as well as in tactical support of landing operations. November saw the Sun Downers continuing attacks on Luzon while launching new strikes on Leyte Island and Yap Island, and preventing shipping in Manila Bay. December was a relatively quiet month, with the only major strike being in support of Southwest Pacific Amphibious Forces during the Midoro Invasion. And finally, January was perhaps the busiest month of all for the VF-11 Squadron, with strikes on Formosa, Pescadores, Luzon, Camranh Bay, Saigon, French Indochina, Kowloon, and Okinawa, as well as two long-range searches of the South China Sea. Of the 103 confirmed victories, the Sun Downers were responsible for 36, and they destroyed more than 35,000 tons of enemy equipment. In two tours of duty (the other being at Guadalcanal), eleven Sun Downers had become aces with five or more kills to their credit.

While the Sun Downers' collective achievements are most impressive, the individual accomplishments of a few pilots are also worth mentioning. Eugene Fairfax was the Commanding Officer of VF-11 with 4 kills to his credit, and much of the Sun Downers' success can be attributed to him. H. Blake Moranville had six victories, while Jimmie "Doc" Savage had seven as second-in-command of most strikes. James Swope had ten victories with the Sun Downers, which is quite a number, but it is one eclipsed easily by his good friend Charles "The Skull" Stimpson, who had sixteen.

Sun Downers Insignia

LDCDR Eugene Fairfax, Commanding Officer of VF-11 (four kills to his credit)

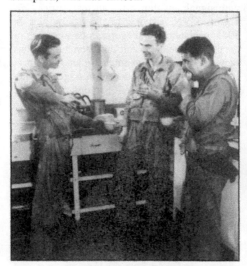

James Swope, Charles Stimpson, and H. Blake Moranville, Sun Downer pilots

Carrier Air Group Eleven (All Squadrons) aboard the Hornet at Ulithi Atoll December 1944. Row 1 L to R: Robcke, Morriss, Meyer, Cardon, Meade, Jones, Oakely, Griffith, Lewis, Sahm, Garlic, Moranville, Tillar, Bethel, Parsley, Willis, Lynch, Shultz. Row 2 L to R: Wolfe, Engle, Richfield, Helmuth, Trendall, unknown, Aubel, King, Dubois, Holt, Wilson, Farley, Lizotte, Williams, Coeur, James, Russell, Higgenbottom, Bourne, Eccles, Kenney. Row 3 L to R: Eft, Cooper, Stimpson, Adams, Ford, Smith, Ramsey, White, Wilson, Lewis, Engmanson, Clements, Bayers, Riera (CAG), Fairfax (CO), Kroger, Yoder, Griffin, Savage, Grau, Chamberlain, Tegge, Earl, Zoecklein, Gallatin, Roberts, Hardy. Row 4 L to R: Crehan, Groves, Crowley, White, Morriss III, Welfelt, Flath, Cyr, Ogle, Ogish, Hyland, Huiner, Myers, Maring, Swope, Boring, Work, Zink, Sisley, Hintze, Sims, Ronsville, Wiley, Schwab, Satterlle, Byerly, White, Saggau, unknown, Jacobsen. Row 5 L to R: Vance, Knott, Richardson, Jesmer, Tonsfeldt, Mudd, Lepianka, Moore, Crowell, Onion, Miles, Edling, Rowland, Sobiar, Bell, Russell, Maier, South, H. Moore, Dewitt, unknown, Bilbao, Olson, McBride, Hayter. Row 6 L to R: West, Brown, Suddreth, C. D. Smith, Warren, McReynolds, Welder, Dickhoff, Chapman, Grosso, McCarron, Boineau, Walker, Nowlin, Beckwith, Koressel, H. E. Smith, Clouser, Erwin, Hayes, Strahan, Campbell, Logan, Cocks.

Officers and Enlisted members of VF-11 aboard the Hornet at Ulithi December 1944. Row 1 (enlisted men) L to R: Butterly, Ryder, Woolsey, Hampton, Saville, Edwards, Rouse, Gluck, Bell, Theimer, Ussery, Berry (with mascot, Gunner), Manthe, Watson, Boyer, Hall, Liston, Mangini, Schaeppekotter, Eaton, Donaldson, Brouillard, Reick. Row 2 (Officers) L to R: Engle, Saggau, Moore, Welfelt, Ogle, Cyr, White, Flath, Maring, Savage, Meyer, Bayers, Fairfax CO, Clements, Sisley, West, Ramsey, Zoecklein, Swope, Brown, Morriss, Work, Williams, Farley. Row 3 L to R: Brookens, Crowley, Morriss 3rd, Crehan, Eft, Lepianka, Sahm, Richardson, Groves, Stimpson, Griffin, Moranville, Boring, Meade, Zink, Hintze, Sims, McBride, James, Hayter, Hardy, Bethel, Lewis, Jacobsen. Row 4 L to R: Knott, C. D. Smith, Jesmer, Tonsfeldt, Mudd, McRenolds, Warren, Crowell, Onion, Miles, Edling, Rowland, Eccles, Coeur, South, Moore, Dewitt, Roberts, Williss, Parsley, Garlic. Row 5 L to R: Wilson, Robcke, Wolfe, Vance, Suddreth, Welder, Dickhoff, King, Chapman, Grosso, Olson, Beckwith, McCarron, Lizotte, H. E. Smith, Walker, Boineau, Clouser, Nowlin, Bilbao, Koressel, Tiller, Byerly. Not pictured: Nelson, Jeffers, Kearns.

Stimpson's sixteen total acknowledged victories were not his only distinguishing characteristics, though; he was the seventh-ranked Navy Ace in World War II. He had already recorded six victories at Guadalcanal while flying Grumman F4-F4, but his most impressive fighting was ultimately to be done flying from the USS Hornet.

On October 14, 1944, his airmanship and heroism were perhaps more apparent and impressive than at any other time of the war. In an air siege against enemy Japanese forces on the coast of the Philippine Islands near Formosa, the flight leader of the eight-plane combat air patrol found his radio inoperable, so Doc Savage took the lead. Soon, though, Savage's compass failed, and Stimpson was next to lead the patrol into combat. What Stimpson did next is now legendary, intercepting and attacking a large formation of enemy aircraft headed directly for the Allied cruiser ship *Canberra*, shooting down at least five—possibly seven—of the fourteen enemy planes destroyed in the attack, his wingman Frederick Blair accounting for three more, and aiding in dispersing the remainder. His triumph was bittersweet, though, as the Sun Downers lost four of their number in the attack including Blair.

As the battle of Formosa was a pivotal air victory for Allied forces, the victories and accomplishments of VF-11 should not be underestimated. The attack on Formosa was so successful, in fact, that after two days American carriers could split up and sent part of their force against Luzon, the ultimate strategic goal for Allied forces. The Japanese saw this split as a retreat and pursued the supposedly fleeing carriers, but too little and too late, as the division in their already-undersized squadron caused them to lose the battle at Formosa.

Stimpson received two Navy Crosses, 2 Distinguished Flying Crosses and an Air Medal for his efforts as a Sun Downer in World War II; he died in 1983 of a coronary seizure at 63 years of age. Fairfax, Swope,

and Moranville are all still alive and willing to tell anyone who will listen about their exploits with the Sun Downers.

Other Sun Downer Aces not mentioned previously are Robert E. Clements (5 kills) and Henry S. White (5). In addition, thirty-eight other VF-11 fighters scored 1-4 kills. They are:

G. G. Anderson (1)
F. J. C. Blair (3)
G. M. Boineau (1)
W. H. Boring (1)
J. S. Brown (1)
G. A. Coeur (1)
K. G. Crusoe (1)
R. F. Cyr (4)
R. C. Dance (1)
N. W. Dayhoff (2)
W. G. Eccles (2)
R. P. Farley (2)
E. Fairfax (4)
R. N. Flath (2)
L. S. Hardy (1)
C. W. James (1)
W. E. Kearns (1)
G. E. Lindesmith (1)
W. E. Lizotte (2)
S. J. Manning (1)
R. McBride (2)
R. McReynolds (1)
A. R. Meyer (2)
H. H. Moore (2)
A. W. Morris III (1)
T. H. Nowlin (1)
J. B. Olson (1)
C. L. Parsley (1)
J. V. Pavela (1)
J. W. Ramsey (2)
J. H. Robcke (3)
W. R. Sisley (2)
M. P. South (2)
J. M. Suddreth (3)
O. H. West (1)
T. St. C. Williams (1)
J. P. Wolf (1)
D. T. Work (3)
J. A. Zink (2)

Charles Stimpson aboard the USS Hornet December 1944

An overview of the significance of VF-11 to the USS Hornet and to Allied forces in WWII would not be complete without a reverent listing of those who gave their lives in service. The following VF-11 pilots were shot down in combat:

George Gordon Anderson (MIA)
John Huston Bethel, Jr. (Crash)
Frederick James Campbell Blair (KIA)
Charles Ray Bratcres (Crash)
Gordon Duward Cady (Crash)
Kenneth Chase (KIA)
Robert Christian Dance (KIA)
Nelson Woodrow Dayhoff (KIA)
Warren De Rolf (KIA)
Samuel Elsworth Goldberg (KIA)
Edward Erwin Helgerson (MIA)
Edward Harold Johnson (Crash: B-17 in transport from his brother's funeral)
Leon Edsel Lee (MIA)
George Edgar Lindesmith (MIA)
William Manniere Mann (KIA)
John James McVeigh (MIA)

George William Papen, Jr. (Crash)
Henry Ptacek (KIA)
Virgil David Roland (Crash)
John Peek Sims (MIA)
Richard Everett Wilson (KIA)

The bomber squadron (VB-11) also played an important part in the success aboard the USS Hornet. Although perhaps less publicized than the Sun Downers, VB-11 recorded some impressive numbers from their September 29, 1944 boarding of the USS Hornet to the completion of their mission on January 22, 1945. During this relatively short period of time, VB-11 flew 490 strike sorties, destroying an estimated 75 grounded enemy aircraft and two in aerial combat. They dropped 368 tons of high explosives and shot over 42,000 rounds of ammunition at enemy shipping, installations, and aircraft. And enemy warships weren't safe from the striking power of VB-11, either; they sank two enemy warships—a destroyer and a light cruiser—and damaged thirteen more. Finally, VB-11 did extensive damage to enemy airfields, twelve in all, as well as harbor installations at Naha, Takao, the Pescadores, Toshien, Manila, Hong Kong, and Kowloon, where one Bomber shot a horse with 20mm fire (it was an accident).

LDCDR Lloyd Addison Smith was the initial Acting Commanding Officer of VB-11, but after he detached on November 1, LDCDR Edwin John Kroeger reported aboard and assumed command, a position he would keep for the duration of VB-11's stay aboard the Hornet. On February 1, VB-11 was transferred from the Hornet to the USS Kasaan Bay at Ulithi Atoll, which they departed three days later for Hawaii and then the United States.

Just as VB-11's contributions to WWII are as commendable as any other squadron's, they too suffered losses among their ranks. The following VB-11 officers and crewmen paid for victory and peace with their lives:

Jack Anderson (Crash)
Richard Glen Aubel (KIA)*
Duane Frederick Brash (KIA)*
William Peter Carey (Crash)
Robert Ronald Cox (Crash)
William Saylor Culver (Crash)
William Herbert Graebner (Crash)
John Phillip Hall (Crash)
Fred Homer Kater (Crash)
Thomas William Ooghe (Crash)
Jonny Wilson Patterson (Crash)
William Malloy Rivers, Jr. (KIA)*
Warren James Sailor (KIA)*
Joyce Eugene Swaim (Crash)
Thomas Jack Warren (Crash)
Marion Russell Young (KIA)*

* Died in combat

Like the Sun Downers and VB-11, the Torpedo Squadron (VT-11) had wartime experience in Guadalcanal prior to their boarding of the Hornet in October; they later regrouped and had been on Hilo Island, Hawaii since April 1944, so they had almost seven months of training and were itching to demonstrate their skills in combat again.

On September 29 VT-11 boarded the USS Hornet; eleven days later they had their first strike, on Okinawa, destroying runways, installations, and buildings in Naha, Okinawa's main airfield. Two days later VT-11 had their first combat strikes, hitting Heito, Einansho, Reigaryo, Takao Harbor, and Formosa. The latter marked their first damage by anti-aircraft fire and first water landing in combat situations. After avoiding losing significant numbers in combat through the rest of October (unlike VB-11 or the Sun Downers), VT-11 returned with the Hornet to port, where they thought they were to get a ten-day rest. After five days, though, they received orders to return to Luzon to launch strikes in support of the Leyte operations. The remaining time until Christmas saw them launch strikes in and on Ormond Bay, Manila Bay, Subic Bay, Luzon, Cabcaben, and Olongapo. After a week-long break for Christmas, VT-11 began what was, as also for VF-11 and VB-11, the busiest and most bloody month of air strikes they were to experience in the war. After sustaining

Robert Crawford, Larry Helmuth, and Gayle Marz, 1944

VB-11 insignia

VT-11 insignia

many injuries and casualties, VT-11 launched four strikes on January 16 against Hong Kong that were largely successful; five days later they struck Toshien and Takao Harbors and Heito Airfield, destroying 21,000 tons of shipping and destroying one ship. January 22 marked their last attack, and quite an inconsequential one at that, as few aircraft and almost no shipping were present.

If Charles Stimpson received much of the acclaim for the Sun Downers' success, then VT-11 pilot Lawrence "Larry" Helmuth must certainly be given the same respect, if for no other reason than he and his crew's sinking of a Japanese cruiser and bomb destruction on the Japanese battleship Nagato, which was forced to withdraw to Japan and never saw future service. Helmuth received a Navy Cross, Distinguished Flying Cross, and an Air Medal for his achievements. His radio gunner, Robert Crawford, and turret gunner, Gayle Marz, also received Air Medals.

On their return to port VT-11 was able to survey their achievements. In all of their major Philippine invasions, sunk 51,400 and damaged 103,900 tons of shipping in their 68 total strikes and 1,845 strike hours. Of course, as stated before, there were casualties. Here are the brave men who gave up their lives in combat or training for VT-11:

Fred J. Baker (KIA)
Rog Balcome (KIA)
Gordy Bell (KIA)
Robert Burgess (KIA)
Paul Chleborad (KIA)
Charles H. Cunningham (KIA)

R. Denniston, LCDR (KIA)
John Ward Evans (KIA)
Glenn Faulk (KIA)
Dowd Hamaker (KIA)
Claude E. Haley (KIA)
Joe M. Hyland (KIA)
Homer R. Johnson (KIA)
Fritz W. LeBlanc (Lost at Sea)
Willie Maier (KIA)
Edwin W. McGowan (KIA)
Robert A. McKinney (KIA)
Norman E.Morgan (KIA)
Burton T. Oberg (KIA)
Laurence E. Sawyer (KIA)
Laurence C. Schiller (KIA)
Eddie P.Spreckner (KIA)
Clint T. Steed (KIA)
William H. Winner (Crash)

Formation flying to celebrate the end of WWII, June 1945

USS HORNET SPECIAL STORIES

The Hornet Goes Through
The Typhoon

by Cmdr. (then Lt.) Ivan F. "Ike"

Andes, USNR Ret.

On June 5, 1945, I was officer of the deck on the 04-08 watch on the USS *Hornet* (CV-12). This put me in a critical and great position to see and experience what happened.

We were cruising at moderate speed and the seas were fairly calm and seemed normal when I relieved Lieutenant Langan who had the midwatch (12:04 a.m.). The *Hornet* was fleet guide in the center of a group of ships consisting of cruisers and destroyers. We were preparing to "top off" the USS *Monihan* at first light since she was low on fuel after serving as "plane guard," a high speed operation which consumed large quantities of bunker oil.

To get ready to receive fuel *Monihan* had pumped ballast water from her fuel tanks and was riding high, like a cork on the seas and making her a bit unstable. She was about 2,000 yards away on our starboard quarter and ready to come alongside when ordered.

Radar had been tracking a menacing looking storm but didn't think it would pose a problem even though it was right on our proposed course. I recall how the wind started to gust and the waves built to dangerous highs. As OOD, I had the captain awakened and appraised him of the threatening conditions. Captain Doyle immediately notified flag plot and Admiral Clark ordered fleet speed reduced to six knots and an emergency turn to starboard. The USS *Monihan* heeled over during the turn and disappeared beneath the waves, with the loss of all hands.

At daybreak the seas had become enormous, making it difficult to control the ship; about all Captain Doyle could do was maintain bare steerage way and try to head into the wind. From my position in the pilot house I remember looking out ahead at mountainous waves which were actually breaking over the flight deck. When the ship pitched down in a trough, one huge wave got under the flight deck over-hang and raised it up, and a second big wave would break over the top and fold it down like limp rabbit ears. A TBM (torpedo bomber plane), which had been tied down on the flight deck forward, broke loose and was tossed over in a cartwheel. This type of aircraft weighed more than two tons. Meteorology estimated that the wind exceeded 125 knots.

The ship passed through the eye of the typhoon, an eerie period of surprising calm, followed by more huge waves while coming out the other side of the storm.

Hornet was to provide air cover for the landings on Iwo Jima next day. When the first plane attempted to takeoff, turbulence, caused by the folded flight deck, flipped the fighter over and into the water; fortunately, the pilot was rescued. Admiral Clark ordered the planes respotted in the forward end of the flight deck and the ship to reverse at best speed. The air group was launched over the stern while backing down at 18 knots. This was the first time this had ever been done.

Since normal air operations were not practical with the damaged flight deck, *Hornet* was ordered to Ulithi Atoll for emergency repairs and to San Francisco Naval Shipyard. With the war ending in August, *Hornet* was pressed into service to ferry troops home.

Guam 1944

by Clint Branham, VT-2

I wrote the following in my cabin several weeks after our first raids on the Mariana Islands. It was inspired by the loss of a friend who was a pilot in VB-2. I was a pilot in the Torpedo Squadron.

Closer even than you lived, you flew
Right wing underlaping left until
The slightest movement of the stick you held
Would scratch the fish like blue-gray belly
Of the plane he flew.
And glancing back, his face relayed his thoughts
As grinning, he patted the metal skin beside him
Motioning, come closer, share my cockpit
But from the surf ringed island far below
Guns nestling in the green, began their blinking,
And echoed in the sky you rode, erupting
Answering fire that changed to dirty puffs of
Black and hung there quivering
And now the grin was gone
And fear was on his face
And yours as the planes
Began their dives - together
The burst that got him rocked you too
The burning smell of powder
Filled your cockpit as well as his
But the jagged scraps of steel that tore
Into his engine somehow passed yours by
The short remaining distance to the earth
You rode with him, wingman still.
Watched his frenzied tearing

At the canopy that cased him
Saw the streaming fire
And smoke his engine breathed
Saw that last tormented scream
For help upon his face
And, helpless, saw him die.

Exposure

by Nickolas Cassano - PHO-M1/c

Following is my experience in the Photo Section of the *Hornet* during the attack and abandoning. At 9:18 on the morning of the 26th, the Japanese planes were sighted and preparations on shipboard were made. We in the lab made ready our cameras and supplies, and all the photographers took their places topside. Our communication system kept us informed, and at 10:00 the attack was in full swing. Our runners worked hard to keep photographers supplied with film, and they brought back the exposed film which we packaged in waterproof containers. Outside the lab we were told it was a 500-pound dud bomb which saved the lab. Our photographers had only one casualty who received a shot in his side and loss of his arm. Frank Regan was next to him with a 16 mm camera they shared. Right after a final bomber attack, orders came at 4:50 to abandon ship.

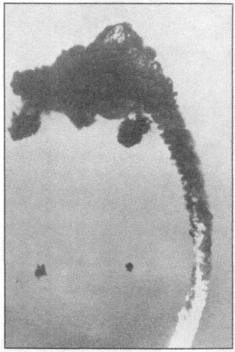

Gunners of the USS Hornet score a direct hit on a Japanese bomber, March 18, 1945.

Vignette from VF-2

by Harry R. Davis

June 24, 1944: Task Force 58, which included the *Hornet*, was lying some 250 miles to the south of Iwo Jima and a strike was launched against Iwo Jima. Just prior to Iwo, a cold front lay across track which had to be penetrated.

Penetration was made by flying low beneath all clouds and breaking clear on the other side, Iwo was in sight, It was immediately noted that the Japanese were launching a strike of their own, as many aircraft were observed becoming airborne and rendezvousing. Lieutenant (jg) "Stinky" Davis's element of four, with other F6Fs from VF-2 entered a climbing spiral to approximately 10,000 feet, then headed into the rendezvousing Japanese.

Stinky was just pulling up from downing a second "Judy" dive bomber when he and others were jumped by many Zeros from above. One Zero was above and dead ahead firing at Stinky, and another was approaching firing position from his left side. The Zero dead ahead made hits on Stinky's cockpit with his 20 mm and 30 caliber guns. Continuing through his pull-up, Stinky fired at this oncoming Zero and noted hits as pieces flew off. After passing each other, Stinky turned to look at his assailant and noted both Zeros going down, one in flames and the other smoking heavily. Some unknown F6F had intercepted the Zero coming at Stinky's left side and shot it down. Stinky's cockpit was a shambles, without a single functioning instrument, and Stinkey had several wounds in the leg and foot.

To this melee the *Hornet* had also launched a TBF as a sort of spotter and air rescue vehicle. This TBF noted several aircraft going down at once, some in flames. A veteran of the European fracas, VF-2s Tex Vinyard, who flew "Spitties" against the Germans from Malta, said this was the most condensed fight he had ever witnessed and it was a wonder more aircraft did not run into each other.

Stinky, besides losing all instruments and radios, also lost all his hydraulics. There was a lifeguard submarine in view to the West, but seas were running heavy from the passage of the cold front and the many whitecaps indicated a wind of maybe 25 knots. This removed a lot of enthusiasm for ditching his F6F by the sub and thoughts of taking a bloody leg into those shark infested waters emphasized a decision not to take a swim.

The melee was over and VF-2 F6F joined up with Stinky and by several hand motions (no radios left) Stinky indicated that the other F6F take the lead home. Back under the front, and a not too enjoyable 200 mile trip back, did give time for landing considerations. No hydraulics meant a dubious landing gear extension. The waters were considerably calmer at the *Hornet's* position, but a gear down or partially down would make ditching a truly hazardous option. No instruments would make an interesting approach to landing at the *Hornet*. The escorting F6F, which turned out to be Kenny "The Kid" Lake, advised the *Hornet* he was escorting an F6F in some sort of trouble without radios. Stinky gambled and used the compressed air

VF-2 planes and pilots aboard the USS Hornet (CV-12).

emergency landing gear extension air bottle. It worked, and his downwind and base leg were flown visually by engine sound and from what felt normal.

The Landing Signal Officer picked him up on base leg and worked him in. Stinky arrived aboard and was helped from his cockpit. His F6F cockpit was so completely shot up and a shambles, that the captain of the *Hornet* requested the F6F be kept on deck for two or three days so ship's personnel could view it first hand, then it was thrown overboard. Some 40 years later at a *Hornet* reunion, Carl Fox, a VF-2 mechanic, advised Stinky that upon close inspection of the F6F, it was discovered that one of the Zero's 30 caliber's had nicked one of the F6F's elevator control cables, and Stinky flew the 200 miles return and came aboard with just a single strand of his elevator control.

Thank God for Grumman ruggedness and Lady Luck!

A Left-Hand Monkey Wrench

by D.A. Giarraputo, QM3/c

Though in the front lines at sea in the Asiatic Pacific, there were still times of laughter and tricks played to pass the time. This is a true story of a seaman second class and two quartermasters of the Navigation Division.

One morning after breakfast, two quartermasters instructed a seaman to find a special tool and bring it to them in their sleeping compartment. The seaman accepted the assignment and went on his way.

When it was time for him to relieve the watch, the seaman could not be found. The junior quartermaster replaced him on watch while the second quartermaster tried to find the seaman. The seaman was in the chow line for the evening meal when the quartermaster finally found him and asked him where he was at watch time. The seaman simply stated that he had looked all over the ship, running up and down ladders and stairs, rested a few times, then being tired had finally given up -

he couldn't find a left-hand monkey wrench. The seaman second class from the Midwest had turned the tables on the two quartermasters from the South.

Memories Of The USS *Hornet* (CVA-12)

by Frederick G. Harvey, Ed.D

As a 20-year-old newly married airman apprentice, I was ordered by NTC Olathe, Kansas, to the USS *Hornet* (CVA-12), home-ported at San Diego, California. This seemed like a coincidental assignment for a young man from Nebraska. My uncle, Robert E. Burton, AM1, had served aboard the USS *Hornet* (CV-8) that was sunk by the Japanese in October 1942 during WWII.

After a short furlough in Nebraska with my new wife and our families, I traveled by train to San Diego, dressed in the winter uniform of "dress blues." I arrived at the train depot in San Diego, walked to the "Nickel Snatcher" for a ferry ride to North Island, then walked to "Quay Wall" where the *Hornet* was docked. I couldn't believe how large the ship was and that it was to be my work place and home for the next 21 months. I reported aboard the *Hornet* and the OD directed me to Personnel for assignment. Being an "Airedale," I was assigned to V-1 Division. Since I knew how to type, I was assigned to the Air Boss's Office as a "Airman/Yeoman" and to the Primary Flight Control Tower during General Quarters and Flight Operations.

At first I enjoyed the excitement of the new assignment, the excitement of the flight deck from the vantage point of "Pri-Fly" and my new home. Getting accustomed to shipboard duty and a ship that could carry all the "needs of a 'ships company' of 2,500 men and a 500 man air-group," plus planes and equipment - all of that on a ship just under 1,000 feet in length. The crews quarters were newly refurbished and clean, the Chow Hall was huge and food was ample in quantity and tasty in quality. The first time at sea was a great experience with the crew at muster and inspection on the flight deck in

"Fueling Around"

Arresting Gear Crew, V-1 Division, October, 1944.

"blues," traveling out of San Diego Bay past Seaplanes at NAS North Island, the Naval Training Center, and past Point Loma to the open Pacific Ocean. The sea was smooth with a slight roll and the breeze was pleasant. Shortly after dismissal, the ship's crews went directly to their quarters to dress in the uniform of the day at sea, "dungarees, boondockers and, of course, the "white hat."

Within a short time, Flight Quarters was called and everyone went directly to their station. I got lost getting to Pri-Fly this time, even after the first introductory visit. The "Air Boss," Commander Berry, USN, was a stern man but friendly. He arranged for another airman to show me what my job was to be. My mentor was an airman with some experience in using the "sound powered" phones and in my new duty. I was assigned to be one of two phone talkers for the air boss and his assistant. I was stationed in the Pri-Fly control tower near the entrance door, but to the furthest "aft" position in Pri-Fly. With the aid of a pair of binoculars I was the visual check to see that the tail hooks on the latest planes of that day were properly working. I would first check to see if the red light on the pilots left wing was on, indicating the tail hook was in its proper position for landing; and second, to visual spot the tail hook in its landing position with a signal to the Air Boss that the "...tail hook (was) down..." He then would give the signal to the LSO that the plane

was prepared to come aboard and the LSO would take control. What an operation. Everything had to be just right and I was now a part of that process. I was learning what a team truly was and how success or failure, life or death, was to depend on the training and quality of that team.

I remained in the Air Office and Pri-Fly for about half the cruise. Flight Quarters was an exciting experience and I had a vantage point that was two hours on duty and two hours off for the duration of flight operations. Flight operations began with the early preparation of plane manipulation on the flight deck in preparing for departures, through the excitement of the planes leaving the ship, through their entire flight time and until they returned to the ship and were secured on the flight deck. Flight operations became a long day or night. But that was the mission of the *Hornet*.

From the operation of and the vantage point of Pri-Fly, you were involved in not only the several thousand takeoffs and slightly less numbered landings during the 16,000 flight hours, a few mishaps or accidents, and the real life action of the flight deck of a modern aircraft carrier in 1955. From that vantage point many lives were seen snuffed out like the "smoking lamp" or aircraft mangled beyond repair. The "Tilley" was generally parked just below Pri-Fly and was frequently used as a "safety barrier" for flight deck personnel when nothing else was available.

I recall a "general quarters" that identified possible enemy planes approaching. Everyone thought that this was probably another "training session" and that we would see no action. Guns and radar were trained to the port bow direction of the ship and everyone was ready and waiting. We had heard stories from the "old salts" about the "good ol' days," but a story was all that they had been up to this point. Suddenly, it was announced that "bogies were approaching" at "11 o'clock, low." Sure enough, two MiGs with "big red stars" flew from fore to aft on the port side at flight deck height and dropped their wings in a salute. What a relief when the bogies were out of sight and the "all clear" was given.

One day I was taking my break from Flight Quarters in the Air Office typing letters and reports from the Air Boss. The Air Office was located immediately below the flight deck, just fore of midships, as I recall. Suddenly, and all at one time, the lights went out, sparks flew all around the office compartment, and there was an extremely loud sound of thrashing, metal cutting, metal flying, and no one seemed to realize what was happening. A buddy in the office at the time, grabbed a battle lantern to look around. Above my desk and chair was a prop from a plane sticking through the overhead ceiling about 2-3 feet. At that point we got scared and quickly found our way out of the office. Meantime, up on the flight deck one of our "Ensign Exterminators," as the white hats called them, had come in for a landing, struck a wheel barrier flipping the AD on its nose, so to speak. The prop had dug into the flight deck, through the wood planking, through the steel under deck (the bottom side was the ceiling of our office) with very little damage to the plane except for the prop. Needless to say, "I was one scared swabby."

Pri-Fly was also the vantage point from which I experienced shipmates from my division being blown off the side by a jet blast, cut-in-two by a port elevator's accidental release, slashed by a prop, and crushed by a plane striking the "tilley" he was using for protection. It was also the vantage point for witnessing many takeoffs and landings and some aircraft accidents during the takeoffs and landings. The *Hornet* lost several pilots during takeoffs with the AD's "Ensign Exterminator" because of the tremendous torque of the prop engine, the AD pilot had to compensate for the torque of the plane's thrust at the time the plane's landing gear lifted-off the end of the flight deck on either a catapult or deck-run launch. Several pilots were lost at sea because the ship could not maneuver clear of the accident site to allow the "Angel" an opportunity to rescue the downed pilot. The Flight Deck during flight operations is a busy place where training is critical and reaction becomes and must be spontaneous. It is not a place for the unskilled or a place for casual observation. Everyone has a job and every job must be done right.

I moved from the "Airedale" V-1 Division of "ships company" to the "black shoe" X Division and became a chaplain's assistant for the Protestant ships chaplain, John Wise, CDR. There was a Catholic and Protestant Chaplain aboard ships company who were responsible for worship service, personal consolation and were also in charge of the Crews Lounge. The excitement reduced tremendously, but the work was gratifying. We provided the on board recreation for the crew with the library, ships radio station, and lounge area. I remember setting up for worship service on Saturday nights, when at sea following the ships movie, if flight operations were suspended. The memorial services for ships crewmen or squadron crewmen killed or lost at sea were memorable and very dignified.

I also remember when bodies were recovered and placed in a "reefer" until the ship returned to port, and how the chow hall attendance would drop off drastically at chow time during this time. It was soon announced that the "reefer" used for the morgue did not contain any food items used by the chow hall; attendance then began to improve. The longest extended "time at sea" was just in excess of 30 days. We ran out of fresh fruits, vegetables, and had limited dairy products available. The replenishing supply ships for fuel and supplies were always a welcome site. But, the most welcome site at sea was the ol' TBM mail plane or "the turkey," as we called it, with letters and packages from home.

All of these memories are everlasting in my mind. I served aboard a great ship and I was a proud crew member of the USS *Hornet* (CVA-12) for 21 months. She was a work place, a home and a haven for all her crew. There were sad times, but there were also many happy times. When I left her in Bremerton, Washington, dry dock, she was being retrofitted for the new angled flight deck, removal of the bow gun tubs to be replaced with a new "hurricane bow," removal of most of the armament on the port and starboard sides, plus numerous other technologies. She went on to recover space capsules and astronauts as covered by national television, and she continued a proud service for many years. I was not to see her again until a professional business meeting allowed me to be in Seattle, Washington. My wife and I crossed the Puget Sound by ferry to Bremerton, to "see where we once lived" in Wherry Housing. We decided to visit the USS *Missouri* that was still in commission and tied up near the mothball fleet at the Bremerton Naval Ship Yard. While aboard the *Missouri*, the Quartermaster pointed out several of the ships docked nearby. Next to the *Missouri* was the *Hornet*, in mothballs. The excitement of coming home was almost overwhelming. I hope to visit her again when she is a "museum of distinction" on the West Coast.

Memories Aboard The USS Hornet

by ACOM William Fred Holloway

NOTE: These are a transcription of memories as recorded by ACOM William Fred Holloway regarding his time on board the USS Hornet (CV-8) during WWII. While the document was not dated, based on the corroboration of his wife, it is believed they were written between his time at the Naval Hospital in Seattle immediately after the Hornet sank and before his medical discharge in late 1944. There are several missing pages or illegible items as noted. At some point the notebook was water damaged, rendering parts unreadable.

Page 1 is missing. ...to take her to sea and see just what she can do and take.

So one morning we went aboard at ole Pier 7 with bag and baggage, in other words ready to go to sea. We pulled out in the bay and anchored, stayed there for a day (what for I don't know) but next day we were under way and out to sea. We went down the Atlantic Coast and around into the Gulf of Mexico. This was where she was to be shaken down. It was too dangerous in the Atlantic with German subs prowling around. We also found they were in the Gulf later on.

The object of a shakedown cruise is to find out what a ship will do; how she will stand up under speed runs; how her fire and boiler rooms will take it and the main thing is to acquaint the new crew with her. As it was with us, our crew was made up of 75% of men who had never been to sea before; so you can imagine how it was and what a beating the other 25% took. But all's well that ends well, which it did. We were down there for 30 days and had a pretty fair crew by that time.

We had one bad accident while we were there. One of our planes (SBC-4s) landed on the flight deck and bounced over the side, the pilot and radioman didn't get out. Most of us didn't find out until later that torpedoes were fired at us.

After she was put through her paces and the skipper pronounced her ready for sea (with a few minor repairs in the Navy Yard which she would get later), we proceeded back to Norfolk. When we got back and tied up at Pier 7, most of the squadron personnel were to go back to the air station. Some were kept aboard for this reason: There were two B-25 Army bombers sitting on the pier. None of the crew knew what they were there for, but later on we would know. They were hoisted aboard and she got underway again and out to sea where the two B-25s were flown off. It was almost dark when she started back in. On the way in one of the lookouts spotted something which looked like a sub periscope. So some of the gun crews started blasting away at it, but the *Hornet* didn't stay around to see if any hits were made. She came on in and lo and behold next morn they found our sub was the mast of a sunken tanker. So much for that.

The ship stayed around there until March 2, then the squadrons went aboard again and we put to sea, headed south to the Panama Canal bound for the West Coast.

Going through the (ditch) is quite an experience in itself. The canal is 50 miles across, through jungles and Lake Gatune. It makes a guy feel kinda funny to be on a 20,000 ton war ship going along with jungle on all sides, hearing the birds singing, seeing crocodiles and things like that. It many not sound any different to you than if you were in a row boat on a river, but think of it - a monster of steel, 880 feet long, 160 feet wide and tall as a seven story building - built for the spans of the oceans and gliding along like she was a raft on a river. You would have to experience it to know what I mean. It took all day to go through so we tied up on the Pacific side overnight.

Got underway next morning, we didn't know where to, but we had a hunch it would be Diego, and it was.

We had a pretty bad accident on the way up. One of the cables which grab the tail hook on the plane when it hits the deck broke. It hit one of the guys in our squadron in the head. He lost one of his eyes and had a fractured skull. He didn't die though.

We went on to Diego and tied up at North Island. Our planes flew to the beach and stayed. The ship and station were right next to each other, so we worked at the station and stayed aboard ship. While we were here we got the new SBD-3, Douglas Dive Bomber. We also went to sea to qualify some Marine pilots in carrier landings, and I must say we had quite a bit of excitement that day. There were about 18 fighters and 18 dive bombers that started landings. Evidently the pilots were very nervous for we had quite a few

V-5 Ordnance TBM Armory. Standing: Hank Castro. Front row: (left to right) T. Dudley, G. Averitt, R. Sieg, R. Pfluger, Joe Nist, C. Sarratt, W. Zellin. Back Row: L. Palella, G. Dittmar, H.C. Valdespino, R. Jensen, G. Guffa, R. Flanigan.

V-5 Division Aviation Ordnance Dive Bomber (SB2C). Front row (left to right) W.H. LaChapelle, Hank Castro, George Guinan. Middle: Jack Hopkins, Melvin Crowder, Robert Jessen, Edward Reese, Klein Fowler, F.J. Rogers. Back: W.A. Tidwell, John Magariello, Edward Hueston, Clyde Holsclaw, Edward O'Neill.

crackups and wave offs. Some of them wouldn't take wave off and would come on anyway, hit the deck and bounce over the side. All in all, I think 10 of them got back to the station. It was so dangerous that they wouldn't let any but necessary personnel on the flight deck.

We went back to the island, tied up and stayed there about a week training the pilots in the new planes.

Then one morn we got underway for 'Frisco; nothing happened on the way up. We entered the bay, tied up at the air station and what do you think was sitting on dock? - B-25s. We started hoisting them aboard as they flew in. In all, we took on 16 of them, then the good old Navy scuttlebutt started flying, and if you have never heard it you sure have missed something. Some said we were taking them to Hawaii; some said to Alaska and almost every place in the Pacific, but no one really knew except the ones in Washington and Jimmy Doolittle. Our skipper had sealed orders.

The ship gave liberty that night and some of the guys went ashore - most of them anyway. Liberty was up at 0800 next morn.

I will take time out here to tell you about a few of my shipmates, the ordinance gang in particular, so we will start at the top in rate and come down. First there was Gibbo, our ordinance chief. He was about 35 years old, had 17 years in the Navy and been around quite a bit. He stuck up for his men and got every break for us he possible could. He was a good leader, but didn't know much about ordnance. All in all, he was a pretty good Joe but will say more about him later.

Then there was Frankie Going. He was our other chief and a big, congenial, good-natured Irishman who was liked by everyone. Most of his 12 years of service time were spent in China and we called him Asiatic, meaning that when we would start a bull session, Frankie would say something like this: "Now when I was in China..." But he knew his ordnance and taught me a lot.

Then we have Schmitt. He was second class ordnance man, and right off I will say he knew his ordnance, although he was pretty overconfident in himself. In his estimation he knew everything. Still he was a good Joe and I had some good liberties with him in Honolulu. He was married and left us before the ship sank. I don't know what happened to him after that.

Then came R.E. Teony. We called him "Mattress Back" because he could always be found in his bunk whenever it was possible for him to be there. He was kinda dudish, didn't know much about ordnance but was still a good guy. One of the things I remember about him is his liking of onions. He was eating them almost all the time. I remember one time we had been to a party in Honolulu and he got pretty swaked up. When we were ready to go back to the ship he was missing and when we found him, he was laying on top of a little shed passed out and had three or four big onions with him.

Then came Al Fone. He was third class, a good guy, but had a tendency to get in trouble. He and I were on the USS *Tuscaloosa* together, and the first time I every saw him a Marine was exercising him on deck. He was in the brig at that time. He and I were transferred together to the *Hornet*. He said he would ship over for another cruise if they would give him sergeant first class, but he missed the ship in 'Frisco and didn't catch up with us until about a month later in Pearl. Didn't know much about ordnance, but he was a shipmate and had a good heart about him. Last I heard of him, he had been sent to the Naval Prison on Maine Island. Hope he doesn't have to stay long.

Then came Nelson, better known as Nellie. He was a big gawky farm boy from Iowa. Clumsy as an ox, a good worker and knew his ordnance. What I remember most about him was his mania for coffee grounds. Every time he came into the armory, he would get him a handful to eat. We all teased him about it. Told him it was going to kill him. In a few days he was in the sick bay all swelled up. We went down to see him and he says "Fellows, do you think the coffee did it?" He was scared it wasn't the coffee though. Don't know what happened to him.

Next we have AOM3/c Cramer S.L. He was my pal and we used to pitch some wicked liberties together. He came from Chicago and knew quite a bit about ordnance. He was a hard worker and all around good guy. We all called him Lou. He had a girl friend in LA that we went to see while we were in Diego and just before the ship sank, he got a letter saying he was going to be a daddy. So we made up about $200 for him to help him out. He went back and married her and

the last I heard they were very happy with a little boy that he was very proud of. Last I heard of him he was in Diego.

Now comes the case of all cases: "Little Joe Copile, the Sad Sack. We are (can't read) Joe, try to swap from UF-8. He came from Brooklyn, got married when he was 15 and was what you would call a typical sailor. The things I best remember about him is his borrowing. I had what was known as a "salty flat hat" and Little Joe would say: "Holloway, hows to wear your flat hat and I need a pair of skivvys and let me use your neckerchief. How about a cigarette, and Holloway, hows to show me so and so about ord?" (Although he was 2/c and I was S1/c), I knew more ordnance than he and I guess you know he had a way about him that you couldn't refuse him these things. He was a little sad sack, but I loved him just the same.

Then there is Dean Harvey Smith. He was just one of the Smith's. Smitty was what we called him and he is Irish. I know because he has a very red nose of which he was quite sensitive. He would get mad when we would tease him about it. His home is in California about 40 miles south of 'Frisco. He could speak Spanish fluently. He went to Ordnance School so he knew ordnance pretty good. The thing I remember most about Smitty is his good nature, his long tongue and his mania to acquire a .45 automatic pistol, which he finally got and lost later on. I remember the time in Honolulu when Smitty and Lou went to the beach on liberty, so naturally they started making all the bars. When time came to start back they were pretty well soused. They decided that they would like to have some pineapples and got about a dozen of them. They carried them in a box and got underway for the ship. But as fate would have it, there was a bar very conveniently located on their way; they agreed to have just one more for it might be a long time before another. So setting their pineapples just in the doorway, they proceeded to get a drink. Then one of them spotted a sailor making away with their pineapples. There were three men and one went one way and the other two went the other way. Smitty went after the two, caught them and proceeded to work them over, which they were also doing to him. In the meantime, Lou had overtaken the one with their pineapples and proceeded to knock him through a plate glass window. By this time a big crowd had collected along with the SP so naturally all of them were taken to SP Station. The Shore Patrol officer told them they weren't locking them up for fighting but for drawing a crowd. It was taboo for a crowd to collect in those days. So along about 6:00 that evening, the SPs delivered Smitty and Lou to the ship and a sorry sight they were. You can imagine how they looked with all the blood, theirs and someone else's, all over their white uniforms. Smitty was kinda beat up about the face. Don't forget he was taking on two of them. So they came on up to the armory and yes, they had their pineapples. Lou and Smitty then got into an argument about who saved the pineapples, etc. You know how a couple of drunks will do. We finally got them quieted down and everything was okay, but the next day our squadron skipper, Lieutenant Commander Gus Widhelm (or maybe it was Whittier?) called them down. It seems that the guys from the station (the ones they had beat up) had made a complaint to their skipper, so naturally it came through the channels to Gus and he asked them, "Did you lick them?" They said "Yes." He just said "Good, just forget it." So much for Smitty. The last I heard from him he was back on some island in the Pacific.

This brings up "Pop" Buckling. He was what we called an old maid. He was on the scholerlistic side and always reading books of autobiography and intellectual stuff. He was down right lazy and wouldn't go the bathroom, or "head" as it was known in the Navy, until everyone else had left them. Couldn't get him to take off his clothes in front of anyone. We used to call him "old maid, grandma," etc. He just grinned and didn't say anything. The last I heard of him he was with Smitty.

Now comes Gartman, better known as "Guts" because he was always eating. His home was in Mobile, Alabama. One day he left some parts out of a machine gun, so this brought the wrath of Gibbo down on him and it was mess cooking for him. The thing I remember about him is on the serious side. The night before we were...(illegible). Some pages missing here.

...we were to push the B-25s over the side and get our planes in operation as soon as possible. We proceeded on toward Japan, but not on a straight course. We were going N-S-E and W. That was to throw off any Japanese subs that might be spotting us. All the time we were com-

ing closer to Japan and were running into bad weather, which was actually good for us as we couldn't be spotted so easily from the air.

About 48 hours from our destination, we left our four destroyers behind. We were to run at flank or full speed into 400 miles and then back. It's not that our tin cans couldn't keep up with us, its that they would have run out of fuel. A ship going at full speed uses three times as much fuel as at cruising speed.

We left them and proceeded with the *Enterprise*, 'Frisco, *Northampton* and *Nashville*. In the meantime, we had the planes all loaded up with bombs, full and ready to go. The weather was overcast and the sea was rough the next morning, of which we were glad to see, for during the night we had picked up two enemy ships. One on port side about 75 miles away, the other on starboard about 50 miles away.

Everything was going fine until about 9:00 then General Quarters sounded. I was down in the chow line waiting for breakfast, so we were rushing to our GQ stations (mine was topside), and when I got up to the flight desk, I saw the *Nashville* on our port beam. She was blazing away with all guns. A Japanese patrol vessel had run up on us. She fired one shot at us and it fell 4,000 yards short. The *Nashville* sank it in two or three rounds, but Admiral Halsey didn't know whether or not they had gotten a message off... (illegible) ...to take any chances, he... (illegible) ...the bombers. We were 600 miles from Tokyo then, so we started launching them. The water was very rough and some of us didn't believe they would all make it off safely; but every last one of them got off without a hitch. We had an accident. One of our plane directors was blown into the prop of one of them and his arm was chopped off at the shoulder.

Soon as all the planes were launched we turned back, and luckily for us, we ran into some more squalls, for we picked up 90 Japanese bombers over us and our planes had sunk two more Japanese patrol vessels, so we ran under squalls most of the day, picked up our destroyers that evening and headed for Honolulu.

When we got to Honolulu, we went into the Navy Yard to have our hangar deck catapult removed. In the meantime, trouble was brewing down south. We took on fuel and supplies and in company with the Big E and our cruisers, we started that way. The carriers, *Yorktown* and *Lexington*, were down there already and as it is known now, they were in a battle which was

known as the Battle of Coral Sea. We were two days late in joining, so the battle was over when we got there. The *Yorktown* had one or two bomb hits and the Lexington had bomb and torpedo hits, but didn't sink. The fires were brought under control and she was proceeding back to Pearl when late in the evening an explosion started her burning again. This time she couldn't be saved and our own forces sank her.

We proceeded on to the Coral Sea and prowled around for a day or so. One day a Japanese plane was spotted over us at about 25,000 feet. Our fighter pilots wanted to go up and shoot him down, but the skipper said no. All that day we steamed south; soon it was dark and we turned and headed north under flank speed to Pearl. We later found out why the skipper wouldn't let them shoot the Japanese down. He wanted them to think we were heading for Australia, which evidently they did. We knew there was something big cooking on account of the way we were going back to Pearl. We got in about noon and tied up at Ford Island. The *Yorktown* came in a little later and went on in the yard to be patched up.

Soon as we were tied up, we started taking fuel, ammunition and supplies. The Big E and all the other ships were doing likewise. Something was brewing and it wasn't beer. We knew there was not liberty for anyone. We fueled and took on supplies all night. Next morning we got underway and stood out to see where we rendezvoused with the *Enterprise, Yorktown* and their task force.

Then came what we had all been waiting for. The skipper told us where we were going and what for. He said the Japanese were going to try to take Midway. He told us that we knew how many war ships, how many transports they had, and just how they were going to approach and attack the island. We even knew they had some guns captured on Wake Island and were going to set them up on Midway. He said they were going to make a (illegible) and Dutch harbor to try and draw us off up there, but being wise to them we didn't go.

(illegible)

Our job was to move in behind the Japanese and cut them off from Guam, which we tried to do but for some reason the Army bombed them too soon so they scattered before we could get into position. But they were still trying to get to Midway on the morning of the 5th. The *Yorktown* was attacked by Japanese planes. She had a

Air Group VF-8 aboard USS Hornet, October 1941.

CV-12 Band playing on the hangar deck.

couple of torpedo hits and several bomb hits. Although she was burning badly and listing to starboard, they finally got the fires under control and took most of the crew off her, leaving a skeleton crew to bring her into port. That night a destroyer was tied up alongside her giving power and trying to repair her so she could be towed in. Everything was going fine until a Japanese sub put torpedoes into her and the destroyer. Both of them sank pretty quick.

In the meantime we were chasing down the Japanese. Our planes, with the help of Army, Marine and Navy planes from Midway, were attacking from the 5th to the 7th. The whole force sank four Japanese carriers, two battle cruisers and an indeterminate number of other ships. The *Hornet* planes accounted for one carrier, two cruisers, a destroyer and some transports loaded with troops. Our squadron lost one plane, pilot and radioman, and we might not have lost them if the pilot had done what Gus tried to get them to do. He said for them to wait until he dropped his bomb and pulled out of his dive before they dove in - that way, he would knock out a (illegible) of AA guns, but this pilot (illegible) down and evidently pulled out of his (illegible) radioman. The gunner's name was Bush... (balance of page illegible).

On the 5th one of the *Yorktown* fighters landed aboard the *Hornet*. The plane and pilot were all shot up. The pilot was almost unconscious, so he forgot to turn off the gun switches. When his plane hit the deck, the right landing gear gave way and all the guns started firing. It sprayed a gun mount right behind the island with about 17 Marines on it. Killed most of them and killed the assistant gunnery officer up on the island. He was Admiral Ingersoll's son. Killed several more people there also. The plane was shot up so bad, we shoved it over the side. In a battle the flight deck has to be kept clear.

We chased the Japanese all the way back almost to Guam, then we had to turn back on account of we were in range of their land base bombers. We went back through the battle area looking for survivors. We ran through oil slicks for two days where sunken ships had made

USS Hornet Torpedo Shop Crew, May 1944.

them. We headed back to Pearl and everyone felt pretty good. We had given the Japanese navy its worst licking in all it's history. All the ships were flying their victory flag. We tied up first, then every ship that passed us on the way in gave the *Hornet* three big cheers and we did likewise.

Here I want to say a few words about the way information was kept by the crew while they were on liberty. If someone asked them where they had been, they would say hunting goldfish or gooney birds or something like that. No one hardly ever talked out of school.

Although this memoir ends prior to the battle that sunk the *Hornet* (or the pages are lost), Willie Fred Holloway stayed with the USS *Hornet* (CV-8) until the bitter end of her short life. During the final Battle at Coral Sea and while the ship was under attack, he and a mate wrestled a gun from the ship's armory, mounted it on the side of the ship and brought down a Japanese plane. For this, he was given a commendation

for bravery signed by Admiral Halsey. In stories recounted later, one memory that struck him was that while the ship was sinking (she took on water slowly), he was below decks helping with the efforts to save her. There was a considerable amount of money actually floating out of the men's lockers and bounding on top of the water amid all the turmoil. No one gave it a second glance or bothered to pick any of it up.

My father held something of a grudge against the *Enterpise* (the *Big E)* and her commander. He felt, along with a number of other crewman from the *Hornet*, that the *Hornet* could have been towed and repaired because they were taking on water very slowly. The *Enterprise* was the only ship available that was large enough to take the *Hornet* into tow. It was explained later that her commander had been given orders to leave the area because of the danger of another Japanese attack. Basically the *Hornet's* crew watched the *Enterprise* steam away while they somersaulted off the flight deck onto a destroyer then watched as the *Hornet* was sunk by our own forces. This did not engender tender feelings amongst the *Hornet* contingent,

On the deck of the USS Hornet: (left to right) Brookens, Williss, Meyer, Sims, and Lewis.

Night "Wave-Off".

orders or no, and he still spoke of it on occasion, until the day he died.

Personal notes: William Fred Holloway was born on April 10, 1921, in Sargent, Georgia, the middle son of three born to Carrie and Robert Holloway. He left school in the sixth grade to work in the cotton mills and helped support his family through the Depression. On April 10, 1940, he enlisted in the Navy at the age of 19. After basic training, he was assigned to the USS *Tuscaloosa* until 1942, then to the USS *Hornet* (CV-8) from the time of her shakedown cruise until she sank. After the Battle of Coral Sea, he spent time in the naval hospital in Seattle, then returned to Ordnance School. He was promoted to the rank of aviation chief ordnance man. During this time he met his future wife, Barbara Hammar, and they were later married in Seattle in 1944. Much to his disappointment, his naval career was cut short by a medical condition that necessitated an honorable discharge on December 13, 1944. He returned to Georgia and became a master sheet metal worker. At the time of his death on December 18, 1969, he was a site foreman as well as founder and secretary of the local Sheet Metal Workers Union. He is survived by his wife, Barbara Hammar Holloway, and three daughters: Kimberly Karr, Laura Joan Gelblat and Cynthia Crowder.

The family of William Fred Holloway wishes to express their pride and gratitude, not only for the sacrifices and bravery displayed by Willie Holloway, but all the men who served on the *Hornet* in her many incarnations. If a ship has a heart and soul, it is embodied in the men who serve aboard her. That being the case, then the *Hornet* must have the soul of a brave and true patriot and the heart of a warrior. Your children and grandchildren thank you gentlemen from the bottom of our hearts.

The First Day

by Stanton R. Newkirk

The following was written at sea aboard the USS Hornet during World War II and describes the first day of the Formosa (Tawain) Operation, October 12-13, 1944.

All day we have been expecting an attack. Why not? Our reasoning has it that we couldn't be in a better spot. As it is, we are between Luzon and a group of islands lying to the south of Japan. Ahead is Formosa. Yet the day passed and we have seen just one "Betty," presumably lost.

Walters and I, after the last hop had landed and had been reloaded, started out to give an "Atlantic City" job to our three planes. It was (and is) very windy topside, the sun had sunk below the horizon, and there was a touch of fall weather in the air. As we were walking back to the shack we were shoved by a gunner who was making knots along the flight deck. "Go," you guys, "better hurry!," he flung back over his shoulder. Walters started to run, I guess I was too tired to run anywhere. I glanced up as I walked along and noted that the huge radar antenna was facing starboard, and moving to and fro nervously. The after "40s" were not as yet manned, but gunners were forming a human caterpillar going up the ladder. As I walked on, I saw that the forward turrets were manned and directed starboard. The covers were off of their muzzles. When those boys take the muzzle covers off something is up! I walked over to the deck edge with a feeling of excitement and jubilance. Some fun tonight! Jack, Tommie, Willie and some more of the boys were standing on the catwalk and fairly dancing. "What's the dope, Radar," I said to Jack. He gave a big grin and sang out, It must be a "Betty" 'cause a Zeke don't fly like that." Then he added, "They're coming in around the clock."

I thought he was joking. The island batteries trained to port. Just as I was walking through the hatch a "tin can" and a cruiser opened up some distance off our port side. There were three big flashes of flame, and smoke which proved to be bombs; near misses luckily. I had seen enough!

In the armory, late-comers were giving out the "latest dope." The juke box played on. Cigarette consumption was (and is) enormous. One of the boys lay on a sack, shaking. Over in the corner, Cramer was on on

the "JG Talker" getting a play by play report of the action topside. "They're firing on port and starboard." Can dead ahead is opening up. Two bogies shot down. Hell you can see 'em burning on the water. Christ, they got another one."

Now that the firing was close, nervousness crept out in all of us. Smitty and Willie even stopped playing acey-duecy.

I went up topside to see what was going on. Tracers and 5-inch flashes bloomed off the port quarter in the other task group. There was an occasional 5-inch burst off to starboard. We started to lay a smoke screen. I left.

When I got to the armory, Reese, the Pittsburgh Kid, came in after me. I could see he had a lung full of smoke. He turned around and said complacently, "They're laying a smoke screen topside, that fresh air sure makes me homesick for Pennsylvania."

It's now 20:00. Everyone has calmed down, and reading, sleeping, batting the breeze. *Trumpet Blues* is playing. We are all dead tired. Every now and then someone comes in with the latest stuff. Jack just came in and said that they're firing port and starboard now, and added, "Now the fourth division stand by to receive torpedo off starboard quarter." I'm going up to take a look. Odd that I should change my mine! Our fantail 40s just opened up. The guy on the phones said that the Japanese had dropped a flare back there. The 5-inchers are opening up! Things are hot!

Salty just came in. He was up topside when they were firing. Riley asked him if they got the plane. Salty said, "Damned if I know, didn't stay to find out." Sensible I must say. I don't mind admitting that I'm nervous. Everyone is except Jack, he's asleep. Things will cool off shortly but we'll probably be at GQ all night. Damn! a full day of strikes tomorrow too.

P.S. The rest of the night was alternately quiet and studded with attacks and firing. We had a big chow next morning: Wheatcakes, bacon, grapefruit juice and coffee rolls were on the menu.

Members of VF-11 at Hilo Yacht Club, April - June, 1944.

Flight deck looking aft: FJ4-Bs, F2Hs, AD-6s, AD-7s, and AJ-1 Savages.

The Day The Beast Turned Ugly

by Albert F. Reynolds

The day was July 9, 1944, and I was flying my assigned SB2C-1C "Beast" off the USS *Hornet* (CV-12) on a dive bombing strike against a pill box target on Guam. I was flying wing on Lieutenant Commander Smith in VB-2 Wing B. My gunner was Kermit "Dipsy" Youmans, ARM1/c. As detailed in my report to the Bombing Squadron Two Trouble Board, the left aileron failed on pull-out from the diving run, and my gunner and I were forced to bail out over the fleet where we were both picked up by destroyers and returned to the *Hornet*.

A few weeks after my bail-out, another dive bomber pilot experienced the failure of both ailerons in a pull-out. He was able to land his plane on the newly constructed dirt strip on Guam where our engineering officer, Lieutenant Mike Micheel, was able to examine the bell crank area of the control stick. He found that the dural alloy to which the aileron control wires were attached had failed. This resulted in the loss of all aileron control. In my case, with only the left aileron disabled, the plane was thrown into a violent roll-over, with the aileron stuck at an upwards angle of about 40°. Fortunately, I had been trained in aerobatics in CPTP Secondary by a former barnstormer, George Gerry, who drilled me endlessly on getting the stick forward whenever I was inverted. It was this instinct which took over when my plane was upside down and headed for the deck at the pull-out from my dive.

To finish up, I resumed flying missions on July 19, 1944, in a strike on Guam and flew a final September 7 strike on Palau. After the Palau mission, Doc Stratton found that I had developed viral pneumonia from my immersion on July 9. That finished my combat flying for VB-2. The pneumonia went into pleurisy, then into empyema. By the time I got back to Oak Knoll Hospital in Oakland, California, in October, my chest cavity was filled with pus and I faced re-section surgery which would have ended my flying career. It was my good fortune to have a Mayo Clinic doctor who told me that there was a new medicine called penicillin which might clear up the infection. He injected the medicine directly into my chest cavity. He was right. It took seven months but I recovered completely and served as a test and acceptance pilot at Harry Guggenheim's "Happy Acres" at NAF, Trenton, and at NAS, Floyd Bennett, until my discharge in 1946.

I look back on my duty as a naval aviator and especially my tour with VB-2, as the highlight of my life.

Memories

by Gordon H. Robertson

The period January 1967 to January 1968 when I was commanding officer USS *Hornet* (CVS-12) left me with many great memories. A couple are detailed below. First, some background to put these into perspective.

On March 27, 1967, *Hornet* departed from its Long Beach homeport for a second deployment to the Far East in support of the Navy's mission in Vietnam. It was a 60,000 mile cruise which included 128 days in the Gulf of Tonkin, and ASW exercises in the Sea of Japan and the South China Sea. Liberty call sounded in ports as familiar as Honolulu and remote as Bangkok.

Hornet was a member of Anti-Submarine Warfare Group Three. Embarked was Commander, ASW Group Three, his Staff, and Carrier Anti-Submarine Air Group 57. The Air Group was comprised of Helicopter Anti-Submarine Squadron Two (flying SH3A-Sea King), Air Anti-Submarine Squadrons 35 and 37 (flying S-2E-Tracker), and Detachment 12 of Carrier Airborne Early Warning Squadron 111 (flying E-2A-Hawkeye).

Deploying with *Hornet* as part of ASW Group Three was Escort Squadron Three composed of USS *Bronstein* (DE-1037), USS *Hooper* (DE-1026), USS *Bridget* (DE-1024) and USS *Evans* (DE-1027) and Destroyer Squadron 11 composed of USS *Davidson* (DE-1045), USS *Jenkins* (DD-447), USS *Taylor* (DD-468), and USS *Walker* (DD-517).

The primary mission of *Hornet* was antisubmarine warfare. During the deployment, exercises were conducted with naval and air forces from Australia, Great Britain, New Zealand, Republic of the Philippines, Thailand, Japan and the Republic of Korea. Following deployment *Hornet* was the recipient of the Anti-Submarine Warfare Excellence Award for Anti-Submarine Warfare carriers assigned to NAVAIRPAC during the competitive cycle of January 1, 1967 to June 30, 1968.

Another major mission during the deployment was support of Task Force 77, a powerful force of aircraft carriers and other ships operating on "Yankee Station" in the Gulf of Tonkin. *Hornet* provided around-the-clock surface surveillance, served as a postal center for receiving, distributing, and dispatching mail for TF-77, and provided search and rescue efforts (SAR) with its embarked helicopter squadron. During deployment 91,567 pounds of mail was delivered to other ships. *Hornet* assumed the role of a supply and repair ship for many destroyers, providing everything from a transitor to a 400 pound motor.

The SAR sorties were remarkable. The helicopters, designed for ASW missions, had been modified by the addition of armor plate on the pilots seats and the addition of a machine gun mount with a breast plate in the side doorway. Upon receipt of word of a downed pilot, the hilo rescue crew, having been briefed regarding coastal areas with the lightest enemy anti-aircraft fire capability, would launch immediately for a rescue attempt. All rescue missions were conducted in the face of varying degrees of opposing fire, some very heavy. The squadron accomplished nine rescues of pilots, and had seven other attempts thwarted either by the capture of the downed pilot or because of damage to the helicopter.

In May 1967, a *Hornet* hilo returning to the ship from a mission off the coast of North Vietnam developed mechanical difficulties and made an emergency landing on the cruiser USS *Long Beach*, which was stationed just outside Haiphong Harbor. Attempts to repair the hilo were unsuccessful. In order to salvage the aircraft, the captain of the *Long Beach* and I decided upon an at-sea transfer. Upon rendezvousing, the *Long Beach* captain maneuvered his ship forward of *Hornet*, which was laying to. The stern of the cruiser was maneuvered under the flight deck overhang. With the flight deck crane positioned so that its hook would drop directly down to engage the hoisting sling attached to the hilo, and with hand lines to steady the hilo, it was hoisted aboard with all observers admiring the ship handling skill of the Long Beach Captain. A few weeks later, a second hilo, also damaged, landed on Long Beach. It, too, was brought aboard in a generally similar manner.

One memorable liberty port was Hong Kong. *Hornet* and six of her eight ASW destroyers visited Hong Kong in August. (The other two destroyers remained in the Gulf to provide coastal gun fire support.) At 0600 Sunday, having been in port just two days of an expected seven day visit, we were notified by the port authority that all of our group had to clear our anchorage's by 1,200 that day. An approaching typhoon was a possible threat to the area and our berths were required to provide a safe harbor for merchant vessels. Upon clearing harbor, transiting the lengthy channel and reaching the open sea, destroyers had to be fueled. All were at dangerously low fuel levels because plans were to fuel in port just prior to expected departure time. With the emergency sortie, there was no time to top-off in port.

About 1700 the destroyers, one by one, began to come along *Hornet's* starboard side to receive fuel. Wind and seas were increasing, but the first couple of refuelings went well, each taking somewhat over an hour, instead of a normal 40 minutes. It was soon black as the Ace of Spades, seas had really kicked up, and the wind was about 40 knots. It was difficult to get the lines across, hoses would get part way across and not uncommonly would be submerged en route to the receiving ship. With winds increasing to 55 knots and heavy seas, hoses were pulled loose from the receiving ship, spilling the oil over an already slick deck. Men would be knocked from their feet by water surging across the decks. Fortunately, no one was lost or seriously injured. Refueling of all six destroyers was completed shortly after 0100 the next day. It was one experience that I will always remember, and I feel certain many others will also.

During the landing on Guam in July 1944, on about D+3 or 4, I joined six or seven other pilots of Bombing Squadron Two to make a trip ashore. One of the pilots had a brother attached to a Marine regiment that he believed was involved in the landing. It would be great fun if we could have a brief visit with him! *Hornet* was anchored off-shore for the day for rearming. The coxswain of a rearming barge, which had just off-loaded, agreed to take us ashore en route to his returning to his ship.

In early afternoon, after a fruitless search, we thought it best to return to the little finger pier (the only one left standing within view along the beach) which we used in going ashore. No

rearming boats were running - the only things afloat were the warships anchored well offshore.

After some time, while trying to decide what to do next, Admiral Jocko Clark's barge came to the pier. The coxswain, there to pick-up the admiral, said that he would try to return us to the ship. Soon the admiral and three of his staff came to the pier from exploring ashore. He wondered what we were doing there and how we intended to return to *Hornet*. When told that we planned to catch the next mail boat, his response left no doubt in our minds that he thought we had lost them.

At the coxswain's request, Admiral Clark agreed to let us return with him. The barge could take all but three of us. With the Admiral's permission the barge would return for the remaining three. "Very Well," said Admiral Clark, "but come hell or high water, we're getting underway at 1700." The coxswain did return us to the ship just as *Hornet* was weighing anchor and the last of the gangways was being brought up. We rode the barge as it was hoisted aboard as *Hornet* got underway. We almost joined the Marines that day.

America Strikes Back
The Doolittle Raid

by Earl L. Miller

"What kind of an airplane is that?" someone asked as a group of us watched an airplane which had never been seen on a carrier before being hoisted aboard. "They say its an Army B-25 bomber," someone replied.

The USS *Hornet* (CV-8) was in Norfolk, Virginia at the time. It was not long after the devastating sneak attack on Pearl Harbor by Japanese carrier based planes. The *Hornet* had just been commissioned on October 20, 1941, and was still having finishing touches completed before being battle ready.

Once this newcomer aircraft was settled safely aboard, we looked it over more carefully. It was quite formidable in appearance, with two powerful engines, a gull wing and twin rudders. A pair of machine guns protruded from the bom-

bardiers plexiglass window in the nose and another pair was mounted in a turret atop the fuselage. It was painted in the traditional olive drab of the Army.

The next day we went to sea for some tests during which the B-25 took off with little trouble and was seen no more. We just assumed it was a test to see if forward bases could be reinforced that way and so dismissed it from our minds.

The day came at last when the *Hornet* was declared battle ready and we set forth to join the fray. We were well escorted as we proceeded southward through the submarine infested waters of the East Coast. With much scraping and grinding we barely eased our way through the locks of the Panama Canal then on up the West Coast to San Diego where we had a few days of rest and recreation. From there on to San Francisco Bay where we moored alongside a dock at the Alameda Naval Air Station. Some planes were to be loaded aboard, and since I was not involved in that operation and I was only 30 miles from home, I requested a 48 hour leave. It was granted and I was informed that when I returned the ship would be anchored in mid-stream, that is, in the middle of the bay.

When my leave was up, my parents drove me to San Francisco to where I thought the liberty boats might be coming ashore. Fortunately, we found the place quite easily and there was a *Hornet* motor launch alongside the dock at the time. So we hurriedly said our good-byes and I hopped aboard the launch just as they were ready to shove off. As we headed out into the bay, I could see the *Hornet* at anchor there and she looked beautiful in the morning light. But what were those dark colored planes on the flight deck? They extended from the very forward edge of the flight deck all the way aft until their tails protruded over the after end. As we got closer I could see they were B-25s like the one that had flown off at Norfolk, but these wouldn't be flying off. There was no room for a takeoff run. So we must be delivering them somewhere.

In another day or two, when all supplies had been loaded aboard and everything was made ready for sea, the anchor chain came clunking up through the hause pipe and the *Hor-*

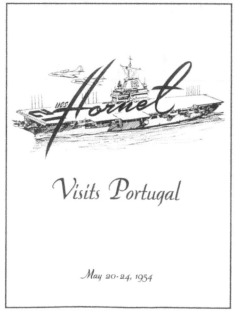

U.S.S. Hornet

Visits Portugal

May 20-24, 1954

今日ハ才嬢サン

Japan

AUGUST '54

U.S.S. Hornet CVA-12

net trembled a little as the screws began pushing her forward on a long and eventful journey. As she steamed through the Golden Gate in broad daylight accompanied by several cruisers and destroyers, no one observing her could imagine what her mission was.

Before the Golden Gate Bridge had faded from sight, the crew was to learn what their next destination was to be. The captain called for the attention of all hands as he made the dramatic announcement over the speaker system. Our mission was to approach within striking distance of the Japanese mainland and launch the B-25s manned by the Army aviators aboard and led by Colonel Jimmy Doolittle. Their objective would be to bomb various strategic targets in Tokyo and other Japanese cities and to proceed to a designated field in an area of China not yet occupied by the Japanese.

As the captain finished speaking, cheers and an aura of excitement permeated the ship. I cheered at the thought of striking back at the Japanese, but it was definitely with mixed emotions as I was well aware of the tremendous risk we were taking by venturing into the home waters of Hirohito's domain. We would need all the help we could get from above to pull this one off.

The leader of the raiders, Colonel Doolittle, was a well-known aviator of racing fame and the holder of records for speed distance and altitude. His crews had been selected from volunteers who were only told they would be going into training for a "secret mission."

Since December 7 the news for our nation had been all bad and the people felt really frustrated at our inability to strike back at our attackers. Such a raid as this would be just the

moral booster that was sorely needed to raise the spirits of the home folks, and for that reason it was considered worth the risk to give it our best try.

As our little task group plowed westward across the Pacific, the mystery of how the planes were to takeoff became apparent. The flight deck crews were put to work moving the planes aft and fitting them together in a pre-planned pattern like a jigsaw puzzle, until the entire forward half of the flight deck was clear. Obviously the planes had been spread out to confuse any possible spies who might be reporting on our departure.

I was able to observe all that was going on because my duty during flight operations was, with the assistance of three others, to replace any arresting gear cable which had been snapped by a landing aircraft. This had to be done as quickly as possible so that landing operations wouldn't be interrupted. Since our own planes would not be involved until after the B-25s were launched, I was free to move about and take note of all the activity.

Our course was plotted well clear of any islands, even Hawaii, and we were headed directly toward Japan. The *Enterprise*, accompanied by several cruisers and destroyers, joined us en route. The *Enterprise* was to supply air cover, searches and anti-submarine patrols. All the *Hornet's* planes had been crammed into the hangar deck space. Some even suspended from the overhead like models hanging from the ceiling of a little boy's room. A photo session was held with some of the bombs lined up in the foreground and the B-25 crews standing or kneeling behind them. The bombs had messages written on them in large letters with various greetings to Tojo. There were also a number of medals fastened to them which some military men had received from Japan and wanted returned.

As the bombs were loaded aboard the planes, we could see that only half the bomb bay was available. The other half was completely filled with a huge auxiliary gas tank. Also there were a number of incendiary type bombs included. They resembled a bunch of sticks held together by straps. When dropped, the straps released, allowed the phosphorous sticks to scatter over a large area, setting fires.

When we were just a few days away from our launching point, we met with an oil tanker for the purpose of refueling all ships. Taking on fuel at sea is a hairy proposition to begin with, but we were going to do it at night. The ship being fueled and also the tanker must hold a steady course side by side and match speeds as well. Then lines are passed across and large, heavy, stiff, black fuel hoses are pulled over to the ship being fueled. These hoses must be bolted to the intake valves on the receiving ship and then constantly monitored, slacked off or taken in, as the distance between the ships changes slightly. Getting all this done on a pitch black night and being vigilant not to show a single flicker of light, which might reveal our presence to the enemy, was a masterpiece of seamanship. The next day the *Hornet* refueled several destroyers while other cruisers and destroyers took on fuel from the tanker. This having been done and the planes all armed and fueled, we were ready to make our high speed run to the launching point for the bombers. The plan being to run all night at high speed toward the target area, launch the planes at dawn and high tail it out of there.

However, you know what they say about the best laid plans of mice and men. The day before the planned launch we were cruising

Pilots and enlisted men of VF-11, Hilo, Hawaii; April - June 1944.

USS Hornet (CV-8) loaded with Army B-25 aircraft on way to raid Tokyo.

Top row (left to right) Wenke, Dow, Powell, San Fillipo, Smith. Middle: Johnson, Wise, Riley, Moss, Lindsley, Brown, Sorenson. Front: Beck, Picirilli, Riffel, Prothra, Jung, Coln, McDonnell, Mossey.

A Lieutenant shines the ship's bell dong with polish on Initiation Day.

along on course, when I heard the roar of a broadside being fired by a heavy ship of the line. I looked in the direction of the sound just in time to see the spout of water rising from the spot where the shells had struck and the smoke of another broadside fired by a heavy cruiser. I couldn't see the target at first, but occasionally caught a glimpse of a dark object in the distance. As the cruiser continued to fire, I could see planes from the *Enterprise* aiding in the destruction with their dive bombing runs. We had the misfortune of running upon a Japanese picket boat, which resembles a large fishing boat. The unequal battle was soon over as the unfortunate vessel was sent to the bottom. The *Hornet* slowly cruised by the spot of the sinking in search of survivors, but only oil and pieces of wooden debris was visible.

In the wake of this event, the officers in charge of the raid were sent scurrying back to the drawing board. It was quite possible that the picket boat had sent a radio alarm signal before meeting its fate. Rather than take the risk of meeting an alerted defense force, it was decided to launch the raid at the earliest possible moment. Since the distance would be much greater, additional gasoline would have to be loaded aboard the planes. This was done by the use of five gallon tins, which must have made the interior of the planes rather cramped for space. While engine covers were being removed and the planes otherwise being made ready for flight, the *Hornet* was proceeding toward Japan at top speed in order to reduce the distance to the target. The wind was increasing and the sea was getting rougher. As the bow plunged into each oncoming roller, the spray would fly the length of the flight deck. The crewmen had to contend with the elements of a pitching deck, strong winds, and a slippery footing.

At last all was ready, engines were started and warmed up, the tie down lines, which had been holding the planes in place, were released, and the first plane, piloted by Colonel Doolittle, taxied to the launching point. The gale was estimated at 40 knots. Add to this the speed of the *Hornet*, which was headed directly into it, and you get an idea of how windy it was on deck.

If the pilots were nervous about taking their heavily laden planes off with such a short takeoff, they could take comfort in knowing that this headwind would add considerably to the lift of their wings in getting them airborne. Colonel Doolittle would set the example by being the first to launch. The bow of the ship was rising and falling with the seas. The takeoff run had to be timed so that the plane would reach the end of the flight deck when it was at its highest point. This was the duty of the flight deck officer who would wave his flag in a circular motion for the pilot to apply full power, and, when the timing was just right, sweep it down and forward to indicate to the pilot to release his brakes and start his run.

Finally that historic moment came when Colonel Doolittle got that signal and his plane went roaring down the deck seeming to gather speed rather slowly, but when he reached the end of the deck he lifted it off very smoothly. Then the bow of the ship dipped and rose up again, and the plane disappeared from sight as though sinking toward the sea. We all watched breathlessly as the bow lowered again, and there was the colonel flying along quite safely. One by one the remaining planes were released from their tethers and taxied to the takeoff point. There were only a few incidents to report on the launching. One of the pilots pulled up a little sharply and bumped his tail skid on the end of the flight deck. Fortunately not to severely, as he soared off as though nothing had happened. Another pilot forgot to put his flaps down, but that didn't seem to have any effect on his takeoff either. The one incident which was most tragic, was when one of the flight deck crewmen was struck on the arm by a whirling propeller. He was releasing the tie down lines and slipped on the wet deck. His arm had to be amputated, but, fortunately, his life was spared.

While the launching was in progress, the B-25s already airborne would make one large circle while gaining altitude. We would watch each one fly over the ships while silhouetted against a lead colored sky and set his course for his individually assigned target.

We wished them God speed, each and every one.

The *Hornet* and her accompanying task force, having completed all that could be done to send the raiders on their way, turned their tails toward Japan and set their course for Pearl at flank speed.

The plane handlers were busy getting the *Hornet's* planes up from the hangar deck, armed, fueled, and otherwise ready for possible defensive action, but we cleared the area without further incident.

Since the B-25s were capable of over 300 miles per hour, it was estimated that they would be over their targets in about two hours. We were all anxiously awaiting the news as to their success. There was an officer who was fluent in Japanese. His duty was to monitor the radio stations in Japan. When it was time for the raiders expected arrival, the broadcasts suddenly turned to panic and pandemonium. There were reports of thousands of people being killed, which, of course, was false, and then the stations went off the air.

We were overjoyed with the knowledge that the surprise attack had been successful, but were concerned for the safety of the daring airmen.

After one more refueling, we proceeded to Pearl Harbor where we saw the destruction left by the December 7 attack for the first time. We moored to a dock on the north side of Ford Island opposite to where battleship row had suffered such severe damage. While provisions were being loaded aboard, portions of the crew were given liberty to go to Honolulu.

Japan was reporting the usual, that schools and hospitals had been bombed. Although the damage done by the raid was not extensive, the boost to the moral of the American populace was incalculable. There was much speculation as to where the planes might have come from. President Roosevelt said "Shangri La," but I don't think the Japanese were fooled for very long. As a result of the attack they had to withdraw many ships and planes for the defense of their homeland.

The early launching may have saved the *Hornet* task force from coming under attack, but it was disastrous for the raiders. Headwinds left them with little fuel as they approached the Chinese mainland. A radio signal which was to guide them to their landing field, never materialized. As their tanks ran dry, some attempted landings in the stormy darkness, while most of them, including Colonel Doolittle, parachuted to safety. Only one plane didn't crash, it landed at a Russian airfield and its crew was detained for the duration of the war.

The Chinese people did all they could to help the grounded aviators to escape, but when the Japanese army arrived, they burned the villages and executed all the Chinese suspected of having given aid to the raiders. Several aviators were captured, tried, and at least one, beheaded by the Japanese.

Colonel Doolittle attained the rank of general before the war's end. He has since passed away, but the remaining survivors of the raid still have an occasional reunion.

The USS *Hornet* (CV-8) at Midway

by Earl L. Miller

In the prelude to the Battle of Midway, events seemed to be moving along quite rapidly. The USS *Hornet* (CV-8) had just returned to Pearl Harbor after launching the Doolittle raid on Tokyo, which took place on April 18, 1942, when a report came in that a task force including three of our carriers was engaged in a raging battle in the Coral Sea. The *Hornet* and a task force of cruisers and destroyers was dispatched to the area to throw our weight into the fray, but the engagement was broken off before we got halfway to our destination.

The Battle of the Coral Sea was the first sea battle fought entirely by aircraft. The opposing fleets never came in sight of one another. A huge Japanese invasion force had been sighted headed southward and it was determined that its intention was to attack and occupy Port Moresby, New Guinea. This strategic port in the hands of the enemy would compose a dire threat to Australia itself. Therefore the Allied forces threw everything in their command against the enemy armada. The Japanese had four aircraft carriers

covering the fleet. The Americans could only muster up three, the *Yorktown, Enterprise* and *Lexington.* When these two forces came within striking distance of one another, both sides launched their attacking aircraft. The battle was a furious one with both sides suffering serious damage to their carriers. The *Lexington* was set afire and had to be abandoned and sunk and the *Yorktown* received considerable bomb damage. Only the *Enterprise* was slightly damaged. The Japanese also lost one carrier with three damaged. At this point the Allies appeared to be the losers, but the Japanese admiral ordered his invasion force to turn around and retreat. So the invasion of Port Moresby was averted and the threat to Australia didn't materialize. This was a great victory for the Allies.

The *Hornet* continued to steam southward and the scuttlebutt was that we wanted the Japanese to find out that we were there. This seemed strange at the time, but later it would all become clear to us. One afternoon General Quarters sounded and at our arrival at our battle stations we learned that a "Bogey," an unidentified, aircraft had been picked up on the radar and was headed in our direction. I was "Talker" on 5-inch anti-aircraft guns five and six at the time, located on the starboard side aft, and was in communication with fire control by headphones. The gun crews and I had been scanning the horizon for the sight of an enemy plane for about 20 minutes, when I saw in the distance a black column of smoke. It emerged from a cloud and descended to the sea. A Kawanishi flying boat on patrol had sighted us, radioed his report, and fallen victim to the guns of the fighters of our combat patrol. I reported what I had seen to fire control and soon we were secured from general quarters. From that day we headed northward toward Pearl.

We steamed slowly into the harbor past the cranes, work barges and tugs. The cutting torches and welding torches sparkled as the workmen worked feverishly around the clock to salvage and repair the ships and other facilities that had been damaged in the December 7 attack. We moored on the north side of Ford Island and proceeded with the routine business of taking on

fuel oil, aviation gasoline, fresh water and provisions.

While all this was going on, there were important and exciting things happening in Admiral Nimitz headquarters.

Our intelligence department had broken the Japanese code and we were translating all their radio transmissions. From these we learned the Japanese were planning a massive attack with the intention of occupying a small island, only six miles in diameter, known as Midway. This island, defended by Marines and Navy, was 3,500 miles from Tokyo, but only a 1,000 from Hawaii. Whoever controlled this island, controlled the entire northern Pacific. So that was its tremendous strategic value.

The intercepted messages continued to reveal Admiral Yamamoto's brilliant plan for conquest. A diversionary force was to attack the Aleutian Islands to draw our attention away from the principal target. A carrier force consisting of the same four carriers used in the Pearl Harbor attack, the *Akagi, Soryu, Kaga* and *Hiryu*, were to bomb the airfield and destroy as much of the other defenses as possible. A second force, consisting of seven battleships, three light cruisers and 20 destroyers, was to follow up and prepare the way for yet a third group consisting of transports with an invasion force of 5,000 troops aboard.

As the *Hornet* and *Enterprise* prepared to put to sea again, a battle scared veteran of the Coral Sea steamed into port. It was the *Yorktown*, which had suffered such severe damage that it would normally take weeks or even months to repair. However, Admiral Nimitz ordered that it be done in three days and it was.

The American counter-forces sailed on May 28, 1942. They took stations 325 miles northeast of Midway and when the *Yorktown* joined up a few days later, the preparations for Yamamoto's little surprise party were all in place.

Long distance search planes, PBYs, were radiating out from Midway trying to locate the approaching fleet, but a weather front was moving along with them, giving them cloud cover which made sighting difficult. On June 2, Dutch Harbor, in the Aleutians, was hit by the diver-

Radar group trained at Barbeis Point NAS, 1945.

sionary force and on June 3, one group of the Midway attack force was sighted. However, it did not include the carriers. B-17s from Midway made a high level bombing run, but no hits were made. Contact was lost over night. Midway was equipped with an early model radar and at dawn of June 4 a large number of enemy planes was detected at a distance of about 60 miles. All aircraft on Midway, fighters, dive bombers and heavy bombers were scrambled, some to meet the attack and others to be preserved from destruction. The source of the attack, the four carriers, was finally spotted. Admiral Nagumo, who had directed the attack on Pearl Harbor, was in command aboard the *Akagi*. At this time he was still unaware that any American carriers were in the vicinity. He thought that he had obtained complete surprise. The squadron leaders of his returning planes reported a second strike would be necessary so he ordered the planes rearmed with the type of bombs used in a ground attack. When the rearming was half completed, the Admiral received a report that American carrier based planes had been sighted. He ordered the planes to be rearmed for action against carriers.

Meanwhile, upon receiving a report of the approximate location of the Japanese carriers, Admiral Spruance, who was in command of the American forces, ordered all carriers to launch planes to the attack.

Aboard the *Hornet* excitement was at a fever pitch. It would be the first time our own planes would be launched to attack the enemy. In the Doolittle raid the Army B-25s were the aggressors.

The words "Pilots Man Your Planes" blared out over the bull horn. The pilots and their crewmen scrambled into their cockpits and strapped themselves in with the aid of their respective crew chiefs. "Stand By To Start Engines" was the next command, followed shortly by "Start Engines." Propellers whirled and engines coughed and spit gobs of smoke from their exhausts before roaring into life. The signal to launch planes came from flight control and the flight deck officer waved the first plane into its takeoff run. It roared down the flight deck and as soon as it had cleared the deck and veered off to the right, the next plane was started on its way. Plane after plane zoomed off into the wild blue yonder in a seemingly endless procession. Stubby little F-4-F fighters were followed by Douglas Dauntless dive bombers with 500-pound bombs slung under their bellies. Finally the large Douglas Devastator torpedo planes lumbered down the deck with long slim "fish" secured below their fuselages. At last all was quiet on deck as the various squadrons from the three carriers formed up and headed toward the target area. I gazed with awe at this huge armada of aircraft the likes of which I had never seen before.

Unfortunately, after having flown the required distance and arriving at the last reported position of the enemy, no Japanese ships were to be seen. The commanding officer of the *Hornet's* torpedo eight, Lieutenant Commander John C. Waldron, correctly estimated their new location. However, after reporting this, he determined that he would be unable to wait for the other planes to arrive to make a concentrated attack. Fuel limitations and the fact that the zeros of the Japanese combat air patrol were diving to

Memorial service for Lt. (jg) E.W. Gallant USNR, August 23, 1955.

the attack, led to this decision. So the order to commence their torpedo runs was given. As the torpedo bombers swooped down to sea level they were pounced upon furiously by the defending zeros. The slow, old model planes were no match for the agile zeros. Soon most were shot down. The few remaining had to slow down even more to launch their torpedoes which were of a type that would disintegrate upon contact with the water if launched at too great a speed. The antiaircraft fire from the ships shot down the last few attackers and all 15 of the Hornet's torpedo bombers were lost. No hits were scored.

However, the gallant men of Torpedo 8 had not given their lives in vain. The zig-zagging and defensive action of the carriers during the attack had interfered with the rearming and launching of their aircraft. Also the Japanese defensive air cover had been drawn down to a low altitude while attacking the torpedo bombers. The remaining dive bomber and torpedo squadrons from the American carriers arrived on the scene about this time. They were able to make their bombing runs with greatly reduced opposition from the air. The Japanese carriers were caught with most of their aircraft still on deck. The *Akagi, Soryu* and *Kaga* were each hit by three or four bombs. Explosions and fire wracked the ships as planes, gasoline and armaments were ignited on both their flight and hangar decks. Many of their experienced pilots were killed while sitting in their cockpits preparing to takeoff. In addition the *Soryu* was hit by at least one torpedo from the submarine, *Nautilus*. These three carriers were beyond salvage and soon sank, leaving only the *Hiryu* still operational.

Aboard the *Hornet*, we launched a new combat air patrol as soon as the first of our returning attack force appeared on the horizon. The fighters and dive bombers circled around and were taken aboard one by one, but we waited in vain for any torpedo planes to show up. We still waited hopefully, but as the time for their fuel supplies ran out, we had to accept what we feared all along, that none would come back. Even as the crews worked feverishly to rearm and refuel the planes, we couldn't help feeling the sadness for our lost comrades. There would be 30 empty bunks in the officers rooms and crews quarters

tonight, and when the action was over, lockers to be emptied and letters to be written to the families of those who fell in the heat of battle.

It was mid-day now and we could just see the *Yorktown* as a spot on the horizon. Small specks could be seen swarming around her like bees around a hive. We knew she was under air attack and we expected to receive the same treatment soon, but none of the planes came in our direction.

The remaining Japanese carrier, the *Hiryu*, had gotten off an attack force of 18 Val dive bombers, six zeros and a number of Kate torpedo bombers. Five Vals got through and made three bomb hits on the *Yorktown*. Four Kates also got through and made two torpedo hits. One plane crashed into the ship.

As this action was taking place, planes from the American carriers were attacking the Hiryu. Four bomb hits were scored and the last of the Japanese carriers went to the bottom.

Despite the severe damage suffered by the *Yorktown*, her crew snuffed out the fires and had her operational in about an hour and a half. However, the victory was short-lived as a Japanese submarine commander had his dreams come true. He fired a spread of torpedoes at the *Yorktown* and obtained several hits. Unfortunately, the destroyer *Hammond* was alongside the *Yorktown* at the time and was also hit. The *Hammond* sank in only a few minutes, and again unfortunately, her depth charges were armed, set to go off at a certain depth. When the sinking ship reached that depth, the charges exploded, taking a tremendous toll of the crewmen struggling in the water.

This was also a death knell for the *Yorktown* as she was no longer salvageable and had to be abandoned. The American carriers too aboard their planes and all flight activities were suspended for the night.

Upon hearing about the disastrous surprise party in the form of an ambush that had befallen his fleet, Admiral Yamamoto ordered a general retreat. We aboard the American ships were eager to follow up and pound as many more of the Japanese ships to the bottom as we possibly could. For this reason we were puzzled and disturbed when, during the night, we found our-

Protestant service at sea, 1955, CDR John Wise, Chaplin.

"Drink, dine, and dance in the EM Club."

selves steaming slowly eastward, away from the battle scene. Admiral Spruance had rightly guessed that the Japanese high command would attempt to lure us within the range of the big guns on the seven battleships in his follow-up contingent, but our admirals didn't fall for this one and wisely chose to proceed with caution as we didn't know the disposition of the enemy fleet during the night.

The following day, two straggling enemy cruisers were attacked. One sank and the other was severely damaged. Also, the battle scene of the previous day was being scoured by PBYs and submarines looking for downed aviators. It was then we learned that among the many rescued, was one of our torpedo plane pilots, Ensign Gay. He had been drifting right in the middle of all the fighting and was able to tell our intelligence department many of the details of the action. He hid among floating debris as the Japanese ships steamed by.

When the final score was tallied, the Japanese had lost four carriers, 332 aircraft and 2,500 men. US losses were one carrier, one destroyer, 147 aircraft and 307 men. Of 41 torpedo bombers dispatched, only six survived.

The USS *Enterprise* continued to serve throughout the war and was present with the *Hornet* five months later when the *Hornet* received her fatal blows at the Battle of Santa Cruz. This occurred only a year and six days after the commissioning of the USS *Hornet*.

Rest In Peace

by Earl L. Miller

The USS *Hornet* (CV-8), accompanied by several cruisers and destroyers, was patrolling off Guadalcanal attempting to prevent the Japanese from re-enforcing their troops on the island. We felt awful lonely and vulnerable out there as we were the only aircraft carrier left in service at the time. The *Lexington* went down in the Coral Seas followed by *Yorktown* at Midway and *Wasp* near Guadalcanal. The *Saratoga* was in repair from torpedo damage and the *Enterprise* from bomb damage. It didn't help that we got word that a very large enemy naval force was on the way to try to force a conclusion to the battle over this strategic island. The report that this armada included four aircraft carriers was par-

ticularly chilling. For several days apprehension over the impending battle was building up when on October 24 we were considerably relieved to be joined by another task force which included the *Enterprise*. This came just in time as on the 25th the enemy force was sighted, but no contact was made.

So then we came to that fateful day, October 26, when the battle was sure to take place. In the blackness before dawn we manned our battle stations. Our planes were already on deck spotted for takeoff, fully armed and fueled. Our combat air patrol was warmed up and took off at the first light of dawn. The *Enterprise* sent out a search group and our planes were held in readiness for a report of contact.

For several hours we steamed along slowly. The gun crews were quiet and apprehensive as the lookouts scanned the horizon. Then, a little after 8:00, the loud speakers blared out, "Pilots man your planes." The flight deck crews scurried about, engines coughed and burst into life. The order to launch aircraft was given and one by one our fighters, bombers and torpedo planes roared down the deck, leaped into the air and formed into Vs as they circled overhead. The long awaited battle was about to begin.

About an hour after our attack force disappeared over the horizon, they sent back word that they were passing large groups of enemy aircraft headed in our direction. Both groups continued on their way without engaging in combat. After hearing this, we rechecked our flash clothes, helmets and life jackets. I was the talker for 5-inch anti-aircraft guns 5 and 7, located in a sponson on the starboard quarter of the ship, so I wore one of those oversize helmets that fit over the earphones.

The *Enterprise* group was about 10 miles from us and had just entered a rain squall. There were scattered clouds over us and passing through an open area I saw a formation of silver colored aircraft. There was no doubt as to their identity. I reported the sighting and within seconds all our ships opened fire. An anti-aircraft cruiser on our starboard beam resembled a volcano erupting as it was almost obliterated from sight by the fire from its guns. I saw one or two planes plunge into the sea on our starboard side, but I couldn't observe everything because there was too much activity going on, and the smoke from our guns sometimes made seeing difficult.

The *Enterprise* was not sighted and the entire attack centered on the *Hornet*. The Japanese had the advantage of a coordinated attack with dive bombers, torpedo planes and strafing aircraft coming at us from all directions, this causing us to divide our targets.

The first bomb that came near us was a near miss, striking the water about 50 feet from our gun position. The second one hit the flight deck about 30 feet inboard from us. We later learned that this was an anti-personnel type and had killed all the Marines manning the 20 mm guns forward of us along the catwalks. Since the 5-inch guns were located below the level of the flight deck, the shrapnel went over our heads, but the Marines were about waist high above the flight deck, so they caught the full force of it. It blew a hole about 10 feet across and also sprayed shrapnel on the hangar deck below killing and wounding a number of men there. Two other bombs pierced the flight deck, but their delayed action fuses did not ignite until they reached the third deck. One exploded in the ammunition handling room for our guns, killing all personnel there. Only smoke came up through the ammunition hoists indicating to us that something tragic had happened there. We continued to use ammo from the ready boxes as we observed smoke drifting over our position from fires up forward. We didn't know it at the time, but the fire was the result of a diving aircraft hitting the forward port corner of the smoke stack, glancing off and hitting the flight deck. One of its bombs exploded on initial contact, destroying the signal bridge. Another bomb exploded when it hit the deck blowing a large hole there. A third bomb was a dud and lay in the ready room compartment just below the flight deck.

No sooner had this happened than we were struck by two torpedoes in rapid succession. They both struck the starboard side amidships. These explosions caused the ship to leap into the air and vibrate violently. We felt like we were standing on a springboard being tossed into the air with each upward movement. The projectiles in the ready boxes were tossed out on the deck and several of us were scrambling about wildly trying to keep them from rolling around and to capture them and get them back in the boxes. This was quickly followed by another fire up forward which we later learned had been caused by a plane flying horizontal to the water and just above the main deck level striking the port side just ahead of the 5-inch battery, shedding its wings as the fuselage penetrated into the forward elevator pit.

The torpedo hits had flooded the forward engine and boiler rooms, causing the ship to lose all power. We drifted to a standstill, the electricity went off and the guns were shifted to manual control. There was no pressure on the water mains to fight fires. There we remained, dead in the water, listing heavily to starboard and smoke billowing up from several fires aboard.

The fast and furious battle had only lasted 10 or 15 minutes although it seemed like an hour. The attack group from another Japanese carrier had located the *Enterprise* group and hit that carrier with two bombs which apparently did no disabling damage. Also the battleship *South Dakota* and cruiser *San Juan* each receive one bomb hit and a torpedo plane crashed into the destroyer, *Smith*. Earlier, while picking up a downed air crew, the destroyer, *Porter*, was torpedoed and had to be sunk by the *Shaw*.

Fortunately the battle seemed to be over for the present as the sky was clear of enemy aircraft. I was sent forward to assist with the bucket brigades which had been formed to fight the fires. As I made my way along the catwalk, I saw for the first time the bomb hole so near to us in the flight deck and the mangled 20 mm guns. The bodies of the dead Marines had been removed. I continued along the flight deck and saw the huge hole left next to the island structure where the dive bomber had crashed into the flight deck. I could even see the unexploded bomb in the ready room.

The destroyers *Morris, Russell* and *Mustin* came alongside to port and passed hoses over to fight the fires. This operation proved quite successful and the fires were soon out. All aviation personnel and all those not necessary to operate or defend the ship were transferred to the destroyers at this time. Our returning attack force, finding their nest untenable, went to their alternate landing sites. Some were taken aboard the *Big E* and some went to Henderson Field on Guadalcanal.

When I was no longer needed up forward, I returned to my gun station via the hangar deck. The destruction was severe. The deck bulged upward like rolling hills in several places where bombs had burst on the deck below. One sad sight was a group of six or eight bodies of hangar deck personnel who had been killed by the same anti-personal bomb that had killed the Marine 20 mm gun crews next to our gun gallery.

A destroyer came alongside aft opposite our guns. I don't know what he was supposed to be doing, but with our ship listing so severely and with the overhang of the flight deck, the gently rolling swells were smashing the port side of his bridge like a dented tin can. He eventually gave up and withdrew.

As we waited in eerie silence, the ship drifting helplessly, we were mostly wrapped up in our own thoughts, wondering if and when another attack would come. We could look down on the fantail below us and see the pharmacist mates putting bodies in weighted canvas bags and dropping them overboard one by one as the chaplain conducted the appropriate services.

Meanwhile the cruiser, *Northampton*, was passing a line up forward in preparation for taking the *Hornet* in tow. The first tow line parted, but a stronger one was passed and we started moving along at a slow but steady pace. Word came that the engineering department was making good progress getting things straightened out down below and that we might soon be able to proceed on our own. This optimism was short-lived, however, as in the late afternoon the dreaded but expected second attack came. Unbeknownst to us the enemy only had one carrier still operational, but they made good use of it. The cruiser dropped its tow line in order to take evasive action and we were left there like sitting ducks. In the center of the bulls eye, so to speak. I looked up and saw directly overhead a dive bomber coming straight down and appearing to be aiming straight at us. I watched in awe as I saw the bomb detach from under the fuselage. I wondered if this one was meant for us, but as the bomb descended I could see that it was going to hit forward of us, and then, miraculously, it seemed to drift to starboard and didn't hit the ship at all. It was a near miss as I saw the plane pull up out of its dive in so sharp an angle I didn't think it was possible. I didn't see if he escaped, however, because, I had to turn back toward the ammo ready box and that's when the third and last torpedo hit. All of a sudden it got dark and a tidal wave of water mixed with oil cascaded down upon us. The ship went into its springboard imitation and once again I was busy trying to keep projectiles from bouncing out of the ready boxes and trying to keep the ones that got away from rolling about the deck.

We had only just recovered from this when we saw a plane coming straight at us at about the same level above the water as we were and at a right angle to our keel. We were looking straight down his gun barrels and once again it seemed like we weren't going to make it. Strangely enough he didn't fire, and as he came closer, we could see he was a

USS Hornet Basketball Champs, 1944.

The Royal Family.

The Royal Admiral and his royal pirates come aboard.

King's wife and daughter do the honors.

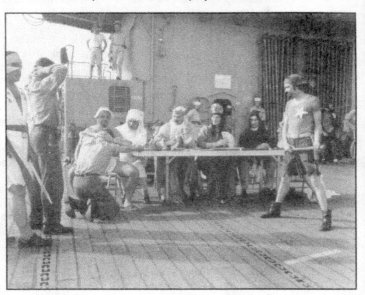

A polywog kissing the Royal Baby's belly on Initiation Day.

little higher than we were, but if he dipped his nose just a little, he would plunge directly into our gun gallery.

We held our breath as he whooshed overhead so low I thought he might hit the port side of the tilted flight deck, but he didn't. His engine was idling and I could see the arm of the rear seat gunner resting on the rim of the cockpit. I contacted the talker on the port side guns and asked if he had crashed. He affirmed that he had indeed crashed in a most spectacular way. To this day I am at a loss to figure out what was happening there. Was the pilot dead or wounded? Why didn't he fire his guns? Why didn't the rear seat gunner fire? Why was the engine only idling? Did he intend to crash into us and then chickened out? Obviously we'll never know the answer to those questions.

That ended that attack, and while we wondered what would happen next, we could look over the side and see a gaping torpedo hole just forward of our position. We could see broken pieces of crates drifting out of the hole so we assumed it had hit a storage compartment, but we learned later that it had also flooded the after engine room and ended all hope of getting under way again.

Finally in the early evening the order came to abandon ship. A large Japanese force was headed in our direction and the admiral wanted to complete rescue efforts by daylight and get the rest of his task force safely on their way. So we all went down the ropes and nets dangling over the side and began swimming away from the ship. Actually it was drifting broadside to the wind and moved away from us quite rapidly. We were all kind of scattered out, but started swimming toward a life raft we could see with some people in it. I remember looking down into the crystal clear water and wondering if there were any sharks around, but I couldn't see anything and presumed they would have been chased away by the explosions. I was still wearing my oversize helmet, so assuming I wouldn't need that anymore, I took it off and allowed it to drift away. Looking back toward the ship, I saw a group of horizontal bombers passing over. Remembering what I had heard about what a bomb blast could do to people in the water, I was concerned, but apparently I was far enough away as I didn't feel anything when most of their bombs exploded in the water. One bomb hit the starboard after cor-

ner of the flight deck. If we had still been aboard, we might have suffered some injury from that.

I arrived at the raft and we all clung together there awaiting rescue. I was still wearing my flash clothes and was soggy and waterlogged and soaked with oil. Soon a destroyer came along and we all clamored up the nets that were hung over the side. It was very difficult with our heavy clothing and fatigues. After all, we'd had a rough day. I had barely gotten a hold on the net when the destroyers screws churned over full speed ahead, but with the help of crew members, I made it aboard.

Our rescue ship was the USS *Barton* and the crew was very helpful in aiding us to get into the shower like sardines and scrub some of the oil off of us. We were also told to take any bunk that was unoccupied. We were well aware that there was still danger of more action, but felt a lot safer being on the outer edge of the target area. We were asked to stay below decks for our own safety and so as not to hinder the action of the crew in case of another attack, but we just had to see what was going on. However, we were headed off over the horizon while two destroyers stayed behind to fire torpedoes and projectiles in an effort to hasten the demise of the *Hornet*. But the old girl just clung to life and the destroyers had to leave while she was still afloat. Documents obtained after the war stated that two Japanese destroyers found her burning furiously and sank her at about 1:30 a.m. on October 27 and thus ended the battle of Santa Cruz.

As our task force sped away in the darkness of the night, flares could be seen on the horizon as the Japanese air force searched for us.

I awoke the next morning to find that someone had helped himself to my dungarees. The only thing that could be found for me to wear was a flash suit.

In the following days the *Barton* was dispatched from the group to go to the Great Barrier Reef to rescue some PBY crews who were stranded there for lack of fuel. That mission completed, the *Barton* proceeded to join the rest of the force at Noumea on the island of New Caledonia. We were taken ashore there and went in line through a large tent where we were given the necessities of life like toothpaste, brushes and razors. From there we were transported by truck to a plateau area of the island where a camp had been set up for us. We were issued blankets and assigned about six men to a tent. Some had cots, but most slept on the ground, me included. The first night I felt something crawling around in the blanket with me. Was it a scorpion, tarantula, snake or what? I let the others know that nobody was going to get any sleep until I found out what it was. Someone had a flashlight and it turned out to be a rather large but harmless bug. We all named our tents. Ours was "Torpedo Junction" from the tune *Tuxedo Junction* which was popular at that time.

After about a week, we were all given new assignments. Some were distributed to other ships in the fleet and others were sent back to the States to form nucleolus crews for new ships being built. I was in the latter group and steamed home on the former Matson liner *Monterey* which had been converted into a troop ship. Upon our arrival in San Diego, we learned that the gallant ship which had taken the *Hornet* in tow, the *Northampton* had capsized and sunk at the battle of Tassafaronga on November 30, 1942.

After a few days liberty in the good old USA, we received our orders and were told to report on New Years Day, 1943. So I spent that Christmas at home.

I reported in to the Philadelphia Navy Yard for assignment to a new light carrier still under construction, the USS *Princeton*. That was like a man floating on a raft being rescued by the *Titanic*. Leyte Gulf, remember.

All USS Hornet (CV-8) survivors aboard the USS Nassau (CV-48).

Men from the USS Hornet and BP NAS coming home July, 1946.

USS HORNET VETERANS

THOMAS B. ADAMS, born Sept. 16, 1919, Detroit, MI. Joined the USN in May 1941 and was assigned to the USS *Hornet* in October 1944. He served as a pilot, TBF, attached to VT-11.

Memorable experiences include the battle at Leyte Gulf and four strikes on Manila Harbor.

Actions while at sea include Formosa, Oct. 12-15, 1944; Leyte Gulf, Oct. 18-21, 1944; Manila Harbor, Nov. 13-14, 1944; Hong Kong, Jan. 12-17, 1945; and China Sea anti-sub patrols from the *Hornet*, August-October, 1944.

Discharged in December 1945, with the rank of lieutenant commander. Received the Navy Cross, Distinguished Flying Cross, Air Medal and Presidential Unit Citation.

Married to Mary E. and has three daughters: Janis E., Julie A. and Kathleen M. He is a retired chairman of Campbell-Ewald Co., Detroit, MI, Michigan's largest advertising agency.

FRANK AGUIRRE, born Aug. 25, 1934, Wilmington, CA. Joined the USN in October 1953 and was assigned to the USS *Hornet* in January 1957. He served in R Div. as an apprentice. While at sea they lost one screw near Taiwan and then went to Yokosuka, Japan.

Memorable experience was his entire cruise.

Discharged in October 1957. He received all sea service awards. Played football for the Yokosuka Seahawks and the Washington Redskins.

Now lives in Guadalojara Jalisco, Mexico, and is working on his Ph.D. in psychology. He is divorced; has four children; and eight grandchildren. He has received a thank you letter from the King and Queen of Thailand.

WILLIAM R. AHO, born Dec. 19, 1933, Fitchburg, MA. Joined the USN during the Korean War in June 1951 and went to boot camp at Great Lakes, IL. He served as ship's company there until 1953 and was transferred to the USS *Hornet* as it was being recommissioned at the Brooklyn, NY, Navy Yard. He was aboard for the shakedown cruise, with port calls in Cuba, Haiti and the Dominican Republic.

Released from active duty in September 1954 and then served until 1959 in the USNR where he was promoted to PN1.

Graduated from Fitchburg, MA, State College in 1958; received his MA and Ph.D. degrees in sociology from the University of Notre Dame; and was a college and university professor for 25 years. Retired in 1995 and now lives in Providence, RI.

RAYMOND L. ALLISON, born June 25, 1941, Newcastle, PA; moved to California in 1954. He attended boot camp at San Diego; served aboard the USS *Hornet* (CVS-12), fireroom #2, hells half acre,

from 1960-62. The *Hornet* was the only ship he ever served aboard in active duty. He also did a Wespac cruise and was in dry dock with the *Hornet* at Bremmerton, WA.

Discharge was extended four months due to the Cuban Blockade by President Kennedy. He was on board the ship with three brothers: Jerry, Jessie and Jack Timberlake. They kept the *Hornet* gang together by marriage: Jerry (Twigpuddle) married one of Allison's sisters; Jessie married another of Allison's sisters; and a shipmate, John (Junior) Cartwright married his wife's cousin. Allison married his USN sweetheart, Sharon, and they have three sons and four grandchildren. He is currently working as a maintenance engineer and resides in Escondido, CA.

PORTER F. AMMERMAN, born Nov. 1, 1922, Altoona, PA. Joined the USN Nov. 20, 1940, at Pittsburgh, PA; attended boot camp, Newport, RI; served on the USS *Hornet* from the time it was commissioned until it was sunk. He ran the "gedunk" and made many gallons of ice cream every night.

Most memorable experience was probably going topside to watch Gen. Doolittle pin his Japanese Medals on the bombs to be used to bomb Tokyo.

After serving six years in the USN he joined the Coast Guard, retiring in January 1964 as a chief warrant officer.

He and wife, Lillian, have three children and six grandchildren. He worked for the Hayward California School District for 15 years before retiring in 1979. He worked many years with the Boy Scouts of America. He and his wife love to travel in their motor home, and have driven to Baja, AK, and the original 48 states.

IVAN F. ANDES, born June 29, 1919, Akron, OH. Enlisted in the V-7 program in 1940 with a training cruise to Guantanamo on the USS *Arkansas* (BB-33). Attended Midshipman School, Northwestern University; commissioned ensign; and was assigned to the USS *Saratoga* (CV-3), March 1941 as junior gunnery and deck officer.

In September 1943 he was ordered to commissioning detail on the USS *Hornet* (CV-12) as assistant 1st lieutenant and senior watch officer. He was OOD during the kamakazi raid and typhoon damage to the flight deck.

Awarded the Presidential Citation and 12 Battle Stars for service in the Pacific. Released from active duty in August 1945 and joined IBM in Akron, OH, and the local organized Reserve unit. Recalled to duty during the Korean conflict and was stationed at the San Francisco Naval Shipyard as hull officer, Reserve Fleet Group, refitting ships for service.

Rejoined IBM, after release, in San Francisco office, December 1953. Married high school sweetheart Louise, October 1943. Retired from IBM with 38 years of service in June 1983, and lives in San Jose, CA.

SALVATORE J. ANGELICO, born Dec. 15, 1934, Salem, MA. He enrolled in the NROTC program at Tufts University where he received a civil engineering degree and was commissioned in the USN in June 1956. Attended Damage Control School in Philadelphia before reporting to the USS *Hornet* in San Diego, CA, September 1956. He served as the A Div. officer until his transfer to the Civil Engineer Corps in October 1958. He then served as assistant officer in charge, Public Works Transportation Center, Treasure Island; Public Works Officer, Naval Air Facility, El Centro; and Assistant Public Works Officer, Naval Air Station, Lemoore.

During his civilian career, he held various engineering and construction contracting officer positions with the Chance Vought Corp., Grand Prairie, TX; NASA, Sandusky, OH; and the USN at the USMC Air Station, Yuma, AZ; Naval Air Station, Lemoore, CA; Naval Station, Rota, Spain; and the Area Construction Office, Jacksonville, FL.

He has been married to the former Eleanor Ann Quinn of Salem, MA, since 1956, and has two children. He is presently retired and resides in Hanford, CA.

JACK D. ANTLE SR., born Aug. 19, 1919, Sumner, OK. Joined the USN on June 16, 1940, ship's cook 3/c, who saw Jimmy Doolittle's 15 bombers take-off on their way for Tokyo and later survived the sinking of the aircraft carrier USS *Hornet* on Oct. 26, 1942.

Received the WWII Victory Medal, American Campaign Medal and Asiatic-Pacific Campaign Medal.

After release from active duty on April 22, 1946, he worked driving a truck for a moving company. Moved a family from California to Ottumwa, IA, where he met Arlene Nichols. They married in St. Louis in 1950. Worked as a magnaflex casting inspector at Sivyer Steel Corp. for 30 years and is now retired and resides in Davenport, IA. He is loved by 13 children, 21 grandchildren and seven great-grandchildren.

JOHN N. ANTONELLI, born Jan. 17, 1933, Brooklyn, NY. Joined the USN Aug. 31, 1951; was assigned to the Fox Div.; was assigned to the USS *Hornet* in 1953; and participated in the Korean Conflict.

Memorable experiences include their Mediterranean cruise; crossing the equator, June 25, 1954; and all the different countries they saw.

Received the China Service Medal, Good Conduct Medal, National Defense Service Medal, Presidential Unit Citation and European Occupation Award. He was discharged Aug. 30, 1955.

Married Pat O'Connor in 1953, and has three children and seven grandchildren. He is retired from the Dept. of Sanitation of New York City and the US Postal Service. He collects baseball, football and boxing memorabilia and enjoys gardening.

DOMINICK APRICENO, born Feb. 28, 1924, Berwick, GA. Served boot camp and ship's company at Sampson, NY, June 1943 until he was assigned to NAS Norfolk, VA, in the same year. He served on the USS *Hornet* from October 1943-February 1946, as a radar operator.

Participated in all the actions from March until the typhoon broke the bow of the flight deck and they had to return to Hunter's Point for repairs. He was on leave in Berwick, PA, when the war ended.

Returned to the *Hornet* while it was being fitted with bunks to ferry troops back to the States. Discharged from Bainbridge, MD, in February 1946.

Married and has three children and four grandchildren. He is semi-retired and working in the family jewelry store.

JAMES ARMSTRONG, enlisted in the USN in August 1943; attended boot camp at Sampson NTC; then was assigned to the USS *Hornet* (CV-12) in October 1943. Was assigned to the 4th Div., a 20 mm gun division, all through the war. He was wounded in his right arm with GM3/c E.R. Alexander in May 1945 at Okinawa. Was transferred to V-2 Div. and K-I Div. and was in radio gang following the war and also while the ship was on "Magic Carpet" duty, bringing troops home from the Pacific.

Discharged at Lido Beach, Long Island, NY, March 19, 1946. Graduated from "vets" Vocational School, Troy, NY, air conditioner/sheet metal course,

1950; and spent 40 years in the sheet metal worker's union. He currently resides in Gloversville, NY.

KENNETH B. ATWOOD, born Jan. 7, 1918, Dighton, MA. Enlisted in the USN June 22, 1942, at Boston, MA, and went to boot camp at Newport, RI. He was assigned to NAS Norfolk, VA, at transition training squadron Atlantic (Big Boats); CASU-21, Oceana, Creeds, Pungo, Mantoe, Chincoteague; all outlying fields in Virginia; CASU-22, Quonset Point, RI, Torpedo Sqdn. 9, USS *Essex*.

Reported aboard the USS *Hornet* on Dec. 19, 1943, until their return in July 1945, at which time he was transferred to CASU-6, NAS Alameda, CA.

Discharged at Boston, MA, Dec. 13, 1945. Received the WWII Victory Medal, American Area Medal, EAME w/star, Philippine Liberation Medal w/ 2 stars, Asiatic-Pacific Medal w/9 stars, Presidential Unit Citation w/star and Good Conduct Medal.

Retired as plant engineer of a textile firm in 1983 after 43 years of employment. Has been married to wife, Ruth, for 50 years; has twin daughters; and now resides in Rehoboth, MA.

ARNOLD BARKER JR., born April 19, 1924, Chattanooga, TN. Joined the USN at the age of 17 on April 26, 1941, at Nashville, TN. Went to boot camp at Norfolk, VA, in Plt. 113; attended Aviation Metal Smith School, Pensacola, FL; and was assigned to the USS *Hornet* (CV-8) in VF-8 at Norfolk, VA.

Assigned to flight deck handling crew until September and was assigned to mess cooking with his battle station at number three elevator on the hanger deck, where he was when the *Hornet* was lost. Transferred to Fleet Reserve in November 1960. Achieved the rank of ADR1.

Married Gladys Roberts in 1962. Retired from Olan Mills Photo Processing Plant; and currently lives in Chattanooga, TN.

JESSE BARKER, born Feb. 1, 1916, Newton, UT. Attended flight training, Pensacola, FL, April-September 1941; ensign and pilot, June 11, 1942; and commanding officer, VF-93, in the USS *Hornet* world cruise, 1954.

Memorable experiences were the battles of Midway, Guadalcanal, Eastern Solomons and Korea.

Spent 32 years in active duty as a dive bomber pilot, day fighter and night VN. Peacetime duty was test pilot, NATTC Pax River; executive officer, CVA-19 and commanding officer, NAMT Group. Received the Distinguished Flying Cross (3) and Air Medal (7). Retired in June 1973 with the rank of captain.

He is married; has three children; and enjoying retirement.

JOHN ROBERT BATES, born March 28, 1923, Portsmouth, OH. Joined the USN Feb. 25, 1941, and was assigned to the USS *Hornet* when it was first launched in 1941, assigned to Supply Div.

Served aboard the *Hornet* during the battles of Coral Sea, Midway and Santa Cruz, where the *Hornet* was sunk on Oct. 26, 1942. He was picked up by the USS *Mustin* (DD-413) and was assigned to Guadalcanal, Auckland, NZ and PC-1138. In October 1944 at Nomea, New Caledonia, he was assigned to the USS *Zeilein* (APA-3) until January 1945. Was sent to Naval Hospital at San Leandro, CA, where he received a medical discharge in April 1945. When the *Hornet* was sunk, his hands and arms were burned so bad he was the last man to be picked up out of the water.

Received the WWII Victory Medal, American Defense Service Medal, American Campaign, Asiatic-Pacific Campaign, Presidential Unit Commendation Ribbon, Philippine Defense/Liberation/Independence Ribbon. Discharged April 24, 1945.

Has two children, four grandchildren and two stepsons. Married Katherine Kay Runyon at the USS *Mustin* (DD-413)/USS *Hornet* (CV-8) reunion at Lake Tahoe in 1991. Worked at AAA Auto Club of Southeastern Ohio, retiring in 1990. Refereed football and basketball for 45 years, his last game was in February 1996. He passed away on Feb. 27, 1996, at the age of 72.

ROBERT A. "ART" BEARD, born Feb. 15, 1926, Fremont, OH. Enlisted Aug. 9, 1943, and was aboard the USS *Hornet* when he was commissioned on Nov. 29, 1943. Was stationed with the 2nd Div. taking care of mount 6-8 open mount.

Memorable experiences were the three typhoons: Oct. 4-8, 1944, Dec. 18-19, 1944 and June 5, 1945. Many hours were spent at GQ.

Received the Asiatic-Pacific Medal w/9 stars, Philippine Liberation Medal w/2 stars, American Area Medal, WWII Victory Medal and Presidential Unit Citation. Discharged March 20, 1946.

Married Feb. 15, 1947; has five children; 16 grandchildren; and four great-grandchildren. He retired from Whirlpool Inc., Clyde Div.

JOHN S. BERGERON, born Jan. 1, 1942, Chicago, IL. Joined the USN Jan. 9, 1961, and was assigned to the USS *Hornet* in June 1961. He was assigned to S-1 Div. and worked in GSK.

Memorable experiences were two Wespac cruises; the overhaul at Hunter's Point, SF. While at sea they were called out of Hong Kong to get on-line for readiness at Bay of Pigs.

Received the Good Conduct Medal. Discharged Jan. 8, 1965.

Married and has three children. He is a credit manager for a division of Tyco Intl.

WILLIAM FRANK BERGQUIST, born May 1, 1916, Great Falls, MT. Joined the USN Dec. 13, 1934, and was assigned to the USS *Hornet* (CV-8) as a signalman 1/c. Served basic in San Diego, graduated in 1935, and was stationed in Pearl Harbor, 1937-38. He was killed in action on Oct. 26, 1942.

He was posthumously awarded the Purple Heart to his family. His wife, Sylvia, survived until Nov. 9, 1991. His children, Ronald (58) resides in Sacramento, CA; daughter, Ellen (56) resides in Modesto, CA. His children were ages four and two respectively at the time of his death. His hobbies included singing and radio singing performances. The family requests that anyone surviving who may remember him please contact Ellen Tatoyan (209-527-8562).

ALLAN BERGROOS, born Dec. 21, 1926, Queensville, Long Island, NY. Joined the USN March 17, 1938, and was assigned to the USS *Hornet* in 1939. He participated in WWII and Korea. He suffered a head injury in Vietnam and lost all his memory and is still recovering.

Discharged June 7, 1973, with the rank of captain. Received the Medal of Honor and the Distinguished Flying Cross.

He is a retired chemical engineer.

MARCEL BICHARA, born in 1924 in Geneva, Switzerland. He received a French Government bursary (1960) to work at the French National Center for Telecommunications Studies (CNET), Paris, France, on microwave components used in low power radar's.

On receiving his Ph.D. from Paris University, France, he went to Switzerland as head of the electronics department of Bern University. Later he left Switzerland and joined Texas Instrument where he worked on various types of hand-held Beacon and Doppler Effect microwaves and infrared radar's. Among them, the one used in the LEM of Apollo 11, hence his presence on the USS *Hornet* (CVS-12) at the time of the module's retrieval on July 24, 1961, Pacific Ocean.

He returned to Geneva, Switzerland, where his is a microwaves consultant for a number of banks and international organizations as well as an external physics lecturer in various universities.

HAROLD F. BILHEIMER, born Feb. 23, 1921, Bethlehem, PA. Joined the USN in June 1943 and was assigned to the USS *Hornet* in August 1943. He served as a five-inch gun turret, gunnery officer, 20 mm, 40 mm and five-inch mount.

Memorable experiences include the first strafing attack; manning the 20 mm; a sailor next to him in the cat walk being hit by Japanese fighter bullets dying and being buried at sea.

Received the American Service Ribbon, Asiatic-Pacific Area Service Ribbon w/9 BSs, EAME Area Ribbon w/2 BSs and the Philippine Liberation Ribbon w/2 BSs. He was discharged in June 1946.

Married Shirley Kunsman Bilheimer. He is a retired school administrator.

WALTON H. BORING, born Sept. 27, 1922, Crouse, NC. He learned to fly in the CPT Program of 1941 and 1942. Given his choice of service, he chose

the USN and received training at Olathe, KS, and Corpus Christi, TX. On July 7, 1943, he was designated a naval aviator.

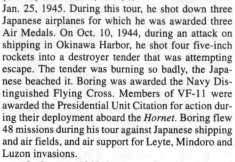

He was assigned to Fighting Sqdn. 11, know as "The Sundowners." The squadron served aboard the USS *Hornet* (CV-12) from Oct. 1, 1944, to Jan. 25, 1945. During this tour, he shot down three Japanese airplanes for which he was awarded three Air Medals. On Oct. 10, 1944, during an attack on shipping in Okinawa Harbor, he shot four five-inch rockets into a destroyer tender that was attempting escape. The tender was burning so badly, the Japanese beached it. Boring was awarded the Navy Distinguished Flying Cross. Members of VF-11 were awarded the Presidential Unit Citation for action during their deployment aboard the *Hornet*. Boring flew 48 missions during his tour against Japanese shipping and air fields, and air support for Leyte, Mindoro and Luzon invasions.

In January 1945, he returned to Alameda and new orders assigned him to NAS DeLand, FL, teaching new navy pilots combat flying and tactics. He was released from active duty in October 1945, but joined Reserve Sqdn. 66E forming at NAS Atlanta, GA. He was called to active duty in the fall of 1952 and assigned to Fighting Sqdn. 171, in Jacksonville, FL, flying the twin jet F2H-3 *Banshee*. The Korean War ended and he was released from active duty Sept. 5, 1953. He returned to North Carolina with his wife, Edith, and two sons, Tony and Jeff. He is retired and now lives in Asheville, NC.

JAMES R. BOWMAN, born Dec. 11, 1923, St. Louis, MO. Joined the USN in April 1942 and was with VT-11 from September 1943 to October 1945; on the USS *Hornet*, October 1944-January 1945 as a TBF pilot. Participated in Okinawa, Philippines, Formosa, Hong Kong and the South China Sea.

Released to Organized Reserved in January 1946. Was recalled to active duty in April 1951 until April 1953. Returned to Organized Reserves until retirement in 1983. Received the Air Medal.

Married Barbara and has two sons, Theodore and Andrew. Retired after 36 years with the railroad industry as a civil engineer.

LOUIS A. BRADLEY, born Dec. 23, 1923, Ashland, PA. Joined the USN March 3, 1943, and was assigned to the USS *Hornet* Dec. 7, 1943. Served as an aviation ordnanceman, aircraft gun mechanic and explosive handler.

Memorable experiences include the Mariannas turkey shoot; the succeeding night aircraft retrieval; and the action off Formosa, Oct. 12-16, 1944.

Participated in all action from the first Palau raid in March 1944 to and including the Leyte Gulf in October 1944.

Received the Presidential Unit Citation, American Theater, Pacific Theater, Philippine Liberation, Good Conduct and WWII Victory Medals. Discharged April 8, 1946, with the rank of AOM1/c.

Married and has four children. He is retired.

DONALD C. BRANDT, born Dec. 21, 1923, Cincinnati, OH. Joined the USN in June 1942 and was

assigned to the USS *Hornet* in March 1944. He was a member of Air Group 2 and served as a fighter pilot.

Memorable experiences include being shot down at Guam and rescued by a submarine.

He participated in the air strikes as a fighter pilot from March-September 1944.

Received the Purple Heart, Distinguished Flying Cross and Air Medals. Discharged in November 1945 with the rank of lieutenant(jg).

Married for 50 years (1996) and has two children, Kenneth C. and Mary Ann. He is a retired civil engineer in heavy highway construction. He is presently Vice-Chairman Board of Directors, USS HORNET Club, Inc.

CLINT BRANHAM, born Dec. 23, 1921, Louisville, KY. Joined the USN in February 1942, and was assigned to the USS *Hornet*. Served as a pilot for VT-2.

Memorable experiences include the 1944 actions from Palau through the Philippines.

Received the Distinguished Flying Cross and Air Medal. Discharged in October 1945 with the rank of lieutenant commander.

Married Else and has five children. He retired as pilot from Pan Am.

ORBIN L. BRANTHOOVER, born June 29, 1927, Rimersburg, PA. Joined the USN April 2, 1945, and was assigned to the USS *Hornet* in August 1945. Served in Div. V-5. Discharged July 15, 1948.

Memorable experience: In January 1947 there were still some of them attached to the *Hornet* (CV-12). They had been living on APL-10 (Casa Maria), APL-11 and in the Hunters Point Barracks buildings at various times. On the morning of Jan. 15, 1947, Chief Boatswain Mate Wheelus said to him, "How about you and Jeff (S1/c Jefferies) raising the Colors today," which they did. Their marines had been long gone. They both were honored to have been selected to raise the Colors on the *Hornet* (CV-12) on the last day that she was in commission.

Married Helen and has a son, Jeff. Retired from Honeywell, Inc.

CHARLES W. BROOKS, born July 20, 1921, Mansfield, LA. Joined the USN July 2, 1941, and was assigned to the USS *Hornet* Oct. 20, 1941. He was assigned to the Fighting Aid Sqdn., VF-8; and personal steward to RADM G.D. Murray; and commander of TF-17.

Memorable experiences include being rescued by RADM G.D. Murray when the *Hornet* (CV-8) sank; and being present when the Japanese surrendered Sept. 2, 1945.

Participated in the battle of Midway, Wake Island, Water Canal, Santa Cruz, raid on Tokyo and Coral Sea.

Received the Good Conduct Medal, WWII Victory Medal, Presidential Unit Citation w/3 BSs and American Defense. Discharged Dec. 29, 1945.

Married Lee Audrey Scranton Brooks and has

five children: Charles, George, Denise, John, Dwight; and 11 grandchildren. He is founder and director of Charles W. Brooks Youth Organization, Inc., Washington, DC, which is to combat juvenile delinquency, and was founded in April 1979.

ERVIN L. BROWN, born June 8, 1927, Newhaven, IN. Joined the USN Sept. 13, 1945, Indianapolis, IN; attended boot camp at Great Lakes, IL; and then was assigned to the USS *Hornet* in 1946. He served with the 6th Div. as a gunners mate striker.

Memorable experience was getting the ship ready for the Mothball Fleet while on board and the ship was being decommissioned.

Received the WWII Victory Medal. Discharged Aug. 11, 1946, then served in the USNR until Aug. 11, 1954, with the rank of S1/c.

Married to Ruth Ann for 44 years and has three grown sons: John E., Jeff and Terry; daughter-in-law, Deena; and two grandchildren, Kelleye and Christopher. He retired from the US Postal Service after 30 years as a letter carrier.

D.C. BRYSON, born Feb. 16, 1925, Walhall, SC. Joined the USN Aug. 7, 1943, and was among the first crew assigned to the USS *Hornet* and is a plank owner. Served with the V-1 Div. as an airplane pusher with the rank of S1/c. He participated in nine major actions in the Pacific.

Discharged Jan. 4, 1946, with the rank of S1/c. Received the American Area Campaign Medal, Asiatic-Pacific Campaign Medal w/9 stars, Philippine Liberation Ribbon w/2 stars, WWII Victory Medal and the Presidential Unit Citation w/star.

JAMES F. BURNETT, born in June 1942, Hunt County, TX, was raised and attended school in Grand Prarie, TX. He joined the USN in December 1959 and completed recruit training in San Diego and was ordered to the USS *Hornet* (CVS-12) and assigned to V-3 Div. He served on the *Hornet* until discharge in 1963.

Returned to the USN through a Reserve Program and in 1967, as ABH2, became regular active duty status and ordered to the USS *Hornet* and was assigned to V-1 Div. Served on the flight deck for over three years completing two Wespac cruises and the Apollo 11 mission. In 1970, after completing the decommissioning of the *Hornet* he was transferred to shore duty in Mississippi. He continued his USN career until he had a heart attack in 1981. He then retired as a senior chief petty officer.

After a second career in the building business in the building business, he is now fully retired to his wood working hobby and lives in the country outside Campbell, TX. He has four children and five grandchildren.

DAVID E. BURTON, born July 28, 1947, Fredericksburg, VA. Joined the USN in April 1966

and was assigned to the USS *Hornet* in September 1968. Served as a welder, SFM2.

Memorable experiences include seeing the Far East; the Apollo 11 astronauts; and President Wilson.

Participated in action at Yankee Station off Vietnam Coast and TF-71 off Korean Coast.

Received the Meritorious Unit Commendation Ribbon, National Defense Service Medal, Armed Forces Expeditionary Medal (Korea), Vietnam Service Medal, RVN Meritorious Unit Citation, RVN Campaign Medal w/1960 Device and Gallantry Cross.

Married and owns a small trucking company and does long distance hauling of van freight.

DONALD LEE BUSKE, born Sept. 24, 1934, Rochester, MN. Joined the USN Nov. 17, 1951; attended training at Great Lakes, IL; and was assigned to the USS *Hornet* in August 1953, to the No. 2 fire room as a boiler tender.

Memorable experiences include the recommissioning of the *Hornet* on Sept. 11, 1953.

Following the 1953 recommissioning of the CVA-12, the ship was moved to Bayonne, NJ to install the top mast. Their first sea trial resulted in a cracked hull (three places) from a full or flank speed maneuver from port to starboard or vice versa. They returned to Bayonne dry dock and held tight with chain falls under three knots. Following repairs they sailed to the Caribbean for their shakedown. The twist and damage to the hull must also have warped a shaft as all future full/flank runs produced heavy vibrations to the aft part of the ship giving a new meaning to the phrase "shakedown cruise."

Received the National Defense Service Medal, Good Conduct Medal, Korean Service Medal, UN Service Medal. Discharged Nov. 16, 1959.

Has been married to Kathryn for 40 years and has one son, one daughter, two grandchildren, two brothers (one Navy, one Air Force) and three sisters. Retired from IBM in 1991 after 35 years of service. He is currently a part-time driver for a local trucking firm. He enjoys traveling, woodcarving, singing, golf, fishing and the *Hornet* Club.

STANLEY O. BUTCHER JR., born May 14, 1925, LaFrank, WV. Joined the USN Aug. 18, 1943. He was assigned to the USS *Hornet* (CV-12), gunner, 4th Div. Other stations were NRS Clarksburgh, WV, NTS Great Lakes, IL, RS So Annex, NOB, Norfolk, VA; USN RS, TRI and San Francisco, CA.

Discharged May 12, 1946, with the rank of cox. Received the Pacific Theater Ribbon w/9 stars, American Theater Ribbon, WWII Victory Medal and Philippine Liberation Ribbon w/2 stars.

Married Letta Butcher and has one daughter, Frances A. Woodmancy; two sons, John A. and Gary D.; and one granddaughter, Ashley M. Butcher. He retired as a machinist from Guterl Steel Co., Lockport,

NY. Was a member of the USS *Hornet* Club, Navy Marine Club Ship 110, VFW, American Legion, Masonic Lodge, Wrights Conners Sports Club, National Rifle Assoc. He enjoyed hunting, fishing and going to many of the ship's reunions. He passed away July 30, 1995.

JOSEPH CAGLIONE, born Oct. 5, 1917, Rutte, MT. Joined the USN Aug. 15, 1939, and was assigned to the USS *Hornet* Feb. 28, 1944. Served VT Maintenance as chief.

Memorable experiences include combat action on CV-12. He was also on board CV-12 during her entire WWII operations.

Received the Presidential Unit Citation, Good Conduct w/3 stars, American Defense, Philippine Presidential Citation, American Theater, Asiatic-Pacific Campaign w/9 stars, Philippine Liberation w/2 stars, WWII Victory Medal, China Service, Korean Service, UN Service, Vietnam Service w/4 stars and RVN Campaign w/Device. Discharged Sept. 30, 1969.

He was a volunteer in a VA clinic. Joe passed away in May, 1998.

REUBEN B. CAROTHERS, born Jan. 11, 1929, Sulphur Springs, TX. Attended boot camp at NAS Dallas, 1951; OCS, Newport, Rhode Island, March 1953; and was assigned to the USS *Hornet* in October 1953. Served as V-4 division officer in 1954; assistant CIC officer and air early warning officer, 1955-56.

Memorable experiences include the around the world cruise and Hainan incident in 1954 and the Wespac cruise in 1955.

Received the American Defense, European Occupation and China Service Medals. Released from active duty in October 1956 and retired from the USNR in March 1973.

He is married (Jane) and is currently working in oil and gas, Real Estate and investments.

NICHOLAS P. CASELLA, born April 26, 1922, Santa Clara County, CA. Joined the USN in July 1940 and was assigned to the USS *Hornet* in 1941. Served as AMM3/c, gunner, bomber for VT-8. He was also selected to attend school for the first TEFs at Grumman Aircraft Factory in New York before the battle of Midway.

Memorable experiences include the battle of Midway; Tokyo raid; and the South Pacific Battles.

Discharged in July 1946. Received two Presidential Citations while with the VT-8/TF-16.

After USN retirement he was able to get a college education and spent 30 years in his career as an art director, motion picture technician and business architectural arts and graphic arts, inventor. At the present he is working at creating a youth organization and does volunteer work in the community. He currently resides in the beautiful hills of California Gold Country.

JOHN CLAIBORNE CASH, born Sept. 20, 1919, Oceanside, CA; graduated from San Diego High School, June 1938. Enlisted in the USN Dec. 8, 1939; attended boot training at NTC San Diego, CA, Company 39-43; and served as a radio striker on board the USS *Moffett* (DD-362), and a number of other destroyers, with COMDESRON 26 Flag. Later COMDESRON 26 changed to COMINRON 2, on board the USS *Hopkins* (DD-249/DMS-13); attended Fleet Radio School at destroyer base in San Diego, 1940-41. On Dec. 7, 1941, at sea near Johnston Island on board the *Hopkins* he later participated in Guadalcanal landing and other war operations in the South Pacific until July 1943.

In September 1943, as RM2/c, he was transferred to new construction on USS *Hornet* (CV-12), at Norfolk, VA. The *Hornet* was then sent to the Pacific area and participated in major war operation from March 1944 to June 1945. The *Hornet* was in Naval Yard Hunter's Point, San Francisco, when the war ended in August 1945. Cash was promoted to chief radioman in June 1945.

In November 1945 he was transferred to San Diego for discharge, however, he re-enlisted with duty at NAVCOMMSTA 11th Naval District. In 1948 he transferred to Tsingtao, China for duty with COMSERVRON 3, on USS *Piedmont* (AD-17), USS *Sierra* (AD-18), and USS *Dixie* (AD-14), and with COMGEN FMF WESTPAC.

In September 1949 he received orders for duty with Naval Security Group and was transferred to NSG Headquarters in Washington, DC. During the next 20 years had COMMINT and COMSEC assignments with the Naval Security Group at Armed Services Security Agency, Arlington, VA; NAVRAD FAC(S), Yokosuka and Kami Seya, Japan, 1950-53; NAVRADSTA, Bainbridge, WA, and NAVCOMMSTA, San Diego as instructor CT School, 1953-56; NAVSECGRUACTY, Bremmerhaven, Germany, 1956-59; NAVSECGRUACTY, Fort George G. Meade, MD, 1959-62; NAVCOMMSTA, Honolulu, NAVSECGRU Dept. Wahaiwa, HI, 1962-66; NAVSECGRU ACT, Skaggs Island, Sonoma, CA, 1966-69.

Retired Dec. 31, 1969, with 30 years and 23 days of active duty service, with the rank of CWO4. Received the Presidential Unit Citation, Navy Unit Commendation, Good Conduct Medal, Asiatic-Pacific Area w/10 stars, American Area Medal, WWII Victory Medal, China Service Medal, Navy Occupation Medal, National Defense Service Medal, Korean Service Medal, UN Service Medal, Philippine Liberation Ribbon and Navy Commendation Award and Medal.

In 1970 he returned to San Diego and attended college and worked as a photographer and audio-visual specialist, retiring in 1989. Married Margaret McCune Andrews, Oct. 19, 1949. They have no children.

NICKOLAS CASSANO, born May 25, 1913, Cleveland, OH. Joined the USN Jan. 31, 1942, and was assigned to the USS *Hornet* May 10, 1942, and served as photographer in the photo lab and scouting with the 8th Sqdn. His first duty was photographing damage on base and ships in harbor.

Transferred to aircraft carrier *Hornet*. After action he was assigned to carrier *Manila Bay* (CVE-61) on Aug. 30, 1943. It took much work to set up the photo lab. The ship was commissioned Oct. 5, 1943.

After several actions, was sent to San Diego for critical repairs. He was then transferred, Feb. 10, 1944, to Pensacola, FL, to teach photography at the Photo School. After six months he was put in charge of a lab at Whiting Field and finished the war there. He was discharged Aug. 27, 1945.

Retired from photography and is now enjoying it all!

RAY J. CASTEN, born Oct. 5, 1918, Great Falls, MT. USNA Class of 1942. Served in the USS *Helena* (Cl-50), 1942-43, Guadalcanal-Solomon Islands Campaign with primary responsibilities for ship's navigational pilot during GQ. Engaged in three major night battles, several sorties, shore bombardments and air attacks. Became instrumental in the early formulation and employment of CIC tactics.

After the loss of the *Helena* in the Kula Gulf, he was assigned to the USS *Hornet* (CV-12), then under construction at Newport News, VA. He was personally assigned by Capt. Miles R. Browning the key navigational-piloting responsibilities during fitting out and subsequent assignment of the *Hornet* to the Pacific Fleet (TF-58). Participated in the Marshall Islands, New Holandia, Palau, and Truk Island operations.

Received the Presidential Unit Citation, the first Navy Unit Citation, Asiatic-Pacific, American Defense, American Theater and WWII Victory Medals.

He became a multi-engine command pilot. Retired from the service in 1962 to engage in military-civilian aviation and space related program contracts. Married to Irene and they are both now retired and residing part-time between Canada and the Detroit, MI.

Most memorable experiences aboard the USS *Hornet* concerned a plethora of extraordinary personal conflicts with Capt. Miles R. Browning, too numerous to mention here, but previously revealed in his book *USS Helena: The Machine Gun Cruiser'* and now covered in detail under a forthcoming sequel describing mishaps aboard the USS *Hornet* (CV-12) during its maiden days under his command.

WALTER CHILDERS, born Jan. 24, 1925, Elkhorn City, KY, Pike County, the fifth child, second son, of John Childers and Elsie Bowling Childers. Enlisted in the USN on Aug. 11, 1943, at Paintsville, KY, Johnson County, he went to boot camp at Great Lakes, IL, and was assigned to the USS *Hornet* (CV-12).

He participated in service March 29 to May 1, 1944, Palau, Holandia, Truk, June 11 to Aug. 5, 1944, Mariannas, Bonins, Yap; Sept. 6-24, 1944, Philippines,

Palau: AG-2 (VF-2, VB-2, VT-2, Part of VFN-76); Oct. 10-Nov. 22, 1944, Ryukyus, Formosa, Philippines, Luzon; Dec. 14-16, 1944, Luzon; Jan. 3-22, 1945, Philippines, Formosa, China Sea, Ryukyus; AG-11 (VF-11, VB-11, VT-11); Feb. 16-June 10, 1945, Japan, Bonins, Ryukyus: AG-17 (VF-17, VBF-171, VB-17, VT-17).

Received the Presidential Unit Citation, WWII Victory Medal, American Area Campaign Medal, Asiatic-Pacific Area Campaign Medal w/7 stars. He was released from active duty March 3, 1946.

Married Beulah Johnson Nov. 8, 1947, and reared three children: Brenda Lou (b. Oct. 8, 1948), Deborah Kay (b. Aug. 27, 1950) and John Cole (b. Jan. 7, 1952). Beulah was deceased on April 21, 1994. Brenda married David Lawrence Mitchell (b. Dec. 15, 1947), Oct. 17, 1971, and has one daughter, Shelly Kay (b. July 17, 1981). Deborah married Gary Lee Adams (b. Sept. 3, 1949), May 10, 1969, and has two sons, Scott Michael (b. Feb. 15, 1972) and Brian Wesley (b. Sept. 21, 1977). John married Becky Lewis in 1972 and they have one daughter, Kimberly Cole (b. Sept. 21, 1974). John and Becky divorced and then married Lisa Ann Drexler (b. May 1, 1960) May 16, 1981, and they have a daughter, Jessica Renee (B. July 25, 1983).

He retired from General Motors Jan. 1, 1977, after 30 years of employment. He also worked 10 years with his son at his auto-body shop. For 12 years he was active in the IUECIO, serving as financial secretary of the union Local 755. Also serving as the president from 1994-96 of the Local 755 Delco Products Retirees Council and holds membership in the VFW of the US and Masonic Lodge 755 AM&FM of Trotwood, OH. Married his school days sweetheart, Maine Jewell Salvage (b. Jan. 3, 1929) June 24, 1995, in East Point, KY, Johnson County, and resided between Dayton, OH, and Prestonburg, KY. Walter passed away August 15, 1997.

JAMES ALTON CHINN, born July 29, 1917, Lemoore, Kings Co., CA. Joined the USN in November 1941 and was issued orders to start aviation training in a V-5 program scheduled to begin Feb. 2, 1942, at the Oakland Municipal Airport. Upon completion of the training at Oakland he reported to Corpus Christi where as a member of the Class 5B-42-C (C) he graduated as ensign on Oct. 8, 1942.

Reported to the USS *Hornet* in February 1945 in the Pacific Ocean. He had previously trained, gone on the Shakedown Cruise, and sailed to Hawaii with VB-17 aboard the USS *Bunker Hill*. He saw action in the Pacific at Nauru, Kavieng, Eniwetok and Truk. VB-17 was returned to Alameda to be reformed and given further training at Fallon Nevada. The squadron sailed to Hilo and returned to the action in the Pacific where they boarded the USS *Hornet*. They bombed the islands on the way to Tokyo including Iwo Jima. After the flight deck was damaged in an hurricane the ship returned to Alameda and Chinn received orders to report to NAS Jacksonville. The war was over and he was assigned to inactive Reserves.

He retired from the Reserves on July 29, 1977, as commander, USNR. For his action, he received ribbons for the Pacific and Asiatic Theater of war aboard the USS *Bunker Hill* and the *Hornet*. He received two Distinguished Flying Crosses and the Air Medal w/5 stars.

After the war he married Barbara Deibert and they raised three children. He attended USC graduating with a doctor of pharmacy degree and eventually they owned the La Ondra Drugs. They now enjoy retirement at Bishop, CA, where they are active in the community and enjoy equestrian activities. Their travels have taken them to Mexico, Alaska, Italy, Jamaica, Europe, Russia and Africa plus they have explored the national parks and other areas in the United States.

STEPHEN G. "CK" CICKAY, born Feb. 5, 1923, Perth Amboy, NJ. Enlisted in the USN Dec. 9, 1942, at New York City; attended boot camp at NTS

Great Lakes, IL. Assigned to radio NTS, University of Chicago, IL, and Naval Radio Station, Annapolis, MD. On Oct. 27, 1943, joined the USS *Hornet* (CV-12) Group at Newport News, VA, commissioned Nov. 29, 1943, became plank owner, and shoved off post-haste to Pacific Theater.

Transferred from the *Hornet* to staff of commander, second carrier task force (Vice Adm. John S. McCain) on Aug. 19, 1944, to USS *Wasp* (CV-18) at Eniwetok; Nov. 17, 1944, to USS *Hancock* (CV-19), at sea; and on May 18, 1945, to USS *Shangri-La* (CV-38) at Ulithi. On July 8, 1945, transferred at sea to USS *Rescue* (AH-18) for medical reasons. Discharged after war ended at USN Special Hospital, Asbury Park, NJ, Jan. 11, 1946.

Authorized for the following Medals: Asiatic-Pacific Campaign Medal w/SS and 3 BSs, Philippine Liberation Ribbon w/2 BSs, Navy Commendation Medal, Presidential Unit Commendation Medal, Navy Unit Commendation Ribbon w/star, American Campaign Medal, Navy Good Conduct Medal and WWII Victory Medal.

He is retired from New Jersey Federal Government Computer Systems Administrator who has traveled world-wide, and has three children and three grandchildren. Presently residing in New Jersey, Pennsylvania and California. He and his wife moved to Jupiter, FL, in 1980, and currently resides there as of 1997.

JAMES A. CLARK, born May 9, 1934. Joined the service June 1, 1943; attended boot camp, San Diego, CA, August 14; and was assigned to M Div., main engine room, until May 1957.

Most memorable experiences were the world cruise in 1954 crossing the equator. He participated in the ships overhaul in Bremerton, WA.

Discharged in May 1957 at Treasure Island.

Married his first wife, Janice, in December 1954, while home. Janice passed away in June 1992. He and his present wife, Kay, celebrated their fourth anniversary on August 21. They have five children and nine grandchildren. They enjoy traveling, fishing, dancing, cooking and eating. He has worked for the city of Crete for 40 years, retiring in September 1997. He started out as a light plant operator and worked his way up to superintendent then to his present position of operations superintendent. Looking forward to retirement and hopes to spend some time with grandchildren and enjoying his hobbies of bird watching and if time permits get a few things done around the house and yard. They live on a small acreage and enjoy it very much. They look forward to the *Hornet* reunion every year.

NELSON W. CLARK, born Feb. 17, 1933, Coleman, MI. Joined the USN Nov. 17, 1952, and was assigned to the USS *Hornet* in July 1953. Served in the pipe shop as a pipefitter.

Memorable experiences include working on the

marine strainer up on the island during flight operations. The plane got wave off and nearly hit the island in the South China Sea in 1954.

Received the National Defense, European Occupation, China Service and Good Conduct Medals. Discharged Nov. 16, 1956, with the rank of FP2.

Married Donna and has four children and seven grandchildren. He is presently a heavy equipment operator.

ROBERT A. CLARK, born July 17, 1922, New York, NY. Joined the USN Nov. 6, 1942, and was assigned to the USS *Hornet* in January 1945 during his first tour and again in July 1955 during his second tour. Served as pilot, VBF-17; photo pilot, VFP-62.

Memorable experiences include the first carrier attack on Tokyo February 1945, 360 aircraft in a massive "group grope!"; April 1945, chased enemy "jack" inside DD screen, shot it down, but got hit by 40 mm shell in tail by own *Hornet* marine gunner; March 19, 1945, on fighter sweep to inland sea, met by 60 enemy fighters at 20,000 feet, eight out of 20 hellcats shot down, got two enemy fighters that day.

Received three Distinguished Flying Crosses (shot down six enemy aircraft) and eight Air Medals. Transferred to inactive duty Sept. 28, 1945. Attended Wesleyan University at Middletown, CT, on the GI Bill, 1946-50. Went back on active duty in February 1951 to fly F9F Panthers in the Korean War aboard the USS *Antietam* (CV-36); med cruise on O-in-C, photo det. on *Randolph* (CVA-15) in 1957. Retired as lieutenant commander in 1965.

Married Darlene and has a daughter, Terri (31). Robert and Darlene reside in Mount Vernon, VA (30 years), and Terri lives in Reston, VA. Worked as a civil servant in the Navy Department. Enjoys playing tennis, strolling the Potomac Shore line, gazing at stars and comets, smelling the roses, HEY, what else!

ALICK J. CLARKE, born Oct. 2, 1904. Joined the USN Jan. 2, 1923, and was assigned to the USS *Hornet* in August 1939 serving as senior CSK in charge of supply department. He was assigned to a battle station in charge of ammo, handling crew, AA, and .51 cal. ammo.

Memorable experiences were during attacks on the *Hornet* (CV-8), he and the chief commissary steward Jesse Ward, noticed that there was no drinking water on the hanger deck, except in old wooden kegs which was not fit to drink. Jesse said there should be water in the galley. Alick had a five cell flashlight, and they went down to the passageway not knowing if they could make it there and back due to bombings. However, they took a bucket and started down the ladder and into the passageway to the galley. They encountered nothing of consequences and carried water back to the hanger deck. Then everyone else was able to do the same. A lieutenant(jg) recommended them for an award (Navy Cross) but the lieutenant colonel said they were not on guns, so he canceled it. After abandon ship he was picked by the destroyer USS *Mustin* and later transferred via breechs boy to the USS *Northampton*.

Transferred to the USNR when the war ended in 1945. He is now retired. He is married to Marie L. Clarke.

ROBERT E. CLEMENTS, born Aug. 4, 1916, Buena Vista, GA; graduated from South Georgia in

1935. After a year in the US Army he entered the USNA graduating in 1940. He served on the USS *Pennsylvania* from 1940-42 as the communications officer. After flight training he reported to the USS *Hornet*, 1943-45, as executive officer of VF-11.

During his duty on the *Hornet* he recorded how tremendously proud he was of the squadron, the ship's crew and his plane, the F6F. He served in campaigns and battles at Pearl Harbor, Midway, Coral Sea, Okinawa, Leyte, Luzon, Formosa and China Sea.

Received the Presidential Unit Citation, three Air Medals, two Distinguished Flying Crosses, Defense Victory, Philippines, American Theater and Pacific Theater. He logged 240.1 hours in combat and 66 missions. He shot down two Zekes, one Tojo, and two Oscars thus becoming an "Ace." After numerous tours of duty from Philadelphia to Jacksonville he retired with the rank of captain in December 1968. He enjoyed golf and wood working.

Capt. Clements died of cancer on Aug. 16, 1989. He is survived by his wife, Eleanore; daughters, Pat and Billie; grandchildren, Chris (now in Navy Pilot School), Debra, Stephen and Deborah; and one great-grandchild.

GERALD A. COEUR, born Dec. 16, 1921, Eureka, CA. Joined the USN April 15, 1942, and was assigned to the USS *Hornet* in October 1944 serving as a VF pilot in Fighting Sqdn. 11.

Received two Air Medals. Discharged in December 1945.

Married to Georganne and has three children: Connie, Marcia and Jeff. He is retired.

ERSKINE H. COFFEY, born to Massie and Siddie Coffey on April 20, 1934, in Montebello, VA. Joined the USN in 1943 and went to boot camp at Bainbridge, MD. Was assigned to the USS *Hornet* in August 1943. He was a 1st Div., five-inch, 38 gun, #4 mount, known as a powderman. Achieved the rank of seaman first class SV V6 USNR. He was in all the action that the *Hornet* was in from 1943-45.

One of the things he remembers is that a tanker came long to refuel the *Hornet* and all of a sudden the lines were taken away. The tanker went one way and they headed straight. They kept their course straight so that they could be near the planes. Around three

p.m., they launched planes against the Japanese fleet. At dark the planes were coming back, while circling the ship to land, some ran out of gas. Some planes landed on other carriers, some in the water. Men ware standing around praying for those pilots to land safely. They picked the men up out of the water. They lost some planes but he does not remember losing any men. This battle was called the battle of the Philippine Sea or turkey shoot. Also the day one airplane came out of the sky so close that he thought it would hit the ship. He dropped to his knees praying and all of a sudden one man shot down that plane, they called it the kamikaze attack. He remembers thanking God for taking care of them. He remembers his mother saying, "Son, we will be praying for all of you." God answered mom's prayer.

They had a band that was called the "Happy Hour." Their names were Fisher, Nathan Redman, himself and two others. They also had passengers on the ship. One man's name was Orcie Taylor, from Nelson Co., VA. He was on the LST-747 ship. Seaman Taylor had special amphibious training. He sailed from the Philippines to California for a 30 day leave, then discharged.

Coffey was honorably discharged from the USN Dec. 13, 1945. Awards received were the Presidential Unit Citation and the Silver Star.

He went home, went to work, became a heavy equipment operator. Started his own business in building golf courses in the US and Canada. He is retired at this time. He has two sons, the oldest served on the USS *Douglass H. Fox*, 1964-68. The youngest son worked with him building golf courses. Both are heavy equipment operators. Also has one daughter, two stepdaughters, six grandchildren, one step-granddaughter and five great-grandchildren. He is proud to have served on the *Hornet* and still proud of it today.

CHARLES COLE graduated from Gardiner High School, Gardiner, ME, 1943; and joined the USN. He was aboard the USS *Hornet* (CV-12) on the day it was commissioned, in V-1 Div. He served aboard the *Hornet* until the war ended, 1945.

Married a girl from his graduating class and resides in Gardiner.

LAWRENCE J. CONLEY, born June 4, 1925, Lancaster, PA. Joined the USN July 13, 1943, and was assigned to the USS *Hornet* in October 1943. He served in the CIC Center as radarman. He participated in action in everything east of Pearl Harbor to Japan. He received the Asian Medal.

Most memorable experience was when they were caught in the China Sea typhoon.

Married Emma and has two daughters, Denise and Cheri, and two sons, Lawrence Jr. and Jere Conley. He retired from gas/electric utility as new development and new homes representative on Sept. 1, 1990.

ERNIE E. CONNOR, born Dec. 8, 1929, Manchester, KS. Joined the USN in January 1951. Was assigned to the USS *Hornet* (CVS-12) ship's company in February 1968 and served as the CCA officer responsible for night and instrument departures and recoveries. Had a totally outstanding CCA crew, conducted ASW flight operation around the clock and in between worked in many carqual periods as the west coast ready deck.

Deployed to the Tonkin Gulf and Yankee Station and to the sea of Japan for show of force when a

RC-121 was shot down by the North Koreans. Most memorable deployments were as the recovery ship for Apollo 11 and 12 moon missions. Apollo 11 recovery near Johnson Atoll had President Nixon and most of his cabinet on board for the recovery.

Enlisted in 1951 and commissioned under the LDO program in 1962. Served as a lieutenant aboard the *Hornet*. Retired as a commander in 1982. He received numerous campaign and Vietnam ribbons.

Associated with an engineering consultant firm until 1993. Play a lot of golf and flight simulation on his computer. Life could not be any better. His son, Mike, retired from the USN in 1995, as a chief air traffic controller and lives near with his children. His daughter was an Army nurse for five years and still retains a Reserve commission.

JOHN THEODORE "TED" CROSBY, born July 30, 1920, Eureka, CA; grew up and educated in the Oakland, San Francisco Bay area. Entered USN flight training in May 1942. Assigned to forming fighter squadron VF-18 at Alameda, CA, as a carrier qualified ensign, July 1943. VF-18 flying F6F Hellcats was sent to the Pacific as part of Air Group 17 aboard the USS *Bunker Hill*, joining the 7th Fleet at a time which started the comeback of the USN in the Pacific.

Striking Rabaul Harbor, the taking of *Tarawa* and attacking most of the islands of the West Central Pacific, VF-18 was then relieved and returned to the US to reform as VF-17. Returned to combat aboard the USS *Hornet* in January 1945. The *Hornet* aircraft flew strikes against Okinawa supporting the invasion and conquest of the island. Many strikes were made on japan including the Japanese Fleet at Kuri Harbor sinking much of it. Attacked Tokyo in support of the invasion of Iwo Jima and participated in the sinking of the battleship *Yamato* and much of its task force.

The big day was April 16, 1945, while on protective cover of a picket destroyer north of Okinawa. Many bogies were reported approaching from the north, Crosby's four plane division started climbing north. At flight level 20 a group of 12 enemy mixed types of planes was sighted, still higher. At this altitude only division leader Lt. Wooley and Crosby were in pursuit, other members having had oxygen and mechanical problems. Upon reaching bogies altitude, 25,000 feet, it appeared to be a group of kamikaze being led by modern "jack" fighters. Lt. Wooley attacked the rear of the group and the lead "jacks" turned into Crosby who met them with the Hellcat superior fire power. After a series of attacks Crosby had accounted for three jacks, one Zeke and one val., becoming a one mission instant ace.

He returned to the USN following WWII, assuming many JO assignments, officer in charge of the first GCA units, and USN Line School in 1949, photo-recon work, leading an umber of flight detachments with the 6th Fleet Mediterranean area, updating US world photo intelligence, then to Korea, in 1952 aboard the USS *Tarawa* in charge of a detachment of photo F2H Banshees.

Retired in June 1969 with the rank of commander. Received the Navy Cross, three Distinguished Flying Crosses, nine Air Medals and two Presidential Unit Citations.

His wife, Lucille, passed away in June 1989. He has one son, a Navy lieutenant in Vietnam. He is retired and restores antique cars.

MELVIN J. CROWDER, born June 9, 1923, Dunsieth, ND. Joined the USN Dec. 12, 1942, and reported aboard the USS *Hornet* Dec. 23, 1943. He was stationed to flight deck, aviation ordnance. He participated in action from the Marshall Islands to the end of the war.

Memorable experiences were being a member of the crew of the best ship in the USN and serving under Adm. JJ (Jocko) Clark.

Discharged Feb. 4, 1946, and joined the Reserves from 1947-52. Received the American Theater, Asiatic-Pacific w/9 stars, Philippine Liberation w/2 stars, Good Conduct and Presidential Unit Citation.

Married to Delores and is retired.

JAMES J. CROWLEY, born June 12, 1924, Ellsworth, MN. Joined the USN on Sept. 25, 1942, and was assigned to the USS *Hornet* in October 1944. He was stationed with VF-11 as a Hellcat pilot. He participated in action in the Philippines, Formosa and the China Sea.

Released from active duty Dec. 19, 1945, then retired from the Reserves in 1968. Received the Air Medal.

Married to Mary and has five children and eight grandchildren. He is retired.

HARRY R. DAVIS, born July 23, 1920, Oakland, CA, attended San Francisco Junior College until 1941. Gained the nickname "Stinky" from a well known comic strip Toonerville Folks and then reinforced name in the USN by a swimming fiasco one night in Biscayne Bay, FL.

Started flying in 1939 privately, then college CPT appeared as a financial blessing, and obtained his private license in 1940. Had taken advanced courses and passed written for commercial license in late 1941. Signed up for the USN on Dec. 8, 1941, but did not get called until January 1942.

Served with VF-2 aboard the carrier USS *Enterprise* (VF-2 was substituted for VF-6) the air group assigned. One month plus aboard the VCL USS *Monterrey* on temporary duty and then rejoined VF-2 for cruises aboard the USS *Hornet*.

After discharge from the USN in late 1945 he enrolled at UC Berkeley. In 1947 he obtained his commercial instrument license and spent the next 33 years with world wide airlines and retired in 1980. Started a manufacturers representative agency for engineered products. Holds three Distinguished Flying Crosses, seven Air Medals, two Presidential Unit Citations and a Purple Heart.

Has two sons and his original wife, Lorraine, of 49 years this date.

JOHN MACK DAVIS, born March 8, 1921, Gordo, AL. Joined the USN in July 1942, and was assigned to the USS *Hornet* from September 1944-February 1945, as a TBF pilot with VT-11. Participated in action at Formosa, Luzon, Okinawa, Leyte, Manila, China Sea, Hong Kong and Samar.

Memorable experiences include after the battle off Samar, with gunner R.A. Willis and radar operator Fred F. Wilson, landed on the *Hornet* and out of fuel in arresting gear.

Discharged in September 1945. Received the Navy Cross and two Air Medals.

Married Alta and had two daughters, Nan and Joanne and two sons, Carroll and Don. He retired from FAA and is living in Tuscaloosa, AL.

WILLIAM J. "BILL JIM" DAVIS, born Aug. 31, 1920, Memphis, TN. Joined the USN in December 1938; assigned to the USS *Helena* in September 1939; aboard the *Helena* at Pearl Harbor, Dec. 7, 1941; forced to abandon ship after *Helena* torpedoed and sank during the battle of Kula Gulf, July 6, 1943.

Reported to the USS *Hornet* (CV-12), Sept. 19, 1943; was in charge of the automatic telephone system; battle station was IC room; promoted to CEM in May 1944; in charge of flight deck electrical systems; and was assigned to battle station of flight deck.

Most memorable experience was while anchored at Eniwetok Island, June 1944. During a movie on hanger deck there was a stampede of men, moving away from the sound of a fire extinguisher accidentally activated, believing a bomb was about to explode. There were deaths and injuries in melee.

Transferred for commissioning to ensign in August 1944; engineering officer, LST-343, November 1944-December 1945. Discharged in January 1946. Joined the USNR unit in 1946; was recalled to active duty during the Korean War, January 1951, as assistant tech training officer, NAS Atlanta. Discharged in February 1954.

Served as Tennessee State Senator from November 1970-November 1982. Worked as an agent for State Farm Insurance Companies, Covington, TN, since 1957.

WILLIAM N DELL, born Oct. 14, 1936, Tiffin, OH. Joined the USN on June 16, 1954, at Detroit, MI; went to boot camp at Great Lakes, IL; attended Dental Technicians School at Great Lakes; and was assigned to NATTC, Norman, OK, upon graduation. Reported to the USS *Coral Sea* at Norfolk, VA, in March 1956; Mediterranean Cruise, 1956-57; sailed around South America to Bremerton, WA, for decommissioning in May 1957. Released from active duty at Naval Amphibious Base, Coronado, Ca, on Aug. 30, 1957.

Attended college upon release and graduated in 1961. Spent 20 years as construction manager in Ohio. Presently resides in Phoenix, AZ, and is employed in the construction industry.

MELVIN E. DELZER, born March 15, 1927, Hague, ND. Joined the USN March 13, 1945, and was assigned to the USS *Hornet* July 5, 1945. Was stationed with the V-5 Div.

His most memorable experience was the "magic carpet."

Discharged July 6, 1946. Received the Asiatic-Pacific, American Area and WWII Victory Medals.

Married and has five children. He is a retired heavy highway contractor.

JOSEPH M. DIANGELIS, born Aug. 15, 1935, Weirton, WV. Joined the USN in 1952 and went to boot camp at Bainbridge, MD. Was assigned to the USS *Hornet*. He boxed and was Bainbridge champ, Mediterranean champ and Air Landt champ. Nickname was "Ohio Whirlwind." Also served on the USS *Lake Champlain* and USS *Alstede*.

Discharged in 1960; raised a family; and joined the US Army Reserves, from which he retired in 1994. Received the Navy Good Conduct Medal, National Defense Service Medal w/Korea and Desert Storm Cluster, Army Achievement Medal, Army Reserve Component Medal, Army of Occupation Medal, Armed Forces Reserve Medal, NCO Professional Development Medal and Armed Service Ribbon.

Married and has five children and nine grandchildren. He is currently enjoying retirement.

FREDERICK E. DILLON, born June 3, 1925, Waterbury, CT. Joined the USN Aug. 24, 1943, and was assigned to the USS *Hornet* in November 1943. He was stationed at the generators.

Most memorable experience was the June 5, 1945, typhoon.

Discharged May 3, 1946, with the rank of MM3/c. Received the American Theater Medal, WWII Victory Medal, Asiatic-Pacific Medal w/9 stars and Philippine Liberation Ribbon w/2 stars.

Married and has one son, one daughter and one grandson. He is retired.

EDWARD J. DOLAN, born May 13, 1927, Chicago, IL. Joined the USN May 13, 1943, and was assigned to the USS *Hornet* in April 1944. He was stationed as plane captain and achieved the rank of MM3/c. Participated in everything the *Hornet* did from 1944-46; he never left the *Hornet*.

Memorable experiences include a typhoon taking off the bow. After the bow was destroyed the Corsair that landed in an emergency landing was the last plane he was plane captain of the Corsair tried to take off from the damaged bow, but flipped into the water.

Discharged in May 1946. Received the Presidential Unit Citation, PUM, ARM, ATM and VM and five Battle Stars.

He is retired and lives in North Carolina in a home he built in 1984, himself. He is 70 years old and feels like he did when he was 20. He has two daughters in Chicago.

NEVANCE ROSS "DON" DONALDSON, born April 14, 1918, Logansport, IN. Enlisted in the USNR Dec. 17, 1941, Oakland, CA. Sent to boot camp, San Diego, CA, and transferred to AMM School, USNAS, Alameda, CA, February 1942. After graduation, transferred to Marine Air Group, Guadalcanal, April 1943. Was senior plane captain for unit of five F4F (Wildcat) fighter aircraft. VF-11 shot down most enemy aircraft in greatest aerial battle fought in Southwest Pacific over Guadalcanal, June 16, 1943.

Returned to the US in August 1943. Attended advanced Mechanical School, Chicago, IL. Returned to VF-11, December 1943. Squadron returned to Fleet to board USS *Hornet* (CV-12) at Manus, September 1944. Principal responsibilities were acting as liaison between squadron and ship's company and continually repairing aircraft including engine changes if combat prevented replacements being flown in.

While in the *Hornet*, participated in battle of Leyte Gulf. Was in TG-38.1 under command of Vice-Admiral McCain. Did not go north with Adm. Halsey. Did attack Japanese fleet on the morning of Oct. 25, 1944, to relieve Taffy CVE units. Per operational intelligence command Pacific Fleet, memo #55, Nov. 24, 1944. "Air Group Eleven strike was one of the longest ever undertaken by carrier aircraft and undoubtedly one of the most important. Damage to Japanese fleet was heavy. Attack was covered by VF-11, five DDs and CA damaged by squadron."

Returned to the States in February 1945. Squadron skipper elected to take a few of them to join Training Sqdn. VF-98, based at Los Alametos, CA, which was his new command. Honorably discharged as AMMP1/c on Nov. 4, 1945.

He is proud to have served aboard the USS *hornet* as a member of VF-11 and had the opportunity to have been aboard the following US ships in hostile waters: carriers *Hornet* (CV-12), USS *Wasp* (CV-18), *Long Island* (CVE-1), *Copahee* (CVE-12), *Altamaha* (CVE-18), *Breton* (CVE-23), *Chenango* (CVE-28), *Kassan Bay* (CVE-69), Seaplane Tender USS *Curtiss* (AV-4) and destroyer USS *Shaw*.

Received the American Theater Ribbon, Asiatic-Pacific Ribbon w/4 stars, Philippine Liberation w/2 stars, WWII Victory Medal, Good Conduct and USS *Hornet* Presidential Unit Citation w/star. Also received commendation presented to Air Group 11 by Adm. Marc A. Mitscher for tour of duty under his command on Guadalcanal. Adm. Mitscher was first captain of first air-crafter carrier named *Hornet* (CV-8).

With his wife, Margie, of 50 years, he has four sons, three daughters, 12 grandchildren and three great-grandchildren. He is recently retired and currently resides in Pollock Pines, CA. He is a member of the USS *Hornet* Club, Inc. and a commander and plank owner of Aircraft Carrier *Hornet* Foundation (ACHF).

JOSEPH M. DORIA, born July 29, 1924, Scranton, PA. Joined the USN June 7, 1943, and was assigned to the USS *Hornet*, March 29, 1944-June 10, 1945, in the Pacific War Area. He was stationed to gunnery.

Memorable experiences were appendicitis surgery being put on hold because of fighting going on top. The surgery was resumed and he healed well.

Discharged Feb. 25, 1946, with the rank of S1/c. Received the Pacific Theater Ribbon, American

Theater Ribbon, WWII Victory Medal, Philippine Liberation Ribbon w/2 stars and Pacific Area w/9 stars.

Has three children, 11 grandchildren and one great-grandchild. Worked as a welder for Foster Wheeler Corp., Mountaintop, PA. Passed away March 2, 1994.

JOHN E. DOUGHERTY JR., born in Wilmington, DE, joined the USN July 31, 1951. He was assigned to the USS *Hornet* in the position of operations and achieved the rank of SN.

Shortly after celebrating his 21st birthday in the South China Sea, they arrived on station July 23, 1954, and relieved the *Tarawa. Hornet* became flagship of TG-70.2 operating in the South China Sea, with Adm. Phillips, commander of the 1st Fleet, embarked on board the *Hornet*.

His duty station was the flag bridge, which provided him with first hand information concerning the following events:

A British airliner out of Hong Kong, was downed by aircraft from the Peoples Republic of China. There were 20 passengers of which five were US Nationals.

Adm. Phillips ordered the Philippine Sea and *Hornet* to launch aircraft, for search and rescue. *Hornet's* station was off the coast of Hainan Island, July 25, 1954. As the search continued their aircraft became entangled with planes from PRC and downed two PRC aircraft; however, during the ensuing skirmish several surface ships from communist countries joined the fight and began firing on the search and rescue aircraft. Several survivors were rescued.

The second event was to cover the French, debacle in Vietnam, it was at this time the use of nuclear weapons appeared on the *Hornet's* deck, along with bombers to deliver the bombs. Adm. Radford's wisdom prevailed and nuclear bombs were stowed away. There were numerous overflights taking place over the PRC, Mainland, plus daily flights over Hainan Island.

Thirdly, *Hornet*, sailed the straights of Formosa for many weeks, keeping the PRC from bombarding the Nationalist islands of Quemoy and Matsu.

Many of his shipmates were not aware of all actions and activities that they were involved in during their five month stay in the China Seas. Notwithstanding his previous remarks, he would like to say that the world cruise enabled him to achieve one of his dreams; that being able to cross every meridian on the face of the earth while traveling in one direction, thus becoming a member of the circumnavigators club. A feat not enjoyed by many in 1954. He is equally proud to have served on board the *Hornet* and joining the Ancient Order of Shellbacks. The most lasting achievement was making real friendships with his cruise mates which have lasted to this day.

JAMES E. DUFFY, born May 31, 1925, Holtwood, PA. Joined the USN Aug. 19, 1943, and was assigned to the USS *Hornet* (CV-12) Nov. 29, 1943. Was assigned to number three fire room as a water tender for B Div. Participated in action against enemy Japanese forces in the Pacific War Area from March 29, 1944, to June 10, 1945.

Most memorable experience was the typhoon on June 5, 1945.

Discharged April 26, 1946. Received the Pacific Theater Ribbon w/10 stars, Presidential Unit Citation, Philippine Liberation Ribbon w/2 stars, American Theater Ribbon and WWII Victory Medal.

Retired from Pennsylvania Power and Light Co. His wife passed away in March 1984.

JAMES ARTHUR DUNLAP, born March 21, 1920, Mt. Ayr, IA. Joined the USN Dec. 16, 1941, and was assigned to the USS *Hornet* in October 1944. Served as SB2/c pilot in VB-11. Participated in action at Okinawa, October 10; Formosa, October 12; Luzon and Leyte, Oct. 19-Nov. 20, 1944.

Transferred to Ready Reserve in September 1945. Received the Presidential Unit Citation and Distinguished Flying Cross.

Married Jean and has three daughters: Judy, Jane and Joan. Retired structural engineer and Navy Reservist.

GAYLORD E. EDLING, born Sept. 10, 1924, Marquette, NE. Joined the USN Dec. 2, 1942, and was assigned to the USS *Hornet* from December 1944-July 1945. He was stationed as a fighter pilot, F6F, VF-11 and VF-17. Participated in all major fleet action during that period with the *Hornet*.

Most memorable experience was when the fly one officer sent him off in the prop wash of the plane ahead of him. Just after leaving the deck and flipping his wheels, he was on his back under the level of the flight deck and he could see the bow of the ship in his mirror. The next thing he knew he was flying just above water and shaking. He had just automatically made a snap roll on take-off and lived (the ship had turned out of the wind to keep from hitting him). He then joined up with his group and went on their mission. After landing a few hours later, his plane captain jumped upon the wing and told him, "you made the neatest snap roll on take-off."

Discharged Sept. 14, 1945, with the rank of lieutenant(jg). Received the Distinguished Flying Cross and five Air Medals.

Married Dorothy Meshier Dec. 28, 1948, and has four sons, one daughter and 11 grandchildren. He graduated from the University of Nebraska in June 1949; worked in sales and management in the petroleum business; and retired in April 1986 from Northern Natural Gas Co.

HOWARD G. ERVIN JR., born May 10, 1918, Hartford City, IN. Joined the USN Aug. 15, 1944, and was assigned to the USS *Hornet* in September 1944. Was stationed with VB-11, dive-bomber pilot (SB2C).

Most memorable experiences were the strikes on Leyte Gulf, Clark Field, Manila Bay; the strike on the Japanese fleet in Samar; several strikes on Formosa; getting hit by AA on strike on Pescadories

Islands and being shot down and rescued by the destroyer USS *Maddox* in the South China Sea. On first strike off *Hornet*, October 1944, he was assigned a 275 mile search close to Okinawa. He spotted a Japanese Val dive bomber. The fighter flying escort on him "smoked" the dive bomber on the first run!

Discharged in February 1947 with the rank of lieutenant. Received the Distinguished Flying Cross.

Married Janet Holliday (author of the *White House Cookbook* and several children's books) and has three sons (two in California and one in Milwaukee). Retired as branch division manager of Corning Fiberglas Corp.

JOHNNY B. EUBANKS, born Dec. 17, 1932, in Bristol, FL. He joined the US Navy on March 4, 1953, and was assigned to the *Hornet* after boot camp. During his time on the carrier, the crew conducted a world cruise in 1954 which included a memorable equatorcrossing ceremony. He was the one showing most of the nightly films aboard the *Hornet*, including movies on the flight deck.

He was among the last of the original recommissioned *Hornet* crew members to leave the carrier in February 1957. Upon his release from active duty with the rank of IC3, he returned to his home town and took a job as an instrument technician for a chemical company. He began working as a Veterans Service Officer for Liberty county in 1959. In 1962, he was named director of veteran services in Leon county, a post he held for 21 years.

Shortly before retiring from the VA, he founded The Calhoun-Liberty Journal, a weekly newspaper that covers a two county area in the Florida panhandle. In addition to his duties as newspaper publisher, he is active in the local chambers of commerce in Calhoun and Liberty county.

Married Rowena and they have one daughter, Teresa.

EVERETT DOUGLAS EVANS, born April 4, 1933, Norwich, CT. Joined the USN in august 1951 and was assigned to the USS *Hornet* in April 1954. He was stationed as a BT and achieved the rank of petty officer 3/c. Participated in the police action in Korea while on the 1954 world cruise.

Most memorable experience was seeing a pilot parachute from a crippled plane and taking movies on his way down.

Discharged in July 1955. Received the European Clasp, National Defense, Korean Service, China Service, Good Conduct and Navy Occupation Medals.

Retired to Leesburg, FL after 36 years with an electric boat (General Dynamics) submarine builders, Groton, CT. Married to Muriel for 41 years and has a son, Douglas; daughter, Lori; and grandchild, Brian.

GLENN R. EVANS, born Feb. 24, 1929, Beaver, PA. Joined the USN Nov. 22, 1950, and was assigned to the USS *Hornet* in March 1951, as a pipefitter. Achieved the rank of AMAN.

Memorable experiences were of the submarine following the ship for three days in the Atlantic Ocean.

Discharged Sept. 20, 1954. Received the National Defense Medal.

He is semi-retired and also works as a transportation construction inspector. He is married and has two sons, one daughter and two grandchildren.

MICHAEL FANOK, born March 3, 1921, in Northampton, PA; joined the US Navy Aug. 11, 1942, and was assigned to the USS *Hornet* on March 12, 1944, at Ford Island.

He was a radioman, gunner trained to fly with his pilot in the SB2C ACFT. Responsibilities were to protect the ACFT during bombing runs, take photographs of results of enemy strikes and anti-sub patrol (ASP). Attained the rank of ARM2C.

Memorable event was during the Pacific Theater, April 22, 1944, Strike Watke Island, New Guinea. Due to anti-aircraft gunfire damage, they were unable to execute a carrier landing. Fanok and his pilot debated whether to parachute from the plane or to land in the water. They chose the sea landing, which he carried out perfectly. He retrieved and inflated the raft and they climbed in. They had two minutes to set sail before the 2C gently joined "Davy Jones' Fleet." As they awaited rescue, he emptied his .38 cal. at some nearby hungry-looking sharks, but he missed purposely. DD Bradford came to their rescue nearly an hour later. His pilot, Hugo Isabella, suggested he stow his helmet inside his flight jacket lest a Bradford crewman "requisition" it as a souvenir. After a vicious storm (but no seasickness), they were transferred the next day to CV-12 without a Navy band to welcome them.

Discharged Dec. 19, 1945, with a the rank of ARM2/c. Awarded the Air Medal twice.

Employed by the Naval Aviation Supply Office in Philadelphia for 33 1/2; currently retired. Three children (all graduates of Drexel University in Philadelphia) and three grandchildren (ages six, three, and one).

PAUL E. FARR, born April 17, 1927, in Fort Wayne, IN, and joined the US Navy April 12, 1945. Assigned to the USS *Hornet* Aug. 1, 1945.

Discharged July 25, 1946, with the rank of seaman 2/c. Awarded the WWII Victory Medal and Asiatic-Pacific Area Campaign.

Has six children and was a engineer and electrician; retired.

CHARLES L. FELLOW, born Feb. 19, 1922, Kokomo, IN. Joined the USN Feb. 4, 1941, and was assigned to the USS *Hornet* in September 1941. He was assigned to fire room #9 and did boiler watches.

He participated in all operations from commissioning to the sinking on Oct. 26, 1942.

Memorable experiences were of the day they were sunk; and when Gen. Doolittle took of for Tokyo in B-25s.

Discharged Nov. 18, 1969. Received the Asiatic-Pacific w/7 stars, American Area, RVN Service, National Defense, Bronze Star, American Defense w/star, Philippine Liberation w/star, Good Conduct w/5 stars, Navy Occupation w/Asia Clasp, WWII Victory, China Service and Vietnam Service.

Married Leila Kise March 23, 1945, and has three children: Elaine, Nancy and David. He is disabled and retired.

OTTO A. FINLEY, born Sept. 11, 1912, near Lacrosse, WA. Reported to NAS Sand Point July 1936 for flight training. Retired from BuPers July 1962.

Reported to pre-commissioning detail USS *Hornet* (CV-12), August 1943. Served aboard until July 1946. Air operations officer during WWII. Air officer, troop officer, navigator and inactivation officer post WWII. Designated naval aviator 1937. VP2, VP45/14, flight instructor and executive officer, TS2B Pensacola; General Line School, executive officer; NAS Whidbey, commanding officer, FASRON 117; commanding officer, NAS Pearl; Armed Forces Staff College, BuNavMat. BiAer. Co. VW-13; Asst. Chief for Records BuPers; Naval Member National Board for Promotion of Rifle Practice 1961-62.

Dir. Competitions NRA 1962-66. International Shooting Rifle Jury Member 1963-75. Farming in West Virginia.

RICHARD J. FITTON, born April 18, 1927, in Hamilton, OH, and joined the US Navy April 1942. Assigned to the USS *Hornet* (CV-12), August 1945. Rank achieved: SKD3C. Discharged August 1946 and is currently Chairman of the Board of First Financial Bancorp and First National Bank of Southwestern Ohio.

OSCAR C. FRESQUEZ, born May 17, 1936, Chamberino, NM. Joined the USN Aug. 6, 1954, and was assigned to the USS *Hornet* Oct. 20, 1954. Was stationed with the 1st Div. as gunner and as a loader on five-inch gun-mount.

Discharged July 7, 1958. Received the China Service and Good Conduct Medals.

He is sixth generation, Spanish ancestry. Retired and waiting for a reunion.

WILLIAM K. "BILL" FULLMER, born June 8, 1932, Los Angeles, CA. Joined the USN Feb. 21, 1951, and was assigned to the USS *Hornet* Sept. 11, 1953. Was stationed on the flight deck as a plane handler, tractor driver and repair.

Memorable experiences include the world cruise in 1954.

Discharged Feb. 18, 1955. Received the National Defense Service Medal, Navy Occupation Service Medal (Europe), Good Conduct Medal and China Service Medal.

Has been married for 38 years and has three children and three grandchildren. Retired from the Los Angeles County fire department as a fire captain after 30 years in 1988. Now lives near San Diego, CA. Rides off-road motorcycles and fly's radio controlled airplanes.

JOHN "WHITEY" GALASYN, born Dec. 9, 1922, Hartford, CT. Joined the USN Nov. 4, 1941, and was assigned to the USS *Hornet* from 1944-45. Stationed as an aircraft mechanic with FS-17; participated in the battle of Mariannas, Okinawa, Philippines, Leyte invasion, Sea of Japan, Coral Sea and Iwo Jima invasion.

Memorable experiences were of WWII, on the *Hornet,* off Okinawa, during the typhoon in 1945; 138 miles per hour winds; and the deck curled up and over the side. Also a deck hand got killed by the propeller of a kamikazi plane that hit the ship.

Discharged Dec. 20, 1945, with the rank of RMM1/c. Received the Asiatic-Pacific w/2 stars, WWII Victory Medal, Presidential unit Citation, American Defense, American Theater.

Has been married for 50 years to Blanche and has one daughter and two grandchildren. He is a member of the USS *Hornet* Club and VFW. He retired as an excavation contractor after 25 years.

ANTHONY GALINDEZ, born Oct. 7, 1936, New York City, NY. He joined the USN Oct. 28, 1954 and was assigned to the USS Hornet Jan. 25, 1955, V-1 and achieved the rank of airman.

Memorable experiences: as elevator operator #1 and #2 elevators was always with safety of aircraft pilot and crew. He was discharged Oct. 27, 1958.

Recently moved to Rangely Co. and hopes to stay active.

PAUL GARBLER, born Jan. 4, 1918, in Newark, NJ and joined the USN on Sept. 3, 1941; assigned to the USS *Hornet* in March 1944. He served with Air Group 2, Bombing Sqdn. 2 and flew scouting and bombing missions.

Memorable experiences include the first and second battle of the Philippine sea. Received two Distinguished Flying Crosses, six Air Medals, Presidential Unit Citation, WWII Victory Medal, American Defense Medal, Asiatic Pacific Area w/4 Campaign Stars.

Discharged in January 1956 with the rank of captain.

Married with a daughter. Semi-retired and does some consulting.

LOUIS P. GARGANO, born Oct. 3, 1918, in Brooklyn, NY. He joined the USN in December 1941. He first served aboard the USS *South Dakota* and the USS *Hornet* (CV-8). In January 1942 he was assigned to the USS *Hornet*, (CV-12), where he served as a seaman first class until his discharge from the Navy in September 1945.

On Oct. 19, 1949, he married Geraldine Speranze. He and Gerald have two sons, John and Gerald; four daughters, Camille, MaryAnne, Joan and Theresa. They have 12 grandchildren. He and his family moved to Pearl River, NY in 1967, their current residence. He retired in 1975 after a 25 year career as an iron worker for the New York City Department of Public Works. He then worked for five years for Prentice Hall in Old Tappan, NJ.

He was a member of the American Legion in Pearl River, NY, the Pearl River Republican Club and the St. Margaret's Golden Age Chapter. He was a usher at St. Margaret's R.C. Church in Pearl River and was volunteer at the Rockland Psychiatric Center and the Hudson Valley Blood Bank.

He passed away on Jan. 5, 1997, at his home in Pearl River, NY. He was 78 years old. He often spoke about his experiences in the USN aboard the *Hornet* and attended the reunions whenever he could. They all knew how proud he was to serve his country aboard the *Hornet*.

ROBERT A. GARRITANO, born Dec. 15, 1931, in Chicago, IL and joined the USN on Sept. 27, 1950. Attended boot training at Great Lakes, IL where afterwards he was assigned MSTS Command and reported aboard the USS *General Randall*, TAP-115. Served aboard the USS *Randall* until August 1953 at which time, he was transferred to USS *Hornet*, (CVA-12), reporting to the chief engineer as the "Oil King."

Since his experience was in engineering, particularly boilers, he obtained a position with a safety valve manufacturer, specializing in the utility market, calling on nuclear and fossil power plants for 25 years.

He retired in 1996 and plans to spend more time with his four children and two grandchildren presently residing in Chicago.

DOMINICK A. GIARRAPUTO, born Feb. 10, 1925, in Brooklyn, NY and joined the USN July 6, 1943; reported to boot camp at Sampson, NY. Upon graduation he reported to the following stations and ships; CASU-21/NH; St. Albans, CASU-21; USS *Hornet*, (CV-12); RS Brooklyn, NY; FAR CH San Diego, CA; USS *Block Island*, (CUE-106); USS *Corregidor* (CV-58). Discharged in March 1946.

While attending college he was recalled for ac-

tive duty in the Korean conflict in January 1951. Earned a Defense Medal and was discharged in September 1951.

Employed by the Dept. of Defense, US Army vessels and was promoted to mate/master on various vessels upon passing the required US Coast Guard examinations.

In June 1972 was transferred to USCG as Water Transport Officer. Returned January 1982 after 38.8 years of Federal Service. Retired from New York Guard as LTC 88BDE.

Memorable experiences were requesting permission to fire ships guns onto an enemy island; Returning from a mission with Capt. A.K. Doyle, they were passing very close to the island they had previously attacked and by passed a few enemy troops on the island. Capt. Doyle thought it was a great idea for the ship's guns to fire onto enemy territory. This would be a first for an aircraft carrier, the request was denied by headquarters.

KEN GLASS, born Feb. 26, 1922, at Dundee, IA. Entered flight training June 4, 1942, receiving his wings at Corpus Christie, TX, January 1943. Completed 33 combat missions aboard the USS *Hornet* from March to October, 1944, receiving the Distinguished Flying Cross, seven Air Medals, the Presidential Unit Citation and five Battle Stars.

Following active duty, he joined the Reserves as a weekend warrior flying out of Grosse Isle, MI, retiring as a captain in 1972. Highlight of his Reserve assignment as commanding officer of an attack bomber squadron was winning the Noel Davis Trophy in 1952.

Accomplishments of recent note include: co-author of *The Hornets* and their heroic men; *Hornet* man of the year, 1993; induction into the Ohio Veterans Hall of Fame, 1996.

Married Rose in 1950 and they have five sons: Kenneth, Richard, Robert, Philip and Paul. All are graduates of Miami University of Ohio. He received a Ph.D. from Michigan State University in 1963. In 1987 he retired from Miami University after serving 25 years as an administrator and professor. Presently Chairman – Board of Directors, USS HORNET Club, Inc.

EUGENE H. GLENN, born Feb. 9, 1924, in Chicago, IL and joined the USN in 1943, receiving his wings on Christmas Eve 1943. He was assigned to Torpedo Sqdn. 2 aboard the USS *Hornet* from June 1944 until the end of WWII. He participated in numerous actions, including the sinking of ships in Manila Bay, Sept. 21-22, 1944. He received two Distinguished Flying Crosses and four Air Medals.

One of his most memorable experiences was seeing the fleet at anchor in Eniwetok Atoll on the day the war ended.

He was released from active duty in 1946 and

retired from Reserve duty in 1975. Gene passed away on Feb. 13, 1996. He is survived by his wife Ann and children: Steve, Tom, Maureen, and Dan.

WALTER P. GODWIN, born Oct. 4, 1926, in rural Whigham, GA and entered the service in January 1945; received boot camp training at Great Lakes, IL; assigned to the USS *Hornet* in April 1945. Was involved in the Okinawa battle and received one Bronze Star.

Was aboard on June 5, 1945, when the ship was damaged in the typhoon that caused it to be sent back to the US for repairs and major overhaul during which time the war came to an end. Served as a member of the 40 mm gun crew. When they went back to sea, they made several voyages bringing troops back to the US; then the ship was prepared for moth ball storage. He left the ship in July 1946.

Married Maggie Davis and they have two children. He has been engaged in farming for the last 50 years. He and his son have been successful farmers in grain, livestock, peanuts, and tobacco. They now own and operate a farm of 1,500 acres.

EMANUEL GOLD, born Feb. 14, 1925, Brooklyn, NY. Joined the USN July 5, 1943, and was assigned to the USS *Hornet* in September 1943. He served as aerographer and achieved the rank of second class.

Memorable experiences were of the Kamikaze missing ship.

Discharged March 9, 1946. Received the WWII Victory Medal, American Theater Medal, Asiatic-Pacific Medal w/9 stars and Philippine Liberation Medal w/2 stars.

He is a retired tech from the New York Telephone Co. He is a widower with two wonderful children and five lovely grandchildren.

CLAUDE M. GOODNER, born April 10, 1926, Arcanum, OH, and graduated in 1944. Joined the USN in January 1945 at Columbus, OH; boot camp at NTC Great Lakes, IL. Served aboard the USS *Hornet*, (CV-12), April 1945-July 1946 in gunnery, 4th Div., 20 mm and 40 mm mounts.

Memorable experiences were of the strikes off Okinawa, typhoon in June 1945, flight deck dropped over the bow, planes and torpedo loose on flight deck, launch planes from the stern.

Discharged from the Navy in 1946 with the rank of sergeant first class.

Retired from General Motors after 40 years as an industrial engineer. Married with three children and five grandchildren.

JAMES GARLAND GRAY, born May 17, 1925, Philadelphia, PA. Joined the USN July 8, 1942, and was assigned to the USS *Hornet* Nov. 30, 1943. Served as a radio operator for Air Dale Ship's Co. Participated in Palau, March 29, 1944 and Tokyushu May 14, 1945.

Memorable experiences include breaking radio silence in Hong Kong Jan. 15, 1945.

Discharged Feb. 22, 1946. Received the Pacific Theater w/9 Battle Stars, Presidential Unit Citation, Philippine Liberation w/2 stars, Good Conduct and American Theater.

Married and has 11 children, 30 grandchildren and two great-grandchildren. He is retired and still loves the ocean. Watches the history channel hoping to see the CV-12.

THEODORE A. GRELL, born Aug. 19, 1915, Detroit, MI. Joined the USN June 14, 1934. Was assigned to the USS *Hornet* in June 1943 as lieutenant in the flight department. Also served as flight deck officer; FOO, V-1 Div. officer; and CDO. Participated in all Pacific action from March 1944-June 1945 when transferred to CNO OP05.

Memorable experiences include the shakedown cruise in the Atlantic and the transit of Panama Canal to the Pacific.

Retired July 1, 1962, with the rank of captain. Received the Silver Star, Bronze Star, Presidential Unit Citation w/star, Atlantic, Africa, Pacific, etc., Medals.

Married Dorothy Prieur and has two daughters, one son, eight grandchildren and three great-grandchildren.

MERLE "MURIEL" LEROY GRIFFIN, born March 26, 1923, in Binghamton, NY and joined the USN April 26, 1943, serving boot camp at Sampson, NY and continued on to Pungo, VA. He was assigned to the USS *Hornet*, (CV-12), TF-58, and went on a shakedown cruise shortly after his assignment. He saw action in Leyte, Philippines and in the China Sea. The *Hornet* went through a typhoon in Okinawa continuing on to engage the Japanese fleet.

His most memorable thoughts were when the Canabera and the Houston were hit. Also, the *Hornet* was attacked at night and flares were dropped, what an awesome sight on the open sea! The sunrises and sunsets were most beautiful when viewed from the open deck of the *Hornet* according to Griffin.

He worked as a propeller technician and received the American Theater Ribbon, Philippine Liberation Ribbon w/2 Stars, Asiatic Pacific Ribbon w/9 stars, and the Victory Ribbon upon his discharge Feb. 8, 1946.

Married Joyce and they celebrated their 51st wedding anniversary June 21, 1997. They have four children, 13 grandchildren and 11 great-grandchildren. He is retired from General Motors and he and his wife enjoy traveling throughout the US and most of all spending their winters in Florida.

DELROY WILSON HAGGIE, born Aug. 28, 1922, in Deerfield IL and enlisted in the USN on Feb. 10, 1942, at NAS Glenview, IL. On October 22, 1943 he reported to Fleet Airwing Nine and on Oct. 3, 1944, to Norfolk, VA for duty, then to BS 15 NAS. On Feb. 14, 1944, he reported to the USS *Hornet*. The following are notes from his journal: February-Panama Canal, Marshall Island, Palau Island, Caroline, Guam, Rota. They picked up R.M. and one half Tweed, Leyte Gulf, Luzon Island. *Hornet* traveled 88, 473 miles during his cruise.

He was released from active duty October 1945 and returned home and joined the Highland Park Police Dept. In January 1949 he transferred from Navy Reserves to Air Force Reserves in Glenview, IL. He was called to active duty in June 1950 and sent to Carswell Air Force Base, Fort Worth, TX where he was a chief investigator- master sergeant.

In 1953 he formed Highland Park Heating Service and was a heating contractor for 35 years.

He was an active volunteer in the VFW, Boy Scouts and Lions and also a lifelong volunteer at the North Chicago Veterans Hospital. He is survived by his wife Pegi and five children; D. Patrick (Karen), Michael (Janice), Dennis, Deborah Ross (Jeff), Barbara Nerini (Larry). He is also survived by his grandchildren: Patrick (Tabitha), Brian, Kevin, Shawn, Kelly (Robert), Valerie, Michael and Christina; and one great grandchild-Kylie.

HARLEY HALL JR., born Oct. 18, 1919, Austin, AR. Joined the USN in 1942, and transferred from the USS *Lexington* to the USS *Hornet*. He inspected planes on the flight deck. Participated in the South Pacific. Discharged in November 1945.

Memorable experiences include a lot of death and destruction.

His wife, Nadine, passed away in 1993. He has a son, Steve. He retired from the Veteran's Administration.

LUTHER PERRY HARRISON, born Sept. 14, 1914, Fort Valley, GA. Joined the USN March 17, 1941, and was assigned to the USS *Hornet* Oct. 20, 1941. He served as an E-1 forward distributor. Participated in action at Tokyo, Coral Sea, Midway and Santa Cruz, where the *Hornet* was sunk, Oct. 26, 1941.

Memorable experiences include being aboard during the raid on Tokyo; and meeting the crew members of Doolittle's raiders.

Discharged March 17, 1947, with the rank of EM3/c. Received two Purple Hearts, Good Conduct, WWII Victory Medal, American Defense, Asiatic-Pacific Campaign, Philippine Liberation and Presidential Unit Citation.

Married in 1946. He worked for a few years as a beer wholesaler in South Carolina, after being dis-

charged; then 27 years with pipe line company. Has three children and two grandchildren. He helps take of his wife, who is in a nursing home.

MICHAEL HARRISON, born Aug. 8, 1919, Scranton, PA. Joined the USN in April 1943 and was assigned to the USS *Hornet* in October 1943. Was stationed with the 4th Div., gunnery, 40 mm forward island and disbursing office. Participated in action at Truk, Iwo Jima, Siapan, strikes on Japan, Ryukyus, Formosa, Luzon and the China Sea.

He was a storekeeper 2/c aboard the *Hornet* on Oct. 13, 1944, operating off the coast of what was then called Formosa (now Taiwan), when the word came: "Bong! Bong!, GQ! Jap twin-engine bomber, port side!" He ran to his gunnery position, the 40 mm just forward of where the admiral was on the island. When he got there, there was no one. He could see the bomber coming low over the water. That Japanese bomber was just skimming the surface of the water. All you could see was a big monster-looking thing coming through. When the first torpedo dropped from the bomber, it looked like a silver whale going in the water. Just missed the fantail. The Japanese dropped a second torpedo, just seconds later. The skipper maneuvered so that one missed, too, and then the five-inch guns on the port side opened up. You saw the plane blow up and fall into the water less than 500 feet away. If the pilot had opened up with whatever guns he had on that plane, he would have wiped out a lot of their crew. Those two torpedoes were the closest they ever came to being hit in action. That bomber was the first plane ever shot down by the *Hornet's* own guns.

Discharged Jan. 16, 1946, with the rank of SKD1/c. Received the Asiatic-Pacific Area Ribbon w/ 7 BSs and the Philippine Liberation Ribbon w/2 BSs.

Married to Dorothy for 56 years and has one daughter, Gloria; five grandchildren and two great-grandchildren. He retired from Chase Bank in 1983. He does puzzles and takes care of his wife.

FREDERICK G. HARVEY, born June 23, 1935, in Kearney, NE and enlisted in the USN on May 10, 1954. Served at NTC San Diego, Company 110; NTC Norman (ANP); NAS/NTC Olathe (ACA); USS *Hornet*, (CVA-12); NAS Miramar (VA-54); and COMAIRPAC North Island.

Hornet duties were: V-1 Division Yeoman air boss's office, pri-fly; X Div., Yeoman 3 Protestant Chaplain. CVA-12 service, WESPAC 1955, Flag Ship COMCARDIVONE; Carrier Air Group Seven; ports of call were Hawaii, Japan, Hong Kong, with operations off the coasts of Formosa and Korea.

Civilian professional life: BA (1962), MA (1965) and Ed.D. (1969) UNL; Nebraska Public Schools, teacher and principal. Superintendent, NSDE; Retired 1993, professor TAMUK, 24 years.

Family: wife Norma; son Larry, architect; grandson, Nathan; and banking daughter Terry. Current plans: full retirement, Aug. 1, 1997.

STEWART L. HASTINGS, born April 25, 1941, Merced, CA. Joined the USN Sept. 20, 1961, and was assigned to the USS *Hornet* in December 1962 as an electricians mate. Attended boot camp, RTC San Diego, CA; served aboard USS *Gregory* (DD-802). Participated in the overhaul at Hunter's Point, San Francisco, 1965.

Memorable experiences include the Wespac cruise in 1962; serving aboard the *Hornet* for two Wespac cruises, 1963-64.

Discharged Aug. 9, 1965, with the rank of EM3. Received the Armed Forces Expeditionary Medal and Navy Good Conduct Medal.

He and his wife, Adrienne, have two children who reside in California. He is a retired civil service employee, 30 years with the VA.

PAUL J. HAYES, born Aug. 11, 1939, Seattle, WA. Joined the USN in 1957 and was assigned to the USS *Hornet* from 1958-60, as flag staff, commander, Carrier Div. 19. He also served in navigation and ASW operations.

Memorable experiences include the typhoons; serving with real WWII and Korean war veterans (many of whom were genuine hero's); and history at sea. Every day was different. The *Hornet* and ship's officers crew always were and always will be one of his life's greatest and favorite experiences.

Discharged in 1960 and was recalled to serve in Vietnam. Was discharged the second time in 1962.

Married to Barbara; has two children from a previous marriage, son, Dany Hayes and daughter, Dede. He is enjoying his 30 foot Bayliner cabin cruiser named "Hornet." You can never take the salt water out of a sailor!

PAUL G. HEATON, born April 10, 1925, at Heaton, NC. He was sworn into the Navy Aug. 13, 1943; attended boot camp at Bainbridge, MD; was assigned to the flight deck of the USS *Hornet* after boot leave; and transferred to hanger control of the USS *Bonhomme Richard* in March 1945. He was discharged Dec. 17, 1945.

Attended Appalachian State University earning a BS, MA and Advanced Certificate. Was principal of Heaton Elementary School, Virginia Carolina High School; Union Grove Elementary School; and North Stanley High School. Retired from school in 1980; drove a tour bus until 1989; presently retired (1996)

and enjoying golfing, fishing, and volunteer work at Britthaven Nursing Home in Albemarle, NC.

KENN "KENN" RALPH HENDERSON, born May 9, 1916 in Pearl River, NY; joined the navy Feb. 4, 1943 and assigned to the USS *Hornet*, (CV-12), on her initial cruise.

Discharged on Oct. 9, 1945, with the rank of photographer's mate second class, USNR. Awarded eight Asiatic Pacific Area Service Ribbons (Bronze Stars) and two Philippine Liberation Ribbons (Bronze Stars).

Before retiring in 1985, he was a manager for 46 years for International Nickel Company and eight years for Technical Reproductions. Past president of the USS *Hornet* Club. Married to Agnes Henderson for 41 years. He has one daughter, Lorranine.

He passed away on Tuesday, March 18, 1997.

STANLEY A. HERGOTT, born April 19, 1925; joined the Navy May 4, 1942, at the federal building, San Francisco, CA. Went to boot camp in San Diego, CA. From there went to school to train as an aviation machinist mate, Navy pier, Chicago, IL; left for Norfolk NAS. Served at various air stations on the East coast. Boarding the *Hornet* as a plane captain with a TBF Sqdn. for her shakedown cruise, this was late 1943. Served aboard her until August 1944, all that time in the air division, working on TBFs.

Finished his Navy duty at Oakland NAS, CA in VR4. The last six months he was assigned to Admiral "Black" Jack Reeves flight crew. Separated from the Navy on Nov. 8, 1945.

Served an apprenticeship as a painter and paperhanger. Had his own business until retiring in 1993, on Maui in the state of Hawaii, now residing in Florence, AZ.

WILLIAM M. HESS, born March 22, 1920, in Pitman, NJ; graduated University of Pennsylvania, Wharton School, June 1941. Went on active duty Dec. 9, 1941, and was assigned to District Intelligence Office, Philadelphia, PA. Reported to the USS *Hornet*, (CV-12), October 1943, at Newport News, VA, on board for commissioning. Served on the USS *Hornet*, (CV-12), until September 1945. October 1945 transferred as navigation officer USS *Roi* (CVE-103).

Released to inactive duty January 1946. Recalled

to active duty Nov. 9, 1951, assigned to Atlantic Reserve Fleet (Florida Group). Released to inactive duty June 1953; commander USNR, assistant navigator, USS *Hornet*, (CV-12). Earned the WWII Victory Medal, American Campaign Medal, Asiatic Pacific Campaign Medal w/1 Silver and 4 BSs, Navy Occupation Service Medal w/Asian Clasp, National Defense Service Medal, Presidential Unit Commendation Ribbon, Reserve Medal, Navy, Philippine Liberation Ribbon w/2 BSs and Philippine Presidential Unit Citation.

Worked in investment banking since 1946. Presently member of the New York Stock Exchange and chairman of the board of Hess, Grant & Company, Inc., Moorestown, NJ. Married with four children, three who reside in California and one in New Jersey and three grandchildren.

TOM HETHERINGTON, born April 21, 1947, in Niagara Falls, NY and joined the USN in January 1966. Served on board the USS *Hornet* for three and one half years from January 1967 until June 15, 1970 when he was discharged in Bremerton, WA, just before the USS *Hornet's* decommissioning. He rose to the rank of ETN-2 and became not only "Senior Salt" in OE division but also supervisor for UHF communications.

He was in charge of UHF communications during the Apollo 11 and 12 recoveries. During Apollo 12, he was able to hear the explosion of the three space craft parachutes and witnessed the craft floating gentile towards the final sea landing. During these missions he also transitioned, with the help of Davey Jones and Neptunis Rex, from pollywog to shellback. What an experience that was. Served off Vietnam for two tours.

The most memorable experience was the TET Offensive of 1968-69 when he watched the fire fights involving our destroyers and the USS *New Jersey*. The sounds from the New Jersey was in fact the proverbial freight train blowing past you at 100 miles an hour. They gave them hell. The entire shore line was alive with an enormous amount of gun fire both from our ships, helicopters, jets and their anti-aircraft guns. The tracers from all the guns illuminated the entire night sky. He stood on the cat walk and wondered how many people, both ours and theirs would not be going home alive.

He remembers the crew members who were medevaced to the USS *Hornet* after a North Vietnamese missile hit our fire support destroyer. He remembers talking to Steve, their medic who said one guy was wounded from the top of his head to his ankles. He and two of his buddies did not make it. The memorial service for these guys, our air crews, and one of their medics will always be one of the most important parts of his *Hornet* experience. You took the bad times with the good and hoped you would make it back in one piece. That's all you could do.

Discharged June 15, 1970, and awarded the Vietnam Service, Republic of Vietnam, Good Conduct, Meritorious Unit Commendation Medals.

He is a program engineer with the Eastman Kodak Co; pursuing masters degree in management. He has two sons, Tom and Scott, three step-children; Jenny, Bob, and Vicki. Married to Maureen.

ELMER C. HEWITT, born June 22, 1923, in the Blue Ridge Mountains of Virginia. Joined the USN in 1942 and received his training at NTS Bainbridge, MD and Norfolk. After completing his training he served aboard the aircraft as a plane mechanic for 18 months in the South Pacific. Following service aboard the aircraft carrier, he was stationed in Hawaii at the Naval Air Base for five months.

During his time he was aboard at the bombing

of Pearl Harbor. He was awarded ribbon bar with star of the Presidential Unit Citation while aboard the USS *Hornet* for extra-ordinary heroism in action against enemy Japanese forces in the air, ashore and afloat in the Pacific war area from March 29, 1944 to June 10, 1945.

He was discharged in 1947. He spent his time working at a weave mill as supervisor.

On Nov. 3, 1950 he married the former Madeline Coffey Hewitt. On Oct. 18, 1951, they were blessed with a daughter, Jackie. In 1983 he became ill with Parkinson's disease. Later he also had Alzheimer's disease. Until his illness, he had enjoyed all his life and talked often of his time in the Navy. On Jan. 12, 1994, he went to be with his Lord.

PHILIP L. HICKMAN,
born June 15, 1947, in Waxahachie, TX and joined the USN June 8, 1965, in Dallas, TX. Went to boot camp at Great Lakes, IL and attended Armed Forces School of Music at Little Creek, VA.

Onboard the USS *Hornet*, (CV-12), summer of 1969 for Apollo 11 Lunar Recovery, as MM2; crossed equator and initiated as shellback. Also served aboard the USS *Newport News*, USS *Springfield*, NAS Corpus Christi, USS *Ranger*, USS *Constellation*, and Danang, RVN. Ended active duty as MU. Now hospital corpsman first class in USNR. Recalled to active duty during operation Desert Storm, to naval hospital, Millington, TN. Also served at naval hospitals in Portsmouth, VA and Pensacola, FL.

Three Navy Meritorious Unit Commendations: USS *Hornet*, USS *Constellation*, Naval Hospital Millington. Served 24 years as registered respiratory therapist (AAS degree); BS degree in Allied Health Education.

Married since 1969; two daughters, one son, and one grandson.

RALPH C. HINSON,
born Sept. 2, 1925, at Bidwell, OH. Enlisted Aug. 17, 1943; reported aboard the USS *Hornet* Nov. 28, 1943, and remaining on board until discharge. Re-enlisted serving on the *Hanks*, (DD-702); *Borderleon*, (DDR-881); *Monrovia*, (APA-31); *Ticonderoga*, (CVA-14); *Farmington*, (PCE-894); two years at Philadelphia Navy yard, *Arcadia*, (AD-23).

Retired from the USN Nov. 23, 1963, as HTL.

In 1990 retired from public works in Streamwood, IL. Medals earned: Presidential Unit Citation, Good Conduct, Navy Expeditionary Medal, American Campaign, South Pacific, Victory, National Defense, Navy Occupation, Philippine Liberation Medals.

Several memorable moments in his mind: carrying his sea bag with the hammock and mattress wrapped around it, up the accommodation ladder. When he got to the hanger deck, saluted the officer of the deck and thought to himself, this is no ship it has to be a building but as time went on the ship seemed to get smaller and he thanked the supreme being for allowing him to be on the greatest team ever assembled for this great republic.

Married to wife, Verna, for 40 years. One daughter, Gail, and grandpa to Jim and Kimberly.

LUTHER J. HOLLOWAY,
born Dec. 20, 1924, and joined the USN in December of 1942; assigned to the USS *Hornet* October of 1943. Worked in the battle station on the flight deck and was assigned to torpedo shop to stand by to load torpedo bombers if needed.

Memorable experiences include the pollywog initiation to trusty shellback and the battle of the Marrianas turkey shoot.

Starting in March of 1944 the summer of 1944 was a hectic time for the *Hornet* and TF-58. March through May they struck the islands of Truk, Palau, Ponape, and targets along the coast of New Guinea with repeated strikes as necessary.

June 11, 1944, they sent strikes on Siapan and Tinian and on June 12 they struck Guam and Rota. June 19 was the battle of the Philippine Sea or known as the "Marrianas Turkey Shoot." Their Fighter Group Two shot down 52 enemy planes. At times ship anti-aircraft fire was suspended due to the danger of hitting their own planes. From their ship they could see dog fights all over the sky.

June 24 they hit the Bonin Island group and their F6Fs shot down 67 planes that day. In just a few months time Fighter Sqdn. Two shot down 223 planes.

During this period of March-July they had no major damage and plane loss was minimal but they did have a terrible accident on deck. A plane, returning from a mission, had a bomb hung up on the starboard wing rack. The pilot attempted to dislodge it with violent maneuvers but it would not come off. It was decided to land the plane, when he landed the tailhook caught, the shock dislodged the bomb. It skipped once and detonated. The plane crew chief was up forward on the flight deck ready to receive his plane and the explosion blew both his legs off. He survived and was removed from the ship, for stateside treatment, as soon as possible. The crew took up a collection and gave him a couple thousand bucks when he left. Not much now days but would buy a lot of pogie bait and gedunk back then. He wishes he could remember his name. He was one gutsy sailor.

While supporting the invasion of Guam, a destroyer picked up a message from the island, by someone signaling with a mirror. It was Radioman 1/C Tweed who had escaped to the hills when the enemy over ran Guam. The destroyer picked him up and brought him to the *Hornet* (Flagship of Task Force 58). They brought him aboard in a Bosun's chair and he was one happy camper.

All dates and numbers mentioned above are sub-

ject to memory loss multiplied by the time factor. Nothing here-to-fore is written in stone.

Awarded the Asiatic-Pacific Medal and Presidential Unit Citation. Discharged December 1945 with the rank of TMV2/c.

Married for 50 plus years and has four children. First son born while *Hornet* was on shakedown. Retired from Boeing Aircraft Company after 39 years of service.

WILLIAM FRED HOLLOWAY,
born April 10, 1921, at Sargent, GA. Joined the USN on April 10, 1940, at Macon, GA; attended basic training at Norfolk, VA; was assigned to the USS *Tuscaloosa*; then the USS *Hornet*, VS Sqdn. 8 in October 1942. Support to Doolittle's raids on Tokyo, fought at battles of Midway and Coral Sea. Commendation for bravery during battle of Santa Cruz. Reassigned to Seattle, WA Naval hospital then NAS Atlanta. Honorable discharge on Dec. 13, 1944 from USNH Jacksonville, FL.

Attended trade school, becoming a master sheet metal worker. Was a founding member of Local 85 of the sheet metal workers union in Atlanta, GA. At the time of his death on Dec. 18, 1969, he was a site foreman and secretary to his union. He is survived by his wife, Barbara Holloway (formerly Barbara Hammar) and three daughters: Kimberly Karr, Laura Joan Gelblat and Cynthia Crowder.

CLYDE ALBERN HOLSCLAW,
born Oct. 3, 1924, in Elk Park, NC and joined the USN Dec. 14, 1942; assigned to the USS *Hornet* Dec. 24, 1943. He was the leading first class petty officer in the aviation Ordnance crew. Their job was loading bombs and guns on SC2C hell-divers.

Memorable experiences: boot camp in San Diego; Aviation Ordnance School, Norman, OK; training with CASU-15 for carrier duty at Norfolk, Quonset Point, RI and Chincoteague, VA (TBF Sqdn.); plank owner USS *Hornet*, experiencing the maturity of the crew from the rookie carrier in early 1944 to the top Exxes Class ship of 1945; surviving the Kamikaze attacks of Okinawa Islands in 1945.

Discharged Feb. 1, 1946, with the rank of AOM1/C and awarded the Presidential Unit Citation and seven Battle Stars.

Upon leaving the service, he earned three degrees: a BS from East Tennessee State University; a MA from Vanderbilt University; and a Ph.D. from the University of Tennessee. Married to the former Lucy Black and they have five children and nine grandchildren. After 37 years of work in public education, he has retired to Amelia Island, FL, where he serves God by giving witness to what he has heard and seen concerning Christ. Served as the USS *Hornet* Club president in 1996 at Jacksonville Beach, FL and also gets to play some golf.

CARL L. HOLSTON,
born Aug. 28, 1921, in Max Meadows, VA and entered the USN May 4, 1943; received his training at Bainbridge, MD and went aboard the USS *Hornet*, (CV-12), Nov. 28, 1943. Served at Norfolk before going overseas in March, 1944. Was in charge of the ordnance store room. When a ship

came along side he manned a line throwing gun. He is a plank owner and was in the 6th Div. with his G.Q. station being five-inch magazines.

He was discharged Feb. 9, 1946 with the rank of gunner's mate third class. Awarded the American Area, Asiatic-Pacific w/9 stars, Philippine Liberation w/2 stars, WWII Victory Medals and the Presidential Unit Citation.

GEORGE J. HOLTON, began his USN career on July 29, 1942. Boot camp was at NTS Great Lakes, IL; afterwards was assigned to the 4th Div. aboard the USS *Idaho* until October 1941. He was then transferred as plane captain and crew chief division aboard the USS *Hornet* during the battles of Coral Sea, the Midway and Santa Cruz where the *Hornet* was sunk on Oct. 26, 1942.

Discharged from the USN in 1949 and enlisted in the US Army so that he could get into Flight School. Retired from the US Army as a CWO-2 in 1962 after 22 years of active duty.

Earned the Air Medal, two Commendation Ribbons, Good Conduct Medal, WWII Victory Medal, American Defense Service Medal, National Defense Service Medal, and Asiatic-Pacific Campaign Medal.

After retiring from the US Army in 1962, worked as a test pilot for Hayes Aircraft Maintenance Company and for Sparter School of Aeronautics at Ft. Rucker, AL. He retired in 1976 and resides in Enterprise, AL.

RICHARD D. HOPEWELL, born July 6, 1925, in Northumberland, PA and entered the USN on July 5, 1943. Attended boot camp in Sampson, NY; was sent from there to Westerly, RI for training. He was then sent to Norfolk to board the USS *Hornet*, (CV-12), and sailed to Hunters Point, close to San Francisco. Sent to get bunks welded on the hanger deck; back to the west coast for bringing Army, Navy, and Marines from islands in the Pacific back to San Francisco. He had charge of a compartment and had so many men to see that they had clean bedding and clothes. Sent to Bainbridge, MD for discharge with the rank of AMM 2C on March 12, 1946.

Earned the Pacific Theater Ribbon w/9 stars, American Theater Ribbon, Victory Medal and Philippine Liberation Ribbon w/2 stars.

Retired with 25 years government service as a mail carrier in Northumberland, PA.

JOHN R. HOPPER, born Dec. 18, 1922, in Glen Rock, NJ. Joined the USMCR on Nov. 6, 1942, and assigned to the USS *Hornet* Nov. 24, 1943. He was a 20 mm gunner, plank owner and orderly-three capts.

Memorable experience include crossing the equator through the canal and Kamikaze attacks.

Discharged Oct. 16, 1945, with the rank of sergeant and was awarded the Philippine Liberation Ribbon w/2 BSs, Pacific Theater Ribbon w/8 BSs.

Married Dolores and they have five children, five grandchildren. He is retired and resides in Ladylake, FL.

RICHARD M. HORKY, born Feb. 1, 1936, in Yonkers, NY and enlisted in the USN March 1953 in White Plains, NY. Attended boot camp at Bainbridge, MD.

Reported aboard the USS *Hornet* in Brookly Navy Yard in 1953. Went on world cruise via Norfolk, VA; went to Mediterranean through the Suez Canal, served in Pacific two tours, with TF 70.2 and 77.

Received the Good Conduct Medal, Navy Occupation, China Service and National Defense Medals while aboard the USS *Hornet*. Got shore duty in NAS North Island, CA, last year, with his wife. Achieved the rank of SN1/c.

His wife was a medical secretary, and he was a heating and air conditioning mechanic. They reside in Murrells Inlet, SC and have two grandchildren, a boy and a little girl, 17 months old. He will never regret his decision to join the USN, because he got a chance to serve aboard one of the best carriers afloat.

KENNETH "KEN" E. HORNUNG, born Dec. 16, 1939, in Dubuque, IA. Joined the USN April 1962 and assigned to the USS *Hornet* in October 1962 as an electrical E Div. officer. Was stationed to the space capsule recovery and cold war games with the Soviet Union.

Memorable experiences include the three peacetime cruises to Wespac. Discharged April 1968 with the rank of lieutenant.

Married Susan and they have two children; Brian, age 20; David, age 16. They reside in Lake Oswego, OR and are the owners of Tanglewood Properties.

EDWARD F. HUESTON, born March 6, 1926, in Philadelphia, PA. Joined the USN June 1943 and attended boot camp at Sampson, NY. Carrier Aircraft Service Unit number 21, November 1943 Norfolk NAS. Assigned the USS *Hornet*, (CV-12), November 1943 to November 1946.

Memorable experiences include crossing the equator March 1944 Shellback initiation; crossing the 180th Meridian, March 1944 and November 1945; received certificate in ancient order of the deep from King Neptune. Also received certificate in the Ancient Order of the Golden Dragon, 180th Meridian (where there is no tomorrow). In 1945 went through typhoon, ship damaged, left Leyte Gulf, homeward bound pennant flying, band playing "California here we come"

after 18 months at sea on a mission of war. After repairs, the war ended, the *Hornet* was assigned magic carpet duty, bringing the troops home in late 1945 to early 1946. Still on board when decommissioned and into Moth ball fleet.

Campaign Ribbons: American Theater, Asiatic-Pacific w/9 stars, Victory Medal, Philippine Liberation w/2 stars, Good Conduct Medal, Philippine Presidential Unit Citation, Presidential Unit Citation w/star.

Has been married to Nancy for 48 years and they have seven children, 12 grandchildren. He is presently retired from the Philadelphia police; life member of VFW, also member of the USS *Hornet* club, attends reunions. Plank owner USS *Hornet*, (CV-12).

CHARLES LEE HUFFMAN, born Jan. 15, 1927, near Hickory, NC. Joined the USN in august 1943, and was assigned to the USS *Hornet* in November 1943, prior to commissioning. Served in the carpenter shop and achieved the rank of carpenter's mate 3/c. He served on the *Hornet* from before it was commissioned through all battles and bringing the injured back.

Discharged in March 1946. Received all the awards awarded to his unit.

Farmed from 1943-80; long distance truck driver, 1957-1993; and retired from driving in March 1993. Married Beckie Whitener, April 20, 1947, and has two children, Dianne and Billy. He passed away on May 9, 1995.

JACK G. HUGHES, born July 15, 1925, Scranton, PA. Joined the USN July 14, 1943, and was assigned to the USS *Hornet* in October 1943, as an aviation machinist mate 2/c. Participated in action at Bonin Islands, Formosa, Guam, Iwo Jima, Keusha, Leyte Gulf, Marrianas, New Caledonia, Okinawa, first and second battle of Philippine Sea, invasion of Philippine Islands, Siapan, Tarawa and Tokyo.

Memorable experience was repelling kamikazi attacks; three typhoons, one of which bent the bow requiring repairs at Hunter's Point, San Francisco, after 18 continuous months of combat.

Discharged March 4, 1946. Received the Presidential Unit Citation.

Married and has two children and three grandchildren.

ALDON T. INGERSOLL, born Oct. 8, 1923, Ilion, NY. Joined the USN June 7, 1942, and was assigned to the USS *Hornet* in April 1944, as a radio gunner, VB-2 in SB2C. Achieved the rank of CAC and ARM2/c. Participated in action at Bonin Island, Guam, Yap, Palau, Philippines and Japanese convoys.

Discharged Jan. 14, 1946, with the rank of ARM2/c. Received the Air Medal, unit citations, etc.

Retired from the State of Connecticut, director administration, DCA, Economical Development, Housing. He has five children and four grandchildren. Currently resides in Newington, CT.

RON "IKE" ISAACSON, born March 15, 1941, in Hayward, CA. He joined the USN on June 16, 1958 and was assigned to the USS *Hornet* in September 1958. Isaacson served on board as boilertender/oil king. He was discharged on March 13, 1962, with the rank of BT2.

His most memorable experiences were two West Pacific cruises and two overhauls in the shipyard in Bremerton, WA.

He has worked at Food Warehouse for 28 years. He has seven children and 14 grandchildren.

HARRY R. "JES" JESPERSEN, born Dec. 3, 1924, in San Diego, CA. Joined the USN in January 1942 and as a combat aircrewman in Bombing Sqdn. 11 flying with then Lt. Edwin M. Wilson, USNR, aboard the USS *Hornet,* (CV-12), participated in carrier strikes from Sept. 29, 1944, to Feb. 1, 1945, on Okinawa; Clark Cabcaben, Nicholson and Nichols Air Fields; Florida Blanca, Olongapo and Manila Harbor on Luzon; and Leyte, in the Philippines; Tinian, Tokyo and Heito on Formosa (now Taiwan); Indo-China (now Vietnam); Taikoo and Kowloon dockyards at Hong Kong and strikes against Japanese Fleet in West Sulu Sea and Sibuyan Sea, Oct. 25-26, 1944, after supporting landing operations on Leyte islands, Oct. 20, 1944.

Memorable events: Nov. 5, 1944, Tailhook shot off at Clark Field, Luzon, and crash-landed aboard the USS *Hornet;* Nov. 6, 1944, portion of tail shot off at Clark Field, plane ditched, picked up by USS *Mansfield,* (DD-728).

Awards/Medals: Distinguished Flying Cross, eight Air Medals, Purple Heart, Presidential Unit Citation, Asiatic-Pacific Theater w/6 stars and others.

Transferred to Fleet Reserve, March 14, 1961, and placed on retired list as of Oct. 1, 1971.

Married (Junko) and retired on Guam, Territory of Guam, USA.

BYRON M. JOHNSON, born May 19, 1920, at Potter, Cheyenne County, NE. Attended Nebraska Wesleyan University, Lincoln, 1938-42, AB degree. Enlisted USN V-5 program at Kansas City on Feb. 6, 1942. Took initial ground school and flight training equivalent to private pilot license at Nebraska Wesleyan University and White Jensen Flying School as part of V-5 program. First class and primary flight training at the newly constructed Naval Flight Training Air Station at Olathe, KS. Advanced training at the Naval Air Training Center at Corpus Christi, TX; designated as a Naval Aviator and received his golden Navy wings in April 1943. First aircraft carrier classification at Great Lakes Naval Air Station, Glenview, IL. Operational training at Miami, FL. Was assigned to Fighting Squadron Two at Quonset Point, RI on July 11, 1943; then completed Advanced Fighter training at the NAS at Atlantic City, NJ.

VF-2 was one of the first Squadrons to be furnished the new F6F Grumman Hellcat fighters. Oct. 7, 1993, Squadron personnel and planes fly to west Coast from Atlantic City. October 12 Squadron aboard

small CVE bound for Pearl Harbor. October en route. Skipper, Lt. Comdr. William Dean called a squadron meeting and advised that he expected fighting two to make the best record ever made by any squadron and that he would volunteer the squadron's services at any time and place, for any type of mission. "And that he did!!!" All types training, support and ferry missions. They became the fighting squadron for Air Group Six, commanded by Lt. Comdr. "Butch" O'Hare, previously awarded the congressional Medal of Honor, went aboard the USS *Lexington* for practice amphibious landings, strafing and coordinated operations with bombers and torpedo planes. Then aboard the USS *Enterprise* to the Gilbert and Marshall Islands strikes and invasion. Nov. 26, 1945, Butch O'Hare was killed in action in the execution of a novel plan to repel Japanese night bomber torpedo attacks on the carrier task force by the launching four night fighting Hellcats and a TBF Avenger, and vectoring the fighters (one piloted by Butch O'Hare) by radar. A large group of enemy bombers were repelled but Butch O'Hare was killed. Big E, Returned to Pearl Harbor on Dec. 9, 1943. VF-2 rejoins their Air Group 2 at Hilo. January 15 and 18. He and fourteen other VF-2 pilots volunteered for temporary ferry duty on the USS *White Plains* and USS *Ialinin Bay.* Ferry duty entailed flying replacement planes to the large carriers as needed in combat zones, and pilots either ferry planes to another carrier that has lost a number of planes or to an island. Tradition is that when launched the jeep transport carrier expected some sort of an air show by the ferrying pilots, either a mock dog fight or a show of aerobatics. Helps morale of pilots and observers. Returned on February 22, after ferrying planes to Rarriers, Tarawa, Roi-Namur and Makin, others to USS *Bunker Hill, Belleau Wood.* On March 6, 1944, skipper Dean received word that Air Group 2 will board the new Aircraft Carrier *Hornet.* On March 9 every pilot in Air Group 2 found carrier qualified boarded the *Hornet.* Will be a part of Task Force, Admiral Marc A. Mitscher in charge. During the next six and a half months the USS *Hornet* is set forth in more detail and Air Group 2 would be in the thick and foremost of Naval Action in the Pacific. The Scoreboard for Fighting Squadron Two and fighting Pacific itinerary aboard the *Hornet* is set out on the attached Chart and Scoreboard. VF-2's

"Rippers" squadron insignia was designed by Walt Disney, at the request of their adoptive angel mother, "Mom" Chung.

In September 1944 they entered San Francisco Bay and sailed under the Golden Gate Bridge. Their trip home a little over a year after their departure.

The Squadron had accomplished what Skipper Dean had envisaged. "Fighting Squadron Two was and is the Navy's best fighting squadron."

They received a rousing welcome home from their adoptive angel mother Mom Chung and San Francisco. The Oct. 23, 1944, issue of *Life* magazine had just hit the stands with a lead feature of six pages of the full circle combat cycle from Makin to Manila, which featured pictures of 26 of VF-2's pilots who had reached the Ace category of five or more enemy planes shot down.

Awards: Distinguished Flying Cross and Gold Star in lieu of second Distinguished Flying Cross; Air Medal and eight Gold Stars in lieu of nine Air Medals; Presidential Unit Citation; inducted into Nebraska Aviation Hall of Fame in 1991; selected as Co-honorary parade marshal and veteran representative for 95

Victory Celebration and Parade, and 50th Anniversary of V-J Day, and the end of WWII, at Omaha, NE 1995; co-signer of 950 prints of "The Home Front" a limited edition lithographs by artist Michael Hagel produced to help build the WWII 50th Anniversary Heartland Memorial in Heartland of America Park, Omaha.

Home on leave and married F. Ferne Evertson on Nov. 26, 1944. Celebrated 50th wedding anniversary with three children: Bryce, Kim and Karen and their grandchildren on Nov. 26, 1994.

Was next assigned to Fighting Squadron 97 at Atlantic City for duty involving flying as a VF type instructor, and was so involved on V-J Day, the day they all awaited and prayed for. Released from active duty at Philadelphia and released from active duty on Aug. 31, 1945.

Began a flight service with his best friend Keith Schwartz, an Army B-17 and 29 pilot and instructor, and spearheaded a new Municipal Airport at Sidney, NE.

Returned to college under the GI Bill and obtained law degree from University of Nebraska, Lincoln, in 1952. Was a weekend warrior and annual duty with Wing Staff 76 during time attending law school. Returned to Western Nebraska and opened Law Office in Gering, Scotts Bluff County, NE. Now the elected public defender for Scotts Bluff County, NE. In second four year term. Plans to seek re-election in 1998 and likes the job and wishes to see the year of 2000 as public defender. Serving one's country is the ultimate and best use of one's time and talents.

HARRY L. JONES, born March 31, 1915, in Houston, PA. Joined the USN March 31, 1942, in Pittsburgh, PA; attended boot camp at Newport, RI and assigned to the USS *Massachusetts* (BB-59), at Boston on May 14, 1942. Served on *Massachusetts* from 1942 to reassignment to the USS *Hornet,* (CV-12), at Newport News, VA; reported to the ship on Aug. 30, 1943.

Stationed in the supply department and saw all the action from commissioning until return to San Francisco in July 1945. Discharged Sept. 23, 1945, with the rank of SK1. Awarded the Campaign Ribbons for the USS *Massachusetts* and the USS *Hornet.*

His wife passed away in 1989. They have two children, two grandchildren, two great-grandchildren. Currently retired.

ROBERT N. JONES, born Oct. 5, 1923, in Exeter, NH. Joined the USN July 7, 1941, at NRS Boston, MA at the age of 17, and attended boot camp at NTS Newport, RI; AMM School (Aviation Mechanics School), NAS Jacksonville, FL October 1941.

Served aboard the VT-8 USS *Hornet* (CV-8) beginning January 1942 at Norfolk, VA. Went through

the Panama Canal to San Diego, CA, then to NAS Alameda, CA where they picked up Doolittle's Raiders. Launched for Tokyo April 18, 1942. Engaged battle of Midway June 4, 1942. (VT-8 lost all planes and crews except one pilot, George Gay) VT-8 got new planes and pilots (TBF) went on (CV-3) USS *Saratoga* to the Guadalcanal invasion. *Saratoga* got a torpedo, VT-8 went ashore onto Esprito Santo till they lost all of their planes to the Guadalcanal support.

Retired from the USN Sept. 15, 1961, with the rank of Aviation Mechanic Chief. Awarded the Presidential Unit Citation, Good Conduct, WWII Victory, American Defense, American Campaign, National Defense, Asiatic Pacific Campaign, China Service, Korean Service and United Nations Korean Medals.

Married Jan. 22, 1950, and has three daughters, three step-daughters, three step-sons. Retired from civilian employment from May 1988.

JOHN "HANK" J. KOPOLKA, born June 12, 1926, in Shadyside, OH. Joined the USN Nov. 3, 1944, and assigned to the USS *Hornet* in July 1945. Stationed as a K-1 Div., radioman, where he was receiving and sending messages to and from the ship.

Memorable experience was on Saturday Jan. 12, 1946, he went ashore to Siapan to see three friends who were stationed there; Frank Circosta, Donald Powell and Bill Brown all from his hometown of Shadyside, OH. The next day Frank and Donald came out to the ship and had Sunday dinner with him. They had a very enjoyable two visits together, very far from home.

Discharged July 6, 1946, with the rank of radioman 3/c.

Married in 1953, now a widower, and has two sons, John Jr. and James; one grandson, J.J. Retired from Ohio Edison Co. after 33 years of service in 1988.

KENNETH K. KAUFFMAN, born Jan. 29, 1932, in Chicago, IL. Joined the USN on Nov. 6, 1952, and attended boot camp at Great Lakes, IL. Co. 366 Pipefitter School at Norfolk, VA, March 1953. Assigned to the USS *Hornet*, (CV-12), July 1953. R Div. Re-commissioned to the USS *Hornet* on Sept. 11, 1953, at Brooklyn Navy Yard. Transferred to the USS *Howard W. Gilmore*, AS-16, Key West, FL April 1954 as FP3. 8th Div. Transferred to the USS *Truckee*, AO-147, October 1955 as FP2 plus Second Class Hardhat Diver. Commissioned *Truckee* at Philadelphia Navy Yard Nov. 23, 1955, FP1, May 1956.

Released from active duty Sept. 19, 1956, at Norfolk, VA. Graduated Embry-Riddle Aeronautical University, June 1958. Graduated Drake University, January 1961. Worked 33 years for Shell Oil Company, Industrial/Commercial Marketing. Retired May 1994. Presently reside with his wife Miriam in Mendota Heights, MN.

HERBERT KAUFMAN, born April 20, 1925, and joined the USN on July 13, 1943; served on the CASU-21, 1943. He was a plane captain and served from the commissioning of the USS *Hornet*, (CV-12), to their return to the US for repairs.

Awarded the Victory Medal, American Campaign, Asiatic-Pacific Campaign, Presidential Unit Citation, Philippine Liberation, Philippine Presidential Citation. Discharged March 1946, with the rank of AMMH2/c.

Married Carol and they have two daughters; Marcelle and Eileen. He is currently retired.

THOMAS M. KEAHEY, born Dec. 19, 1911, Clopton, AL. Joined the USN Nov. 3, 1938. Was assigned to the USS *Hornet* Jan. 13, 1944, as a medic and achieved the rank of CPHM.

Memorable experiences include the typhoon in 1945; Adm. Jocko Clark, Adm. Sample and Adm. Doyle.

Discharged in December 1950. Received the American Area Campaign Medal, American Defense Service Medal w/Clasp, Asiatic-Pacific Area Campaign Medal, WWII Victory Medal and the Good Conduct Medal. Transferred to Fleet Reserve, Class F6, and was released from active duty July 18, 1958, with the rank of HMC.

Married and has two children, Carole and Tom Jr. He has owned and operated Keahey's Moving and Storage since 1960. His wife passed away June 29, 1989.

RUSSELL R. KELLER, born April 10, 1939, Brainerd, MN. Joined the USN on April 30, 1956; was assigned to the USS *Hornet* May 15, 1968 as AIMD A/f and TAD to MAA. Changed from AMS1 to NC1 while a recruiter. Served off Vietnam and crossed the Equator.

Memorable experiences include the Cat shot and landing aboard in COD.

Retired May 15, 1975. Received the Vietnam Service, Good Conduct Medal (4), National Defense, Armed Forces Expeditionary and Meritorious Unit Citation.

Married Marilyn and has son, Gene, daughter, Debbie, step-son, David and step-daughter, Laura. He is a journeyman carpenter.

STEWART KERR, born Dec. 23, 1934, Dickson City, PA. He entered the USN in October 1952 and went through boot camp at Bainbridge, MD. Following boot camp he was assigned to the USS *Siboney* (CVE-112) in B Div. He was transferred to the USS *Hornet* (CVA-12) in June 1953 and served in B Div. and #3 fireroom, attaining the rat of BT2 before leaving the *Hornet* in November 1955. Following service on the *Hornet* he transferred to the USN Civil Engineering Corp. and retired in 1985.

Married Joan on June 8, 1957, and has two children, Lisa Ellen Knauss and Eric Allan Kerr, along with triplet grandsons: Garrett, Logan and Spencer Knauss and another grandson Evan A. Kerr. He is employed as a senior engineering officer in the Engineering Div. for Arkwright, a factory mutual system company.

DAVID C. KILLARY, born April 20, 1925, Burlington, VT. Joined the USN in December 1942,

and went through boot camp at Newport, RI. Attended Naval Air Technical Training School, Millington, TN, and Gunnery School in Pensacola, FL. Plank owner of USS *Petrof Bay* (CVE-80); transferred to the USS *Hornet*, BS 2, rear gunner in SB2C Hell-diver, April 1944. Took part in actions in Marrianas, Bonins and battle of Philippine Sea. In August 1944 he transferred to officer candidate training at Drew and Princeton Universities in New Jersey.

Discharged in April 1946. Received the Distinguished Flying Cross.

He is one of the founders of Pamarco, Inc., in 1946, a machinery and printing roller manufacturer. The company sold in 1986. He is now a partner in Serenco Inc. corrugated box machinery company, 1990 to date. Has been a licensed private pilot since 1951. Married to Janice Sharp Killary. He enjoys sailing, skiing and fishing.

DONALD G. KINCADE, born Oct. 22, 1932, Yuba City, CA. Joined the USN on March 15, 1951, at Yuba City; attended boot camp at San Diego. Was assigned to the USS *Thompson* (DMS-38); did one tour in Korea; prior to returning with the *Thompson* to Korea, in June 1952, he was given a chance to attend fire control technician class A School at San Diego.

Returned to the *Thompson* as an FT3 in April 1952. The police action was winding down, and the *Thompson* was to be decommissioned. Reported to the USS *Hornet* (CVA-12), September 1953 to assist in recommissioning. While aboard, he made FT2, was in charge of the main battery director (SKY 1), later the fore and aft 63 systems (40 mm). They were assigned San Diego as their home port.

Released from active duty at the destroyer base in San Diego, CA, on March 11, 1955.

Went to work for PT&T in Los Angeles, CA, April 1957. After 27 years he retired on a disability in 1983 as a senior engineer. He presently resides in Yuba City. Married for 41 years; has one daughter, two sons and eight grandchildren.

H.C. "DUTCH" KLEPPER, born Oct. 15, 1919, Denton, TX. Joined the USN March 17, 1937; was assigned to the USS *Hornet*, June 15, 1941, pre-commission, Newport News; served as radioman; served aboard the USS *Iowa*; attended Electronics School, Chicago; Teletype School, Maryland; and changed rate to CT. Served aboard the *Hornet* with his brother, Winston Klepper.

Memorable experiences include the voyage to the States aboard the USS *Lurline*.

Married Sue Pate; retired to Jasper, AR. He passed away in November 1990. *Submitted by Winston Klepper.*

WINSTON L. KLEPPER, born Sept. 3, 1914, Denton, TX. Joined the USN on March 17, 1937; and was assigned to the USS *Hornet* pre-commission detail, Newport News, June 15, 1941; and served in the radio transmitter room.

Memorable experiences include the Doolittle raid; battle of Midway; rescue by USS *Mustin* (DD-413); drawing lots for return to the States; and going to Esprito Santos, Tulogi and Guadalcanal, March 27, 1957.

Married Frances Beddon in 1941 and has three children: Sharon, Stephen and Lisa. Was employed by Conair, San Diego, as QC engineer for Atlas missile. Now lives in a retirement home, Morning Star, in Wichita Falls, TX.

EDWARD L. KNOEBEL, born Feb. 19, 1924, Sunbury, PA. Joined the USN on Feb. 20, 1941, and was assigned to the USS *Hornet* with the plane fly deck crew. Participated in action in the coral Sea, Midway and Santa Cruz, where the *Hornet* was sunk on Oct. 26, 1942.

Memorable experiences include being at the same battle station with Bert W. Whited, and both getting hurt.

Discharged Aug. 19, 1960. Received the Purple Heart, Good Conduct Medal, WWII Victory Medal, American Defense, American Area Campaign, Asiatic-Pacific Area, National Defense Service and three Presidential Unit Citations.

Married Bea. After retirement he built a gas station and shop and now just has a salvage yard.

THEODORE C. KOLDA, born Feb. 22, 1947, Vallejo, CA. Enlisted in the USNR on Feb. 26, 1964, at Naval Reserve Center Mare Island, CA, and reported to Naval Reserve Submarine Div. 12-11. Completed Naval Reserve Recruit Training and Submarine Preparatory School at Hunter's Point NSY and Torpedoman A School at Fleet Anti-Submarine Warfare School, San Diego, CA.

Reported to W Div. aboard USS *Hornet* (CVS-12) at Yokosuka, Japan, September 1965, and served in the Western Pacific on Yankee Station during the Vietnam War. Maintained and handled MK-44 torpedo's for embarked air group (VS35, VS37 and HS2) and CRUDESPAC destroyers attached to ASW Group I. This cruise also included a stop in Sidney Australia before returning to Naval Station Long Beach, CA. Later completed a midshipman cruise and ASW exercises in Hawaiian waters, and simulated recoveries of the Apollo space capsule.

Following release from active duty, rejoined Naval Reserve Submarine Div. 12-11 in January 1968 at Mare Island and later earned silver dolphins aboard USS *Blackfin* (SS-322) in October 1969. Assigned to Naval Reserve Submarine Base, Pearl Harbor Detachment 220 at Mare Island January 1972. Assigned to USS *McKee* (AS-41) Reserve Detachment in January 1933. Appointed Command Master Chief, Naval

Reserve Center Mare Island in April 1993. Retired with 31 years of service March 1, 1995.

Earned BS degree in business systems in 1980 from San Francisco State University. Reside in Vallejo, CA, father of two daughters, employed in the information systems division of the California State Automobile Association in San Francisco since May 1968. Cello player in the Solano Community Symphony and active in local sports leagues.

EDWARD E. KOZO, born Jan. 30, 1934; graduated Vo-Tech High School, Beth, PA. Joined the USN June 22, 1952; attended boot camp, Bainbridge, MD, June-September 1952. Transferred to Brooklyn Receiving Station, September 1952 to June 1953, in transit, attached to motor pool waiting for the *Hornet*. Boarded the *Hornet* in June 1953; recommissioned, Sept. 11, 1953; and participated in the shakedown in the Caribbean, September-December 1953.

April 1954, left for the 6th Fleet Med.; June 1954, transferred to 7th Fleet, Far East and made world cruise. Returned in December 1954 to San Francisco; May 1955, shakedown, Pearl Harbor, HI; and six month tour of the Far East again. Returned to San Francisco in December 1955 . Discharged June 23, 1956, Bremerton, WA. Received the Good Conduct Medal.

Retired as an electrical/mechanics maintenance foreman, Beth Steel, Beth PA, after 34 years, in 1985.

IRVIN H. LAMOTTE, born May 21, 1925, Deepwater, NJ. Joined the USN Aug. 31, 1943; was assigned to the USS *Hornet* in December 1943 as supply GSK with the rate of SK1/c. Saw all actions from March 18, 1944, to the June 5, 1945, typhoon.

Memorable experiences include being 18 years old; all strikes, invasions and attacks made on them were very memorable to him; getting married in the Navy Yard. He will never forget his shipmates in S-1 Div. He was the youngest of all and they kept him in tow. Fine bunch of men.

Discharged Feb. 6, 1946. Received seven Battle Stars and the Presidential Unit Citation.

Retired after 40 years with DuPont Co. Married to Audrey for 51 years; have two children: daughter, Janis Cooker in Spain (husband, Robin, in naval aviation); son, Byron, deceased, (wife Anne lives in Carney's Point, NJ); two granddaughters, Michell Cooker and Sarah Lamotte; and one grandson, Bradley. Hopes to visit the *Hornet* in 1997 with grandchildren. He has shared things about the *Hornet*, they will be able to see just how large it is.

RICHARD B. LANING, born Jan. 1, 1918, in Washington, DC, son of Richard H. and Marguarite B. Laning. His father was a Naval surgeon who retied a rear admiral. Graduated Vallejo High School in 1934; US Naval Academy, BSMEE in 1940; University of

California, Berkeley, MS in biophysics in 1950; and US National War College, 1960. Served as AA Div. officer, aboard the USS *Yorktown* (CV-5), 1940-41, in the Pacific and Atlantic; neutrality patrol, radar officer and OOD, USS *Hornet* (CV-8); Doolittle raid and battle of Midway, 1942; then to Submarine School; and married Ruth Richmond with whom he had two wonderful daughters.

From 1943-44 he served on *Salmon* (SS-182), then on *Stickleback* (SS-415) which made last patrol of war going through minefield of Tsushima. In 1945, commanding officer *Pilotfish* (SS-386) which was a target submarine in the Operation Crossroads at Bikini Atoll. In 1946, staff COM1 in Boston, MA, setting up submarine Reserve.

From 1947-50, Graduate School. Studied under nine Nobel Prize winners, University of California, Berkeley. Officer Joint TF-3 conducting nuclear tests. Commanding officer *Trutta* (SS-421), fleet boat operating out of New London. 1951, commissioning commanding officer *Harder* (SS-568); operating in Atlantic in newest "fast attack" boats. 1953-54, OP-365, in Pentagon planning development and production nuclear weapons. 1955-58, PCO and commanding officer, *Seawolf* (SSN-575); developed ASW tactics and set world record, submerged cruise for 60 days. 1959-60, OP-31X, studying new ship construction methods; attended National War College. 1961-62, commissioning commanding officer *Proteus* (AS-19) first Polaris tender; set up facility at Holy Loch, Scotland. 1963, assistant chief of staff (N2/3) commander submarines, Pacific. Retired to become a corporate planner, United Aircraft Corp. This job covered most sciences and technologies of time.

In 1973 moved to Florida, became life member of Orlando Chamber of Commerce. Military decorations include the Silver Star, Legion of Merit, Bronze Star, Commendation Medal, Presidential Unit Citation, Unit Commendation, various campaign ribbons, The Stephen Decatur Award and the Marjorie Sterret Award.

JOHN W. LAUER, born June 24, 1924, St. Louis, MO. Joined the USN June 17, 1942; was assigned to the USS *Hornet* in June 1943; served as plane captain; and was stationed on the flight deck servicing TBF planes. He was on board the *Hornet* (CV-12) from christening to discharge.

Memorable experiences include the christening; shakedown cruise; going through the Panama Canal; then to Pearl Harbor seeing the damaged and sunken ships. Being stationed on the flight deck servicing TBF planes and able to watch planes returning from the first battle of the Philippines; planes low on gas; and damaged planes. The captain turned on ships lights to assist their landings. Some crashed on deck, others into the sea. Seeing ship's gunners down kamikaze's and the combat air patrol (night fighting radar planes) downing incoming Bogeys. captain gave on-going directions to watch in sky. Falling from the hanger deck into the sea while anchored in Ulithi. Meeting famed war correspondent Ernie Pyle night before he left ship and was killed on Okinawa, Easter Sunday, April 1, 1945. The three typhoons. Many battles and triumphant return home.

Discharged Dec. 23, 1945, with the rank of AMM1C. Received the Good Conduct Medal and Presidential Unit Citation w/9 Battle Stars.

Married Laura and has six children. He is retired.

ROBERT B. LAWHORN, born March 24, 1921, Humble, TX. Joined the USN Jan. 8, 1942. After boot camp in Norfolk, VA, he was assigned to the USS *Hornet* (CV-8) right after her shakedown cruise in February 1942. The ship sailed to San Francisco where Doolittle's planes were picked up for the bombing of Japan. He remained on the *Hornet* until her sinking Oct. 26, 1942, in the Santa Cruz battle. His battle station was gun number 13 on the starboard side, forward of the island. He served on the USS *President Jackson* (APA-18) from November 1942-October 1944, attaining the rate of BM2/c. Discharged June 20, 1945.

Retired after 41 years as a journeyman electrician. He and his wife, of 52 years, have two children and two grandchildren, all of whom live in Galveston, TX.

LEROY OLIVER LEMASTER, born Nov. 21, 1937, Twisp, WA. Joined the USN Jan. 12, 1956; was assigned to the USS *Hornet* in April 1956; and was stationed on the flight deck control where he operated the 500 lb. bomb elevator. Discharged in February 1958.

Memorable experiences include the Far East cruise from January-June 1957; meeting a lot of friends, that he still stays in contact with over all these years.

Married to Sharon for 38 years and has three children: Ty, Tressa and Jay; three grandchildren: Sarah and Dustin Lemaster and Dallon Bogart. He is retired after working for the state of Washington for 36 years. He coaches the high school tennis team in Medical Lake, WA.

ARTHUR WILSON LEONARD, born Jan. 7, 1924, Boone County, MO. Joined the USN Jan. 7, 1942; attended boot training at Great Lake, IL; was sent to Philadelphia Receiving Station, Feb. 25, 1942; assigned to USS *South Dakota*, March 20, 1942; was assigned to C&R Div. After his tour in the South Pacific, battle of Guadalcanal and Santa Cruz, the ship returned to Brooklyn Navy Yard for repairs. After his tour in the North Atlantic and the Mediterranean, his ship returned to New York and he was transferred to Newport News, VA, for school. In mid August 1943 he was assigned to the USS *Hornet* in November 1943 until late October 1945.

In late June 1945 the *Hornet* (CV-12) had its flight deck bent by a typhoon and the ship returned to Hunter's Point, CA, for repair.

Discharged Nov. 14, 1947. Received the Navy Unit Commendation, Navy Good Conduct, Presidential Unit Commendation, EAME, Philippine Liberation Medal, Philippine Independence Medal, WWII Victory Medal, American Area Campaign Medal, Guadalcanal Presidential Medal, Expeditionary Medal and Asiatic-Pacific w/2 SS and 4 BSs.

Married Jessie in August 1946 and had five children. He worked in sheet metal and heating. He passed away July 6, 1995.

GORDON H. LEONARD, born May 23, 1924, Torrington, CT. Joined the USN May 26, 1943; was assigned to the USS *Hornet* Nov. 28, 1943; was a plank owner; and served as a deck hand; 20 mm gunner and loader on #1 gun starboard side and master at arms.

While on 20 mm gun watch one very cloudy and overcast day, somewhere between Siapan and Okinawa, he spotted an Emily sea plane break through the cloud formation. He opened up on it with a short burst from his 20 mm. Cmdr. Duerfeldt called down, "What in hell is that guy firing at?" With us was the USS *Wasp*, USS *Iowa*, USS *New Jersey*, two cruisers and several destroyers and nobody else even fired a shot. He believes Duerfeldt thought Leonard had lost his mind. "Must have been a mail plane," he said.

Discharged June 26, 1945, with the rank of coxswain. Received the Asiatic-Pacific w/9 stars and Philippine Liberation Medal w/2 stars.

Married Barbara and has four children and eight grandchildren. He is retired.

EDWARD F. LETSCH, born March 12, 1934, Brooklyn, NY. Joined the USN Aug. 12, 1952; and was assigned to the recommissioned USS *Hornet*, ship's company, 1953; and was assigned to communications.

Memorable experiences include the world cruise and the Far East cruise.

Discharged July 30, 1956. Received the National Defense and Navy Occupation Medals.

He and his wife, Winnie, have four children and four grandchildren. He retired from Suffolk County Police Dept. and is still in the printing field.

LARRY J. LIEBE, born Oct. 7, 1932, Wausau, WI. Joined the USN Oct. 7, 1950; was assigned to the USS *Hornet*, July 1965-September 1967; served as V-6 Div. officer, COD Pilot and aircraft maintenance. He participated in two eight month Wespac tours and rare ship's company centurion.

Memorable experiences include primary fly watch officer and COD flights.

Retired Aug. 30, 1974. Received the Vietnam Service and Meritorious Service Medal.

Married and has four children and nine grandchildren. Managed a retail store; owned a trucking company; and retired to the state of Oregon. He is completely retired and travels in his motor home.

W.L. LINDEMANN, born April 29, 1926, Windthorst, TX. Volunteered for the USN and was assigned to serve aboard the USS *Hornet* (CV-12) in late 1944. He remembers thinking, this is the life—we have running water, electric lights and indoor toilets. None of these things did he have at home. And they did not plant cotton on the ship that had to be picked—another plus for the Navy.

He thought everything was just great until he saw the first kamikaze plane head straight for them. But, thank God, it was shot down just before it could reach them. He thought to himself, "W.L., what have you gotten yourself into now?" The electric lights, running water and indoor toilets did not seem too important any more.

Another incident that sticks in his mind happened in June 1945. The *Hornet* was badly damaged in a big typhoon off Okinawa. They went to Guam to unload their bombs and other supplies, as they were going back to San Francisco for repairs and they did not need them.

They were unloading the bombs from the hanger deck to a barge below with the forward crane. As he remembers, they had unloaded approximately 200 bombs and torpedoes and were picking up four 500 pound bombs. As the crane was swinging them out over the side of the ship, something went wrong with the winch and it would not stop going up. The turnbuckle hit the pulley and the cable snapped dropping those four bombs a distance of 75 feet on top of the 200 already in the barge. Needless to say, none of them went off or he would not be writing this. No one was hurt and the men in the barge jumped over the side.

The *Hornet* was in dry docks in San Francisco when the war was over and all the men on board were given leave. He remembers he was one day late getting back to the ship from his leave. He had met a girl at home that kept him from getting back on time. He had to go before the captain's mast, Capt. Doyle, and Doyle gave him 10 days in the brig on bread and water with one full meal every third day.

He eventually got even with that girl. He married her and they have eight children, 18 grandchildren and one great-grandchild. They have been married 50 years. He is in the oil and ranching business in North Texas.

He was discharged from the *Hornet* in April 1946 with a good friend of his from Muenster, TX, named Joe Tempel, who died eight years ago. He also served at many masses for Father McMahan, a great chaplain. Received the WWII Victory and Pacific Area Campaign Medals.

RONNIE W. "RON" LIVELY, born in October 1942 in Palestine, TX, was raised and attended school in Duncanville, TX. Joined the USN on Oct. 12, 1959, one day after his 17th birthday. He attended boot camp in San Diego and upon completion of recruit training, was ordered to the USS *Hornet* (CVS-12) and assigned to V-3 Div.

Transferred to another ship in 1961. He continued his USN career and in 1966, as an ABH1, was ordered to the USS *Hornet* and assigned to the V-1 Div. Served on the flight deck for over three years completing two Wespac cruises and the Apollo 11 mission. In late 1969 he was transferred to recruiting duty in Arizona.

Retired in 1986 with the rank of CWO4, after completing his masters degree and a second career in law enforcement, he moved to a ranch near Campbell, TX, where he and his wife own a horse and cattle operation. They have three children and three grandchildren.

JOHN E. LOGSDON, born June 7, 1924, Riverside, CA. Joined the USN in September 1941; attended boot training at Great Lakes; joined the USS *Hornet* (CV-9) in December 1941 staying until the sinking during the battle of Santa Cruz. Served aboard the USS *Mt. Vernon* (AP-22) the remainder of WWII.

Memorable experience was of when he was a bugle master. He was standing the bridge watch as they returned from the battle of Midway. As they passed the battleship anchorage on Ford Island, starting with the USS *Pennsylvania*, all of the battle ship gave them passing honors. This was the beginning of Carrier Navy, then end of the battleship Navy. He returned the honors.

Separated at Great Lakes in October 1945. Earned the Good Conduct Medal, American Defense, European Defense, Asiatic Defense and WWII Victory Medals.

Used the GI Bill to attend college and study pharmacy. He got into the manufacturing of ethical drug and nutritional supplement. He has five grown children. John passed away February 15, 1998.

JOHN J. LOLLI, born Aug. 13, 1924, Wayne, PA. Joined the USN just before Thanksgiving in 1942. He was assigned to the USS *Hornet* (CV-12) in October 1943 and played the commissioning for the Secretary of the Navy Knox. Participated in action from Norfolk to San Francisco in 1945.

Memorable experiences: MCing Happy Hours, straddling stretcher of wounded pilot down torpedo elevator to hospital deck, just as GQ sounded!! Playing for DDs as they refueled, choir for Father McMahon, aided start of radio WING.

Discharged July 6, 1946, Long Beach Naval Hospital. Not combat related, ruptured appendix! Received 9 stars, Presidential Unit Citation and the Philippine Liberation Medal.

Met a widowed classmate at Radnor High's 25th reunion. Connie has four children and he has two children (previous marriages) and they have 14 grandchildren and two great-grandchildren. He is retired from Florida schools, still in music and entertaining cruise ships, hotels, condos and nursing homes in Philadelphia area each summer, plus other adventures, such as touring with a circus in Canada, etc.

HENRY L. LONG JR., born March 14, 1926, Brooklyn, NY. Entered the USN V-5 flight program in July 1943, following high school graduation. After completing flight preparatory he transferred and completed aviation radioman gunner training; then back to pre-flight and primary flight training when the war ended. Navigation School became an option that resulted in wings and a commission.

Reported to NATS Alameda, CA, January 1946. Was assigned to the USS *Hornet* in April 1946 to be part of the inactivation of the ship until discharge in July 1946.

Attended Yale University. Married Mary D. Harder in 1948 and has four daughters and eight grandchildren. He spent 42 years in the family paint business (sales) manufacturing products for the nuclear and utility industry. Retired in 1990 in Watertown, CT, where community projects are the present vocation and grandchildren, skating, swimming and care of the homestead are recreation.

PAUL MACKENZIE, born Aug. 17, 1920, Needham, MA. Joined the USN Aug. 20, 1942; was assigned to the USS *Hornet* (CV-12) from November 1943 to November 1944; and was assigned to aircraft ordnance. Saw action at Hollandia, Truk, Yap, Guam, Siapan, Tinian, up the Bonin Island chain, etc.

Memorable experiences include the first Philippine Sea battle.

Discharged Nov. 12, 1945. Received the Presidential Unit Citation, American Area Campaign, Asiatic-Pacific w/3 stars, WWII Victory Medal and Good Conduct Medal.

Married Gloria and has one son, Paul Douglas II and granddaughter, Nicole. Spent his working years in sales and sales management; traveled in jewelry industry; sales in advertising; and sales manager, advertising sales group. He is retired.

H.W. "MAGGIE SKYHOOK" MAGNUSSON, born Oct. 4, 1935, Worcester, MA. Joined the USN Dec. 12, 1952; was assigned to the USS *Hornet* in March 1954; was stationed with the catapult crew; and achieved the rank of airman. He was the hook-up man under the plane's to the catapult shuttle D-Ring cable to airplane and jet's.

Memorable experiences include going from Navy bomber squadron to two different aircraft carriers and four Pacific tours.

Discharged Sept. 28, 1956. Received the Korean Service and China Service Medals.

Married for 34 years and has four children. He is a retired tree clearing contractor living in Edgewater, FL.

CLARK H. MAINS, was sworn in March 7, 1951; attended boot camp, Co. 347, Great Lakes, IL; was assigned to the USS *Orion* (AS-18), sub tender; Class A fire Control School, Washington, DC. In July 1953 he was assigned to the USS *Hornet*, Brooklyn Navy Yard for recommissioning; September 1953 to February 1955, Fox Div.; 1954, round the world cruise, 7th Fleet, South Pacific; and discharged Feb. 18, 1955, San Diego.

Employment included the New York Giants professional baseball, 1955-56; plumber, 1957-68; IBM, Kingston, 1959-90; and retired in March 1990. Married Dorothy Vaught in May 1960 and has a son, Clark (Karen), professional fireman, Kingston; son, Douglas, facilities coordinator, Parsons, Corp., IBM, Poughkeepsie and daughter, Cindy, US Air Customer Service agent, Stewart Airport, Newburgh. He is a volunteer fireman; spent 21 years as fire chief; member of the American Legion; and a baseball and basketball coach and official. He enjoys hunting, fishing and traveling.

SAM S. MALOSKY, born Jan. 26, 1923, Crosby, MN. Joined the USN in October 1942; was assigned to the USS *Hornet* Feb. 1, 1945; stationed with Air Group 17 (VBF-17) as a pilot. Participated in action at Iwo Jima, Okinawa, Japanese mainland, Tokyo, Osaka, etc.

Memorable experiences include the Typhoon in June 1945; the first flight over Tokyo Bay; and taking off fantail due to typhoon damage.

Discharged in September 1945. Received two Distinguished Flying Crosses and four Air Medals.

Married Poppy in 1944 and has two daughters, Sammye and Nancy. Retired from Republic Insurance Group after 43 years.

JOSEPH D. MARTIN, born April 1, 1923, Spartanburg, SC. Joined the USN in February 1943; was assigned to the USS *Hornet* in November 1943; and was stationed with the generator gang. Participated in action at Formosa, Luzon, Leyte, Manila, Iwo Jima, China Sea and Hong Kong.

Discharged Nov. 21, 1945. Received the American Theater, Asiatic-Pacific, Philippine Liberation w/2 stars and WWII Victory Medal.

Married and has three sons, three step-daughters and one step-son. He is retired.

GAYLE K. MARZ, born Nov. 1, 1924, Newport, KY. Joined the USN Jan. 25, 1943; was assigned to the USS *Hornet* in September 1944; stationed as turret gunner and ordnance TBF, VT Sqdn., CAG-11.

Participated in the aerial strikes in the Philippines, Ryukyus, etc.

Memorable experiences include participating in the sinking of a Japanese cruiser.

Discharged June 26, 1946. Received the Air Medal, Presidential Unit Citation, Asiatic-Pacific Area Campaign and Gold Star.

Married Perli and has four grown children and six grandchildren. He is a retired FBI supervisor and does community service.

ALBERT WILBUR MASSE, born Sept. 28, 1923, Providence, RI. Joined the USN May 3, 1943; was assigned to the USS *Hornet* in October 1943; stationed to gasoline detail; and achieved the rank of ABM2/c. Participated in action at Marrianas Turkey Shoot; first battle of the Philippine Sea; ship lashed by typhoon; second battle of Philippine Sea; strikes on Central Luzon, Subic Bay, Mindoro invasion and Okinawa; ship investigated center of typhoon; and taking ship to California due to damage; from June 1944 to June 1945.

Memorable experiences include a time they were landing planes coming in from an air strike. As they were fueling, planes were still landing, coming back from the air strike. All of a sudden tracers started flying over his head, and a plane landed without disarming or switching off his guns. Another experience was being forward of the twin five-inch gun turrets on the starboard side, waiting for the last flight to come in. All of a sudden GQ sounded and the five-inch gun turrets started to swing and lower to horizontal. He moved to the catwalk where a cameraman was standing, because a Betty-torpedo bomber was coming straight at them. Starboard started to fire and their gunners started firing at it. When the action started the cameraman had disappeared. The gunners did shoot that twin engine Betty down off starboard. One of the proudest days of his life was in May 1995 when he received an invitation from Capt. Dodge, commanding officer of NAS Alameda, CA, for "the last cruise of the USS *Hornet*." She was docked at Hunter's Point and was going to be towed by tugboat to NAS Alameda. It was the thrill of his life to once again be standing on the deck of "his" *Hornet*.

Discharged Feb. 27, 1946. Received the WWII Victory Medal, American Area Ribbon, Asiatic-Pacific Area Ribbon w/9 stars, Philippine Liberation Ribbon w/2 stars and Presidential Unit Citation.

Wife, Connie (former secretary of USS HORNET Club, Inc. 18 years) is presently secretary to Board of Directors. Al's free time is devoted to handling the club's Ships' Store orders. They have five children and eight grandchildren.

Retired to Florida, working part-time at Winn Dixie supermarket; member of Warm Mineral Sprigs Archeological Society; member and usher at San Pedro Church; member of Holy Name Society; member BPOE Lodge 2632 and American Legion.

WILLIAM B. "BRAD" MATTHEWS, born April 14, 1925, Lakewood, NJ. Enlisted in the USN on March 5, 1943; attended boot camp at NTS Bainbridge, MD; received electronics training; and was assigned to CAG-11 which boarded USS *Hornet* at Manus Island in September 1944. Participated in action at the battle for Leyte Gulf, attacks on Okinawa, Formosa, Northern Luzon and the China Coast.

Most memorable experience was witnessing the loss of Lt. Ed Helgerson during preparations for catapult launch on Oct. 14, 1944.

He was honorably discharged on March 5, 1946. Was awarded the Presidential Unit Citation, Good Conduct, American Theater, Asiatic-Pacific Campaign, WWII Victory and Philippine Liberation Medals.

Retired as a senior engineer from IBM Corp. in 1989 and presently resides in Gaithersburg, MD, where he and his wife, Gloria celebrated 50 years of marriage Christmas Day 1997. They have two sons, Brad Jr. and Richard and five grandchildren.

GEORGE HERNY MAYNOR, born Jan. 11, 1923, Tampa, FL. Entered the USN at Macon, GA, May 7, 1941; attended 11 weeks of boot camp at Norfolk, VA; and went aboard the USS *Hornet* to be commissioned Oct. 20, 1941. Served aboard until the *Hornet* was sunk Oct. 26, 1942. Served as plane captain and was assigned to GQ. Participated in action in Tokyo, Doolittle raid, 1942; battle of Coral Sea; second phase of Guadalcanal, 1st Mar Div.; Midway battle; and Santa Cruz, where the *Hornet* sunk, Oct. 26, 1942.

Memorable experience was when the word was given "stand by to abandon ship" the air groups went first. The destroyer came along side and they went aboard. On the last attack by a Japanese plane, they strafed the port side of the ship. One sailor was wounded and he was next to him, standing.

Discharged April 28, 1947. Received the American Defense, American Area, WWII Victory, Presidential Unit Citation, Asiatic-Pacific, Good Conduct, Expeditionary Medal and Doolittle Raiders Medals.

Married Betty and has three grandchildren and one great-grandchild. He and Betty are both retired; have one hobby; and seven years of caregivers.

KAYE LEMOYNE "MAC" MCDOWELL, born Aug. 25, 1925, Pittsburgh, PA. Joined the USN Aug. 6, 1943; served boot camp, USN 2C, great Lakes, IL; assigned to the USS *Hornet* March 14, 1956, to March 25, 1957; assigned to the air department and administration/personnel with the rank of yeoman. Participated in action at Western Carolina, Leyte, Luzon, Okinawa operations, Korea and Vietnam.

Memorable experiences are too numerous. He served on six carriers and one battleship and as a USN recruiter.

Released from active duty on Feb. 18, 1963 and transferred to the Fleet Reserve. On Dec. 1, 1972, he was honorably discharged from the USN and retired,

thereby completing 30 years of active and inactive service to his country. Received the American Theater, Asiatic-Pacific w/7 stars, Good Conduct Medal (5 awards), WWII Victory Medal, Presidential Unit Citation w/2 stars, Philippine Liberation w/2 stars, Navy Occupation (A), Korean Service w/2 stars, UN Service Medal, National Defense Medal, Korean Presidential Unit Citation.

The day after he was released from active duty he went to work for Wells Fargo Bank as chief special agent in their investigations department, where he remained for 20 years, retiring on March 1, 1983. Married Veronica and had three children: Robert K, Candace G. and John W. and two grandchildren, Ashely E. and Robert L. He passed away on June 6, 1994. *Submitted by Veronica McDowell.*

GEORGE W. MCFEDRIES, born June 22, 1916, Oak Park, IL. Joined the USN Sept. 26, 1941; and was assigned to the USS *Hornet* Feb. 1, 1945, as a pilot, VF-17. Participated in action at Iwo Jima and Okinawa operations; also the Gilbert Islands operation where the USS *Liscome Bay* was sunk on Nov. 24, 1943.

Memorable experiences include the typhoon of June, 5, 1945, which damaged the ship and sent them home.

Discharged Sept. 20, 1945, with the rank of commander. Received the Distinguished Flying Cross and five Air Medals.

Married and has three daughters, three granddaughters and three grandsons. He is enjoying retirement and reminiscing sea stories and the nice things in life.

HARRY ELLIOT MEATYARD, born Jan. 17, 1920, Mobile, AL. Was drafted into the USN in May 1944; was assigned to the USS *Hornet* in December 1944; served as plane captain; and achieved the rank of seaman 1/c. His assigned was F6F Hellcat #2. The engaged in strikes on the Philippines, Formosa, Tokyo, Iwo Jima, Kobi Japan and Okinawa. Ulithi was the fleet anchorage.

His plane was hit. Shrapnel came through the side, causing minor injury to the pilot. Another of his planes went in the "drink." Both plane and pilot were lost. They were refueled by tankers at sea. Sometimes one of their planes would tow targets for gunners to practice firing on. In notes he described one liberty when they went ashore on Mog Mog (island where supplies were stored) as "just a bunch of inebriated sailors." A typhoon severely damaged their flight deck, and they headed for San Francisco.

Memorable experience was the shuddering of the *Hornet* when a bomb dropped by a kamikaze barely missed them. Their marvelous gunners, as usual, did not miss.

Discharged Jan. 17, 1946. Received the American Campaign Medal, Asiatic-Pacific Campaign Medal, WWII Victory Medal, Presidential Unit Commendation, Philippine Liberation Medal and Philippine Unit Citation.

Became a line crew foreman for an electric utility. Enjoying retirement after 40 years, nine months with a power company. Married to Shirley and has one daughter, three sons, seven grandchildren and two great-grandchildren. They reside on the East Fowl River in Mobile County, AL.

JACK MELLOTT, born Aug. 3, 1926, Fort Loudon, PA. Was sworn in the USN Aug. 25, 1943; went to boot camp, Bainbridge, MD; aboard the USS *Hornet*, which was new; helped load the ship; shipped out in February 1944 for the Pacific. He was on mount #1, 5:38 gun.

Memorable experiences were seeing some of his buddies buried; one day standing on the catwalk outside his gun and nine Japanese planes got through their radar. It dropped a bomb and he saw it explode right below him in the water. They went to Ulithi to reload ammunition and food. They were watching a movie, he was sitting in front of the officers on the deck, there was an ammunition barge between the *Hornet* and the *Bennington*. The *Yorktown* and the *Rudolph* were the too. The nine Japanese planes came in without being detected and flew across the *Bennington* and across the bow of the *Hornet* and hit the *Randolph*. Things started to explode and he ran to his gun.

Discharged March 17, 1946. Received the Asiatic-Pacific w/9 stars, Philippine Ribbon w/2 stars and the Presidential Unit Citation.

Retired in 1988 from the federal government after 41 1/2 years. Married and has two children, two grandchildren and two great-grandchildren.

SPERO J. MELONIDES, born Dec. 31, 1932, Chicago, IL. Joined the USN May 12, 1952; was assigned to the USS *Hornet* in May 1955; assigned to Air Group CAG-7, VA-72, as a plane captain.

Memorable experience was working on the flight deck and taking a ride in a AD5N sky raider.

Discharged May 3, 1960. Received the Navy Good Conduct Medal, National Defense Service Medal, Air Medal, AF Outstanding Unit Medal, AF Commendation Medal, Combat Readiness Medal, Air Reserve Meritorious Service Medal, South Asia Service Medal, AF Longevity Award, Armed Forces Reserve Medal, Small Arms Expert Marksmanship, Kuwait Liberation Medal and numerous other state awards.

After the USN he became an aircraft and power plant mechanic and worked for United Airlines for one year; then went into sales of bakery/dairy product for 22 years. Retired from civilian work in 1992. He joined the Air Guard in January 1971 as a staff sergeant; became an air crew member, first on the KC-97L, then on the KC137 A/E. His job was a boom operator; served as an instructor evaluator and senior NCO of his unit. This was the 108ARS/126ARW at O'Hare International Airport. In the 22 years of flying as a part-time he accumulated 5,248.9 hours and his travel was world wide. Summer camp for the first seven years was at Frankfurt, Germany, but the most interesting part of his career was near the end. His unit was activated for Desert Shield and Desert Storm. He and his crew flew 30 combat support missions out of Saudi Arabia. He serviced USAF, USN and other foreign aircraft that needed fuel. This was the highlight of his USAF/ILANG career. After the war he became a boom instructor and taught TDY at various USAR and Guard installations. He was lucky to be able to serve until he hit 60 years of age. He retired as a chief master sergeant. since then he as taken it easy for the last two and one-half years. He has been working as a driver for a company called Auto Drive Away. He delivers autos and trucks all over the world.

Married Francis and has three sons: John (LT CMDR, USN) surface warfare and helicopter pilot;

Stephen (CAPT), USAF pilot, KC-135A/E/R; and William, a college student.

WILLIAM MESSAROS JR., born Aug. 2, 1933, Elyria, OH. Joined the USN Aug. 20, 1951; was assigned to the USS *Hornet* in February 1954; and worked on the flight deck.

Memorable experiences include pulling into New York Harbor; going through Suez Canal and Liberty; typhoons; and their ship's planes shooting down two Chinese planes.

Discharged Aug. 15, 1955. Received the China Service, Navy Occupation (Europe), Good Conduct and National Defense Medals.

Married Shirley and has two daughters, Kim and Becky, and five grandchildren. He retired from the US Postal Service after 31 years. He is very involved in the American Legion.

PAUL LOUIS MEUNIER, born Oct. 12, 1923, New York, NY. Joined the service Aug. 19, 1941; was assigned to the USS *Hornet* Oct. 1, 1941; and served on the signal bridge as a signalman.

They knew Hitler had to be defeated, so several he and several friends enlisted in the USN at Great Lakes on Aug. 19, 1941, before Pearl Harbor! His four years, two months and two day tour of duty took him to Norfolk, VA; boarded the USS *Hornet*; tested B-25 take-offs; through the Panama Canal; to San Diego; and loaded B-25s at Alameda, CA. On the *Hornet* they carried Doolittle and his B-25 bombers to within 500 miles of Japan, then went on to the battle of Midway. After Midway, his communications duty assigned him to Pearl Harbor Navy Yard, Palmyra Island, back to Pearl Harbor and finally home to Great Lakes. He would do it all again for his country!

Discharged Oct. 21, 1945. Received the Asiatic-Pacific w/BS, American Defense w/BS, Good Conduct and American Area Medals.

Married Juanita on June 12, 1948, and has two daughters, Barbara and Nancy. He is retired, living in Florida on beautiful Lake George.

CARL DUANE MILLER, born June 1, 1942, Marshalltown, IA. Joined the USN in June 1959; was assigned to the USS *Hornet* on June 7, 1962; served as a plane captain and weapons loader and ordnance shop, VS-35; and achieved the rank of AO2. Also

served aboard the USS *Princeton* and the USS *Yorktown* (CVS-10).

Memorable experiences include losing Helo (HS-2), June 22, 1962, and Richard F. Miller, ATC, losing his life in the same.

Discharged in June 1963; transferred to USNR, being discharged in June 1965; and re-enlisted until 1991.

He is an engineering assistant for research and development for Fisher Controls International.

EARL L. MILLER, born April 29, 1919, Vallejo, CA. He enlisted in San Jose, CA, on Oct. 3, 1938. After attending boot camp at San Diego, CA, he was assigned to the cruiser USS *Detroit* where he served

three years and achieved the rank of coxswain. In September 1941 he was transferred to the USS *Hornet* in Norfolk, VA. His division was V-1 and their first action was to launch Doolittle's raiders, followed by Midway where their entire torpedo squadron was lost; then Guadalcanal and finally Santa Cruz where the *Hornet* suffered such severe torpedo damage that it had to be abandoned. His next ship was the USS *Princeton* which fought for 18 months before being sunk in Leyte Gulf. He then served at the amphibious training base, Coronado, CA, until discharge in September 1945.

MARK JOSEPH MITCHELL, born Oct. 9, 1945, Passaic, NJ. Joined the USN July 23, 1963; was assigned to the USS *Hornet* in late October 1963; stationed with R Div. as a ship fitter. Served on two Wespac tours. Both times they operated in the Gulf of Tonkin. The referred to it as "Yankee Station."

Memorable experiences include Jan. 22, 1966. They lost four men and one plane. They were shot down over the waters of North Vietnam. The plane was a twin engine prop designated as an S2D. The downing of this plane and the men on board stick in his mind because they were due to head for home soon. In December 1990 they were visiting his family. He found out at the time that his mother father read of his being killed in action in their hometown newspaper. His mother was frantic. The thought that possibly he had re-upped and had not informed her of it. She spent the next 24 hours on the phone in order to confirm hat he was still alive. In fact he had been discharged just prior to the writing of the article in the newspaper and was still on the west coast.

Discharged Oct. 7, 1966, with the rank of SFM3. Received the Vietnam Service Medal and Armed Forces Expeditionary Medal.

He is the third son in a family of six children. His mother is deceased. He has been married to his second wife for over 20 years. Together they raised his son and step-daughter and are currently raising their oldest granddaughter. He has worked for McDonnell Douglas Aerospace in Huntington Beach,

CA, on and off since Oct. 17, 1966. He works in the mock-up and development department. They call this department "The Rocket Shop."

RICHARD A. MOODY, graduated from Gardiner High School, Gardiner, ME, 1943. He joined the USMC and was on the USS *Hornet* (CV-12) the day she was commissioned, and served as a gunner. Served on the *Hornet* from the day she was commissioned until the war ended, 1943-45.

Currently resides in Gardiner. Married a girl from his graduating class.

JERRY F. MOORE, born April 22, 192, Grayville, IL; attended school at Grayville, a vary small high school. Drafted into the USN on June 15, 1943. Reported to Great Lakes and Glenview Air Station June 17, 1943. Received firefighter and aircraft training there, then reported to Norfolk, VA, and Creeds Field, VA, a dive bomber training station with SBD planes. From Creeds to the USS *Hornet* as a plank owner at Newport News, VA, shipyard. The *Hornet* was ordered to join TF-58 in the south Pacific. He worked as a mechanic on aircraft's in the hanger and on the flight deck.

Memorable experience was when Chief Leonard Miles grabbed him, preventing him from falling down elevator one as it was being lowered. The guard rail failed to come up.

Released from active duty at Great Lakes, IL, Feb. 18, 1946. Received the American Area, WWII Victory, Asiatic-Pacific w/10 BSs, Philippine Liberation w/2 stars and Presidential Unit Citation Awards.

Worked at Hines, IL, Veterans Hospital for over 30 years. Retired as an assistant fire chief in 1977 and moved to Hot Springs, AR. He joined the Lake Hamilton Fire Dept. in 1977 and retired as chief in 1991. He and his wife are still living in Hot Springs.

H. BLAKE "RABBIT" MORANVILLE, born Feb. 14, 1923, Guide Rock, NE. Joined the USN in June 1942. On Sept. 29, 1944, Ens. Moranville, a pilot in FS-11, went aboard the USS *Hornet* (CV-12) at Manus in the Admiralty Islands. Along with his squadron and AG-11 he participated in combat operations throughout the Western Pacific Theater. During this period Moranville shot down six enemy aircraft, destroyed numerous aircraft on the ground, attacked other targets  on the ground and along with other members of his division attacked and sunk various enemy ships. While on the *Hornet* he was caretaker of Gunner, a Boston Terrier and mascot of VF-11. When ever you saw Rabbit on the ship you almost always saw Gunner along with him.

On Jan. 12, 1945, when the *Hornet* along with the rest of TF-38 were in the China Sea, Rabbit was shot down while attacking the airfield at Saigon, Indo-China. He was a POW and ultimately escaped to Kunming, China and from there was flown back to the States.

He made a career of the Navy and retired in 1964. In 1946 he married and is still married to Mary Sheridan Sherwood, they have two grown sons and four grandchildren. Following his retirement from the Navy he worked at Western Oregon State College and retired as Dean of Students. He presently lives with his wife of 51 years in Monmouth, OR.

JOSEPH N. MOREAU, born May 23, 1918, Cambridge, MA. Joined the USN April 2, 1943; was assigned to the USS *Hornet* Oct. 11, 1943; and was stationed as MM2/c, no. 2 engine room. Participated in all operations of the entire cruise until October 1945.

Memorable experiences include seeing the USS *Kearsage* on the hull stern before it was changed to the *Hornet*.

Discharged Oct. 12, 1945, with the rank of MM2/c. Received the American Area Ribbon, Asiatic-Pacific Area Ribbon w/8 stars, Philippine Liberation Ribbon w/2 BSs and Presidential Unit Citation w/star.

Married Louise and has a son Joseph C, married to Maria; and two grandsons, Jackson and Zackary. He is retired.

JOHN M. MORTENSEN, born May 24, 1930, Crystal Township, WI. Joined the USN Feb. 5, 1951; assigned to the USS *Hornet*, September 1953-Jan. 28, 1955; assigned to the metal shop with Air Div. V-4; and achieved the rank of AM3.

The *Hornet* sailed from Norfolk, VA, early May 1954 to the Mediterranean Sea and Indian Ocean for operations and in June 1954 joined the Mobile 7th Fleet. After approximately six months of the 7th Fleet operation, the *Hornet* arrived back at San Diego on December 20. Discharged Jan. 28, 1955.

Memorable experiences include crossing the equator at South Singapore and visiting with his father stationed at Subic Bay, Philippines, MCB11, July 1954; and the world cruise while aboard the *Hornet*.

He worked for 40 years at the Andersen Corp. manufacturer. He retired on Aug. 31, 1990. Today he is an active volunteer for community organizations in New Richmond, WI area. Married to Bernadine for 42 years and has three grown children, eight grandchildren.

GEORGE MULLINS, born Nov. 27, 1935, Pittsburgh, PA. Joined the USN May 25, 1953; was assigned to the USS *Hornet* Nov. 14, 1953; assigned to the print shop and ship's newspaper. He was assigned to X Div.

Helped with the ship's paper *Hornet Buzz*; set head lines for the ship's newspaper in the print shop. They needed a printer so he ended up working there until he left the *Hornet* in November 1956. Made the world cruise and went over the equator, made three Wespac cruises and also went with the *Hornet* when the angle deck and hurricane bow was installed in Bremerton, WA. Then to Philadelphia Navy Yard until April 1959 to Argentina, Newfoundland until 1961; then to USS *Fulton* (AS-11), Pax River, MD, print shop; to USS *Bonhomme Richard* (CVA-31); communications center, Pentagon, London, England, print shop, 1968-70; to USS *Sierra* (AD-18); and was assigned as petty officer of the print shop until he retired.

Memorable experiences include crossing the equator and three Wespac tours with the *Hornet*.

Retired Sept. 3, 1974, with the rank of LI1. Received the Good Conduct w/3 BSs, Navy Occupation (Europe Clasp), China Service, National Defense w/BS, Armed Forces Expeditionary and Vietnam Service.

Divorced and has two children, George Jr. and Mary Ellen. He is retired in Pittsburgh, PA, and has his own business, George Mullins Printing. Also works for Triangle Poster Co., printing tickets for carnivals and four color posters.

OTTIE ELMER NABORS, born Aug. 15, 1919, in Greenville, SC. Joined the USN Jan. 9, 1942, at Greenville, SC; assigned to the USS *Hornet*, (CV-8), in January 1942 and held the ratings of BKR3, BKR2, BKR1, CCS and CSC. He was a qualified Naval Investigator and Instructor.

Memorable experiences include being picked up by the USS Mustin after abandoning the USS *Hornet*, (CV-8); the sinking of the USS *Princeton* which he was on; and shore duty at Sasebo, Japan.

Awarded the American Area, Good Conduct Medal w/5 stars, Asiatic-Pacific w/7 stars, Navy Occupation Medal, China Service, Philippine Liberation, Philippine Defense, Korean Service w/3 stars, National Defense, United Nations and WWII Victory Medal.

Married Bertha and they have one son, Ottie F. (Fred). He was a policeman for the City of Seaside, OR for 19 years. Retired as a Detective Sergeant in 1979. Lived at Knappa, OR for 17 years on small ranch. Now resides at Westport, OR.

STANTON "BUD" NEWKIRK, born July 4, 1924. He served in the USS *Hornet* during WWII and received an honorable discharge from the USN in 1947. Newkirk earned BA degrees in psychology and English at Miami University, OH, 1948.

From 1948 until retirement in 1987, he worked for Champion International, Hamilton, OH and Chicago, IL. He has 35 years employee relations management experience.

Newkirk is member of several civic and professional affiliations. He is married and has two daughters. He lives in Hamilton, OH.

DAVID E. NIELSEN, born March 20, 1941, in LeMavs, IA and joined the USN Jan. 7, 1960. Assigned to the USS *Hornet* in October 1960; stationed as 14-Div. Hyd. He was a mess-cook for 90 days and then repaired and operated plane elevators.

Memorable experiences were liberty call in Yoko, Japan; Subic Bay; and Henekay. He hocked his high school class ring in Japan, returned a month later and got the ring out of hock.

Discharged April 1, 1990, with the rank of FN E-3. He spent 30 years, two months, 24 days in the USN.

He is a used car manager in West Hills Honda, Bremerton, WA. Married to Donna F.

JOSEPH "JOE" B. NIST enlisted in the USN in late 1943 using his brother's name since he was only 16 years old. Attended boot camp and Gunners Mate School in Great Lakes then went to Hawaii on a fleet replacement ship. Here he joined the USS *Hornet* and spent the next two years in the Pacific battles.

One of the many memorable occasions was the typhoon Easter Sunday on the way to Okinawa where 100 feet of the flight deck was destroyed.

Awarded the American Area, Asiatic-Pacific w/ 6 stars, WWII Victory, Philippine Liberation w/2 stars, and the Presidential Unit Citation. Discharged in May 1946.

He has been married to Dolores for 48 years. They have two sons, one daughter and four grandchildren. He is retired from the H.J. Heinz Company.

LARRY R. NITCHMAN, born May 26, 1940, Gary, IN. Joined the USN on May 29, 1957; served in the flag office, COMCARDIV-19.

Memorable experiences were the two Wespac cruises and being at sea August 1959 trying to evade Typhoon Ellen.

Served 12 years and was discharged May 28, 1963, with the rank of YN3. Awarded the Armed Forces Expeditionary Medal, National Defense, two Naval Reserve Medals.

Married Lois and they have four children, two grandchildren. Two sons served in the USN and daughter in the USAF. He worked 28 years for the city of Burbank, CA; 20 of those years as a police officer. Currently retired.

WALTER I. OKANO, born Jan. 16, 1933, in Los Angeles, CA. Joined the USNR while attending college. Upon graduation, received commission as an ensign and reported aboard the USS *Hornet* in April 1955.

Memorable experiences were while he was on watch at main engine control when the number three propeller was lost (sheared off) while picking up speed to recover planes off of Okinawa; spent approximately seven months in dry dock enclosing the bow, installing and angled deck and making many other modifications and repairs.

Released from active duty March 1957, at Treasure Island. Continued taking correspondence courses and attended Submarine Warfare School in San Diego. Received commission as a lieutenant June 1, 1959. Honorably discharged Sept. 21, 1967.

Married Florence and they have two daughters, Cathy and Cindy. Retired Feb. 1, 1993, after working 38 years as an electrical engineer.

KENNETH MORRIS OLSON, born Feb. 20, 1934, in Los Angeles, CA. Joined the USN August 1952 in the USNR-R on VF 776 NAS Los Alametos, CA. Went on active duty Dec. 3, 1956 with VF-94 NAS Moffett Field, CA; assigned to the USS *Hornet*, January 1958 at NAS Alameda, CA as a plane captain flying FJ-3 Furys.

Memorable experiences were the typhoon in the South China Sea; all the ports of call.

Discharged December 1958; January 1959 he went back to VF-776 at NAS Los Alametos. Jan. 26, 1968, was called back to active duty with VA776 for one year. Was stationed at NAS Los Alametos; NAS Lemore and NAS Fallon. Spent some time on the aircraft carrier *Ranger* and carrier *Quals*. After being discharged, went back into the Naval Reserves with VA776. Ended his Naval service with VC-13 at NAS Miramar with the rank of ADC-E-7.

Married to Myra, who has passed away. They have two children, one son and one daughter, 28 and 30 years old. Retired from the US Postal service and has a 30 foot boat and motor home. He does a lot of camping and fishing.

LYMAN E. PARKHURST enlisted in 1955 and served at BuPers, NAS Glenview; NMCSSC/JCS; VQ-2. Appointed ship clerk 1966. Ordered to the USS *Hornet* as ship's secretary. Capt. Van V. Eason assuming command. After the yard, *Hornet* made a Hawaii midshipman cruise and unmanned Apollo, Saturn pickup near Wake Island. Capt. Eason left early to command *Wasp*, which had run aground. Capt. Gordon H. Robertson became commanding officer.

The *Hornet* deployed to Vietnam March 1967 and was also in a major SEATO exercise, "SEADOG", and visited Thailand and Hong Kong while deployed.

The *Hornet* was dry-docked when the *Queen Mary* arrived in Long Beach. The *Hornet* left dry-dock early to allow the *Queen Mary* in, as she was leaking around her shafts. He left the USS *Hornet* in April 1968. He later served in San Diego; CINCUSNAVEUR London, England and in Maine.

Retiring in 1978 with the rank of lieutenant. He then earned two degrees at the University of Minnesota.

Married Cathy and they owned a resort in Wisconsin for nine years, currently retired.

FRANK PARRA, born Sept. 12, 1930, Queens, NY. Enlisted in the USN in October 1950. Attended boot

camp at Newport and Engineman A School at Great Lakes. In 1951, received fleet appointment as NROTC midshipman and attended Northwestern University, Evanston, IL, receiving degree in mechanical engineering and commission as ensign, USN, June 1955. As midshipman, made summer cruises on *New Jersey* (BB-62) and *William R. Rush* (DD-714); worked winters in Brooklyn Navy Yard as student trainee.

Upon commissioning, ordered to the USS *Hornet*, (CV-12), assuming duties as A-Div. officer. In 1956, while ship was in Bremerton, attended fire fighting, damage control, and ABC Warfare Defense Schools at Treasure Island. In 1957, promoted to lieutenant and assigned as R Div. officer, assistant to damage control assistant, and ABC Warfare Defense Officer. In charge of damage control party responsible for limiting flooding and pumping out flooded compartments resulting from the cleaning the sea strainer incident. Also survived the "Fiestaburger" campaign. Transferred to Naval Reserve; released from active duty July 1958.

Returned to civilian life, held various management positions in three different companies, retiring in 1992 as plant manager and chief engineer. Now resides in Valley Cottage, NY.

DAVID ALLEN PAYNE, born June 27, 1921, Murfreesboro, TN. Joined the USN Jan. 25, 1941 at Stevenson, AL and attended boot camp at the Naval Operating Base, Norfolk, VA; went to Aviation Machinist Mate School NAS Norfolk, VA. Assigned to Air Group 8 for the USS *Hornet*, (CV-8), in BS 8; was plane captain on SBD-3.

Action at Sea: Tokyo raid; Midway with *Wasp* (CV-7) when sunk; action around Guadalcanal with raids up the slot on Bouginville and finally the Japanese got them at the battle of Santa Cruz on Oct. 26, 1942.

Memorable experiences include signing his name on Doolittle bombs for the Tokyo raid and leaving the *Hornet* Oct. 26, 1942; a sad day in history. Surely this great ship will go down in history to be remembered as Great.

He left the USN in February 1947 as aviation machinist mate 1/C.

Retired from TVA as electrician after 36 years in 1985.

CLYDE T. PERKINS, born Jan. 4, 1925, Williamstown, PA. Joined the USN June 5, 1943; assigned to the USS *Hornet* in December 1943, a week before commissioning; served as boiler room operator; and achieved the rank of WT2/c. He was a plank owner. He participated in all action with the *Hornet* from commissioning until his discharge.

Memorable experiences include the loss of the bow while in a storm; returning troops at the end of the war; being on smoke watch while under attack.

Discharged April 15, 1946. Received the Asiatic-Pacific w/9 stars, American Area Campaign Ribbon and WWII Victory Medal.

Married Alma and has a daughter, Jane and son, Dewey, and five grandchildren. He is retired.

JACK VINCENT PERRY, born Nov. 27, 1921, Neosha Falls, KS. Joined the USN in December 1941 and was assigned to the USS *Hornet* in October 1944 as a TBF pilot. Participated in action at Formosa, Oct. 12-15; Luzon, Leyte, Oct. 18-20; Manila, Nov. 13-14, 1944; and the china Sea, Hong Kong, Jan 12-16, 1945. Discharged in November 1945, with the rank of lieutenant. Received two Air Medals.

He passed away on Feb. 10, 1996. He left his wife Helen and children: Carol, Robert and Linda. *Submitted by Helen Perry.*

GEORGE G. PETERS enlisted in the USN in August 1942; and was discharged in May 1955. Served one year on the USS *Bogue*, North Atlantic duty, prior to service on the USS *Hornet* (CV-12), January 1944-September 1945. Served on various ships and stations in the next 10 years, but none as good as the *Hornet*.

Memorable experience while aboard the *Hornet* was making wine in the battery locker, hanger deck and almost getting caught by the E Div. officer making his inspection. He probably suspected what they were doing and wanted some. Many other experiences, but will never forget that one.

Upon discharge he worked for a regional airline in aircraft maintenance. Has been retired for some years, still runs his own boat, cruising, fishing, in the Boston area, and doing some traveling. He is the father of eight children; grandfather of 15; and great-grandfather of two. Originally from Yonkers, NY, but has made "beautiful Boston" his home since 1946.

CLAUDE ROBERT PINCKNEY JR., born Oct. 5, 1920, Savannah, GA. Joined the USN Sept. 12, 1940; and was assigned to the USS *Hornet*, (CV-8/CV-12), plank owner, Block Island. Participated in action during the Doolittle attack on Japan and the battle of Midway.

Memorable experiences were all of his six years. He came back alive, and some did not. Thank God!

Has two daughters and one son. He is the owner of Pinckney's Auto Supply and retired.

GILBERT L. PITTMAN, born Dec. 28, 1921, La Crosse, WI, and grew up there. After two years in college he joined the USN in the spring of 1942. Attended boot camp at Great Lakes; Carpenter's Mate School, Treasure Island, CA; then took a pleasure cruise on the USS *Matsonia* to Moumea, New Caledonia. Assigned to the destroyer USS *Mustin* (DD-413) bound for Guadalcanal. In the spring of 1943 he went up to the Aleutian Islands on the *Mustin* for the landings on Attu and Kiska. After that got transferred to new construction on the USS *Hornet* (CV-12). Was a member of the first crew and was on her until V-J Day.

After discharge moved to Wichita, KS, where the four large airplane plants are. He and his brother had a tooling and pattern business there for 36 years. He still resides in Wichita, KS.

ALFRED L. POE JR., born Sept. 10, 1924, Jacksonville, FL. He joined the USN on Feb. 19, 1943, and was assigned to VT-2 in the USS *Hornet* on June 16, 1944, as a replacement aircrewman. His rating at that time was seaman 1/c (ARM). His very first carrier take-off was from the *Hornet* in a TBF on June 20. Poe was the radioman, radar operator and tail gunner and their target was the Japanese fleet. After the attack, the landing had to be made after dark, and his first carrier landing was made on the USS *Enterprise*.

Other actions that he participated in, while assigned to the *Hornet*, were attacks on Chi-Chi Jima, Ha-Ha Jima, Rota, Guam, Yap, Palau, and the Philippine Islands, including a torpedo run during the first attack on Manila Bay.

During his Naval career, he received the Distinguished Flying Cross w/2 stars, Presidential Unit Citation w/star for the *Hornet* and Air Group 2, Navy Good Conduct Medal w/2 stars, Armed Forces Expeditionary Medal for Laos and Vietnam, American Defense Service Medal, Asiatic-Pacific Campaign Medal w/3 stars, WWII Victory Medal, National Defense Service Medal w/star. He retired from active duty with the USN on June 30, 1966.

He is married to Dottie and has three children: James, Sharon and Nora. After retiring from the USN he qualified as a US Merchant Marine officer/ship's master and performed ship deliveries and diving charters. Currently he does volunteer work as a master gardener for the University of Florida Cooperative Extension Service in Homestead, FL.

SEBASTIAN J. POST, born March 28, 1921, Olean, NY. Enlisted in the USN at Detroit, MI, Oct. 30, 1942; went to boot camp at Great Lakes, IL; went to Navy Pier Aviation Mechanic School; then to Philadelphia Navy Yard to Arresting Gear and Catapult School; on to Newport News, VA, assigned to the USS *Hornet* (CV-12). Was the original crew on deck during commissioning Nov. 29, 1943. Sailed with the *Hornet* on her first war cruise. His job was operating #1 arresting gear unit.

The *Hornet* and her crew participated in many phases of the Pacific War. Awards received were 11 Battle Stars and a Unit Citation w/star. Arrived home in June 1945. Left the *Hornet* in August 1945. Separation was in December 1945.

Married and has three children. Retired from GM in 1986.

JOHN R. POTTS, born Jan. 9, 1925, Omaha, NE. Joined the USN Jan. 7, 1943; attended boot camp, Great Lakes; Navy Pier, graduated AMM3/c; one month on the USS *Wolverine*, Lake Michigan; and then on board the USS *Hornet* (CV-12), commissioning day, 1943. Went through Panama Canal, San Diego, Honolulu and out to the Pacific. Stayed aboard the *Hornet* until just after the typhoon that hit them on June 5, 1945. Transferred at sea, boatswain chair to tanker; then on to Guam for flight back to the States and his first leave.

After spending some weeks traveling from Virginia to the South Pacific, with day after day going to GQ to be prepared for seeing a Japanese plane or ship it finally happened. They were cruising along just before they were to join up with the rest of the fleet, and low and behold a lone Japanese plane is all of a sudden off their port side about 100 feet off the water. He gets within a few hundred yards, banks up towards their fantail, loops back and dives down the flight deck, guns blazing. The crew on the flight deck, like himself, being a plane captain, were all yelling "Shoot Him—Shoot Him!!" If his memory serves him right, they had in excess of 100 guns aboard and they were all trying to get him in their sights. Needless to say no one hit him. He strafed the flight deck and took off into the sky. That was his first chance to see the enemy, but it was not his last. After this one incident their gunners never missed another plant that close; they became very, very proficient in shooting down the enemy.

After two months at base in Norman, OK, he was discharged on Nov. 5, 1945.

Spent a few years in the Cardinal baseball farm system, then back to Omaha to finish college. Coached two years at high school level and then into sales work. Retired from Celotex Corp. in 1982 and has spent the rest of these years trying to become a golfer or hacker, whichever. Has lived in Overland park, KS, for the last 24 years with wife, Roz, two children and two grandchildren.

ALLEN DALE QUIRING, born Feb. 2, 1946, Glasgow, MT. Joined the USN Oct. 20, 1965; attended boot camp in San Diego; and Machinist Mate School in Great Lakes, IL. Was assigned to the USS *Hornet* in June 1966 and was assigned to hydraulics with A-

1 Div.; and achieved the rank of MM2. Served two tours off Vietnam and supported operations for the USS *Pueblo*'s recovery from Korea.

Memorable experiences include picking up test capsule for Apollo 11 in 1966 and picking up the Apollo 11 in 1969.

Released from active duty in Long Beach, CA, Oct. 10, 1969. Received the Vietnam Service Medal and three others.

He owns his own tool and die company in Anaheim, building injection molds. He is married and has three children and four grandchildren.

BILLIE H. REDBURN, born Dec. 22, 1921, Hazelton, IN. Joined the USN in December 1939 at Indianapolis, IN; attended boot camp at Newport, RI; Group One Ordnance School, NOB Norfolk; pre-commissioning with VP-56, the first PBM squadron; flew in the XPBM1; plane ordnanceman on no. 6 as seaman 2/c; AOM3/c, February 1941; flew with VP-55 and VP-74 on North Atlantic patrol to NAS Norfolk, August 1941; pre-commissioning of Torpedo Sqdn. 8, Sept. 2, 1941; on board the USS *Hornet* (CV-8) when commissioned; AOM2/c, February 1942; loaded three of Jimmy Doolittle's B-25s for the Tokyo Raid.

At the battle of Midway, hooked up the starting lanyards of the torpedo's on all 15 of the TBDs of Torpedo Sqdn. 8. None of the planes returned so he spend the next three days loading 1,000 pounders on the SBDs of BS 8 and Scouting 8 of the six Japanese carriers that hit Pearl Harbor; four were sent to Davy Jones Locker at Midway.

After Midway as the only torpedo squadron left in the Pacific Torpedo Sqdn. 8 transferred from the *Hornet* (CV-8) to USS *Saratoga* (CV-3) with the new TBF avengers from Grumman Factory for the invasion of the Solomons. Following the battle of the Eastern Solomons *Saratoga* was torpedoed. While dead in the water and in tow by the cruiser *Minneapolis* the TBFs of Torpedo Sqdn. 8 flew off to Esprito Santo ad the squadron personnel and gear were highlined to the destroyer *Grayson*. At midnight, September 20, flew out to Esprito Santo in ADC3 transport with squadron gear, landing at Henderson Field, Guadalcanal at dawn to maintain and arm the six TBFs already there. Turned over the one remaining TBF of Torpedo Sqdn. 8 to the marine squadron relieving them on Nov. 15, 1942. On Dec. 13, 1952, Torpedo Sqdn. 8 was decommissioned at NAS San Diego.

With 15 months of commissioned service his squadron had earned seven Battle Stars and two Presidential Unit Citations; the first unit of the Navy or Marine Corps to be so honored. In January 1943, Naval Air Test Center, Pax River, MD; December 1943, China cruises with VT-4 and VA-2A on USS *Tarawa* (CV-40) and USS *Princeton* (CV-37); med cruises with VA-15 on USS *Coral Sea* (CVB-43); pre-commissioning on USS *Forrestal* (CVA-59) in 1955;

AOCS, 1959; AOCM, 1960; LTJG, 1961; VA-75, 1961; transitioned from ADO to A-6s, 1963; LT, 1963; and retired in 1968.

As a widower for 15 years, living in Virginia Beach, VA, he welcomes information from any of his shipmates, especially those that came back from the Canal.

ERIC THOMAS W. REESE, born Aug. 16, 1914, Lewiston, NC. Joined the USN in March 1934; went to USS *Whiting* (AD-4), 1941; and to the USS *Hornet* (CV-8) to help commission her on Oct. 20, 1941.

Made the Doolittle raid on April 18, 1942; *Hornet*, battle of Midway, June 4-8, 1942; Guadalcanal, August 1942. He was EM3/c to assist in maintenance and upkeep of engineering department and electrical equipment. His battle station was forward engine room electrician. His first torpedo hit on the starboard side of this space. After coming to the hanger deck he assisted two men who where hanging on the rungs of the ladders leading to decks below by pulling them one at a time to the hanger deck. Later they abandoned ship.

In the water he took charge of a life raft; proceeded to work their way to the USS *Mustin* (DD-413). It picked up 337 of the *Hornet* crew.

When he returned to the States, he received orders to the USS *Lexington* (CV-16) commissioning, Feb. 17, 1943. He put it out of commission in 1946. Leaving her in 1947 for shore duty, NAS San Diego, CA; to the USS *Oglethorpe* (AKA-100); then to underway training command; Yokosuka, Japan to Hawaii to San Diego to Advanced Electrical School in Chicago; to *Lexington* (CVA-16); to Pensacola, FL, shore duty.

Retired Nov. 17, 1958. Attended college on the GI Bill and obtained his BSEE. Worked for Conair Div. of General Dynamics, retiring in 1977 as senior engineer. Volunteered with senior programs in San Diego city and county. In 1987 he was elected as senior senator in California Senior Legislature. Served three two-year consecutive terms, retiring in 1993. Today he does handy man work for the people in the community. He and his wife, Lee Flannery Reese, married on Sept. 8, 1942. She taught foreign born students after her BA and MA degrees. She has written and published 10 books since retiring from teaching. They have one son who is married and they have three daughters.

JOSEPH E. REICH, born Dec. 24, 1924, New York, NY. Joined the USN March 16, 1943; and was assigned to the USS *Hornet* in March 1944 as CIC and radar with V-4 Div.; and achieved the rank of RDM2/c. Participated in all battles and campaigns until the typhoon damage. Also served on the USS *Cabot* (CVL-28).

Memorable experiences include meeting two

Navy brothers at Ulithi Harbor; visiting the *Hornet*; kamikaze close calls; 1045 typhoon; and safe return to the States and home.

Discharged in November 1945. Received two Presidential Unit Citations and nine Battle Stars.

Spent 48 years in police work with the New York Police Dept. and West City Police Dept., and is still active. Has been married for 47 years and has five children and six grandchildren. His three brothers served during WWII, one in the US Army and two in the USN.

ALBERT F. REYNOLDS, born May 2, 1921, Derby, ME. Entered naval service Oct. 15, 1942, at Chapel Hill, NC. Designated Naval Aviator Number 4714 at Pensacola, FL, July 27, 1943. Reported to VB-2 at Santa Rosa, CA, Nov. 7, 1943. Served aboard the USS *Hornet* (CV-12) with VB-2 in TF-58.1 from March 11, 1944-Sept. 29, 1944, and participated as a dive bomber pilot flying SB2Cs in Asiatic-Pacific raids, Western New Guinea operations, Marrianas operation and the Western Caroline operation. On July 9, 1944, on the pull-out of a diving run on Agana, Guam, qualified as a member of the Caterpillar Club when the left Aileron of his SB2C was disabled because of structural failure requiring him and his gunner, Dipsy Youmans, to bail out over the Task Force. In 1945-46, served as an acceptance and test pilot at NAF Mercer Field, and NAS Floyd Bennett.

Attended Columbia University upon release from the USN, Sept. 11, 1946, then served as a state department foreign service officer for 21 years. On assignment as a civilian to Army G-2 in Korea in 1950-51, awarded Bronze Star for work with resistance forces in setting up evasion and escape routes to recover downed American pilots. Upon early retirement in 1970 he took up a new career in environmental management in Santa Barbara county, CA, where he still resides in Solvang with this wife of 52 years, Ruth Derby Reynolds. In 1944-45, Ruth served as a Navy WAVE Specialist V Flight Controller with VR-3 at Olathe, KS, and NAS Floyd Bennett.

CLARENCE L. RICHARDS, born March 20, 1924, Columbus, IN. Joined the USN at 17; six weeks training at the NTC Great Lakes, IL in Co. 133; three companies were assigned to the USS *Hornet* and they went aboard about Oct. 16, 1941, and commissioning was on Oct. 18, 1941. He was assigned to communications (visual signals).

One memorable experience was during training in the Gulf of Mexico. Over the speaker came the word, "Richards, seaman, report to the captain on the bridge." He did not even know the captain knew him, and all kinds of things went through his mind. The captain said, "I want you to get a pair of binoculars and sound powered telephones, go up on the radar platform (radar not put on yet) and report everything you see, and God help you if I see it before you do." That changed his life, because he reported all floating objects, colored water, flying fish and birds. He reported land off the port bow. The captain called the navigator to the bridge to check. Land was 300 miles away. Before the B-25s came aboard the radar was installed.

Actions at sea was the Doolittle raid, a tour of the South Pacific, and the battle of Midway. At Pearl Harbor, he and the captain were transferred off the ship the same day. He went to temporary duty to Ford Island Signal Tower. Assigned to Troop Transport, USS *Catron* (APA-71) to the end of the war. Served two tours in Korea.

Retired June 30, 1961, as chief quartermaster (20 years). Received the WWII Victory Medal, American Defense, American Area Campaign, Philippine Liberation, Good Conduct, Asiatic-Pacific, Korean Service, Korean Presidential Unit, UN Service Medal, National Service Medal, National Defense and Navy Occupation China Sea.

Spent from Jan. 22, 1962, to Jan. 22, 1983, with the US Postal Service, retiring on June 30, 1983.

GORDON H. ROBERTSON, born Dec. 27, 1920, Kansas City, MO. Joined the USN in 1942 in the aviation cadet program. He served two tours aboard the USS *Hornet*. One was in 1944 as a lieutenant(jg) in BS @ embarked in CV-12 and a second tour in 1967 in CVS-12 as a captain and commanding officer.

Between those two tours, as he remained on active duty, his assignments rotated between shore and sea duty during which he made several deployments to the 6th Fleet in the Mediterranean. He commanded Heavy Attack Sqdn. 11 in the Atlantic Fleet and the amphibious assault ship USS *Capricornus* (AKA-57) home ported in Norfolk, VA. After 27 years of active duty he retired following an assignment on the staff of the chairman, Joint Chiefs of Staff, at Washington, DC.

Upon retirement from active naval service, Capt. Robertson returned to Kansas City. He was active as a broker of industrial, commercial and investment properties until he again retired in 1981. He is a past president of the greater Kansas City Council, Navy League of the US and a past commander of the Kansas City chapter, The Military Order of the World Wars.

In addition to his wife, the former Frances Hodges of Olathe, KS, he has two daughters and five grandchildren.

Awards received: Navy Meritorious Service Medal, Distinguished Flying Cross, Air Medal w/6 Gold Stars, Presidential Unit Citation Ribbon, American Campaign Medal, Asiatic-Pacific Campaign Medal w/1 Silver and 1 BS, WWII Victory Medal, Navy Occupation Service Medal w/Europe Clasp, National Defense Service Medal w/star, Vietnam Service Medal, RVN Service Medal, National Order of Vietnam 5th Class, and the Vietnamese Cross of Gallantry w/Willow Branch.

LORNE ELLSWORTH ROUX, born April 11, 1918, Montreal, Canada. Joined the USN Nov. 11, 1936; sent to Newport, RI, training station; assigned to USS *Vincennes*, March 1937 to July 1941; and was transferred to the USS *Hornet* (CV-8), July 1, 1941, as an aviation mechanic 2/c, with Fighting Sqdn. 8 until Oct. 26, 1942.

Participated during the Doolittle raid on Tokyo, Japan; battle of Midway; numerous raids on New Guinea and the Solomon Islands; battle of Santa Cruz and the sinking of the USS *Hornet* on Oct. 26, 1942; reassigned to Composite Sqdn. 81 on Dec. 22, 1943, and the USS *Natoma Bay* (CVE-62), TF-24; occupation of Leyte Island, Philippines, between Oct. 17-30, 1944; chased by Japanese fleet off the Somar Islands, October 25-26, 1944; provided cover support for amphibious landings at Mindoro Lingayen, Luzon, Subic Bay, Jan. 3-31, 1945; and provided cover and support during the landings at Iwo Jima, Volcano Island, Feb. 14-March 7, 1945.

Retired May 21, 1956. Received the Presidential Unit Citation w/1 BS, Asiatic Campaign Medal w/6 stars, American Area Campaign Medal, National Defense Service Medal and WWII Victory Medal.

Married Elizabeth and has two children and four grandchildren. Worked in industrial instrumentation until retirement.

DAVID ROYER, born Aug. 1, 1931, Waterbury, CT. Joined the USN July 29, 1951; and was assigned to the USS *Hornet* (CVA-12) in October 1953, in the after engine room.

Memorable experiences include the world cruise and the initiation crossing the equator.

Discharged in July 1955 with the rank of MA2. Received the Good Conduct Medal, National Defense Medal and Korean Service Medals.

Married Linda and has two grown children: daughter in Easthampton, MA, and son in Torringtin, CT; two granddaughters in Easthampton, MA. He has been employed at Torrington Company, Fafner Bearings, for 38 years.

JAMES S. RUSSELL, born July 23, 1913, Fort Worth, TX. Commissioned ensign USNR, March 2, 1942. After aviation ordnance duty in Washington, DC, he was assigned to the USS *Hornet* as V-5 Div. officer in May 1946.

Memorable experiences: repair of battle and typhoon damages and installation of additional armament and catapult. As officer of the deck, morning after V-J Day, authorized the bugler to swing reveille, beautiful job. Magic Carpet Ferring troops. "Mothballing" the *Hornet* and preserving her for future crews.

Awards include the WWII Victory Medal, American Campaign and Philippine Liberation Medals. Released from active duty in October 1946.

Married Margueritte and has two children, James Jr. and Beverly Broomell. He is currently active in masonry and helping hand jobs. Margueritte passed away in 1996.

WALLACE "WALLY" SALAMONY served on the USS *Hornet* from 1943-47 and again 1951-52 as a machinist mate. He put the *Hornet* in and out of commission having the distinction of being the last man to walk off the ship.

He boxed on board ship, had a few fights, then had his nose broken. He saw combat and his buddies commented they would not want to be down below then, but Wall said after being deck, "Never mind, I'd rather be below."

He remembered the typhoon that messed up the bow of the ship, with seas so rough you thought the ship would break in half, bending and cracking at mid-ship. It was as scary as the combat they saw. Another memorable experience was the day a pilot hit the deck trying to land, killing himself and decapitating a deck hand. Wally was standing nearby and became ill.

He was 17 when he enlisted in 1943. After discharge he became a master plumber in Baltimore, MD, and worked in that trade until his death at age 66 in 1992. He left behind wife, Kathleen, three step-children, five step-granddaughters, brother Robert and his three beloved dogs.

JOSEPH SCALZONE, born Feb. 12, 1931, Raritan, NJ. Joined the USN March 12, 1951; was assigned to the USS *Hornet* in August 1953; was stationed AFT as a galley cook. He participated in action at the Straits of Formose and expected to be attacked by Red Chinese.

Memorable experiences include the crossing of the equator; the Cold War; air attack alerts; Typhoon Grace in 1954 in the Sea of Japan.

Discharged March 2, 1955, with the rank of CS3. Received the Good Conduct Medal, National Defense and Presidential Unit Citation.

Married Margaret on Sept. 15, 1962, and has three children. After discharge he did carpentry work for four years; steel work for 13 years; building inspector for 21 years; and retired in 1995.

WILLIAM A. SCHAUB, born Jan. 23, 1924, Parkland, MD. Joined the USN in November 1952, and was assigned to the USS *Hornet* in June 1953. He was part of the recommissioning crew and a plank owner. He was a member of E Div. and was a movie operator, one of the ship's most important jobs.

Departed New York in early 1954 for a world cruise, a journey that took them across the equator.

After a second cruise to Japan, he left the *Hornet* and the USN in November 1956.

Presently works for USAA in Reston, VA. Married to Evelyn and has three children and six grandchildren.

RICHARD D. SCHREUL, born March 9, 1932, Aurora, IL. Joined the USNR in 1950; was assigned to the USS *Hornet* in October 1953; served as a photographer; and achieved the rank of PH3. Discharged in September 1955.

Memorable experiences include the world cruise and crossing the equator.

Has been in the photography business since 1955; Real Estate sales since 1970; and working at ACE Hardware. Married and has two daughters and two grandchildren. Still living in Aurora, IL, to ambitious to retire.

HOWARD "BUD" SCHRODER, born in New Jersey and joined the USN for adventure and a career. After boot camp he reported aboard the USS *Savannah* in 1940. His tour of duty aboard that ship included many exotic parts of call and adventures: Hawaii, Samoa, New Zealand, Fiji Islands, and Tahiti.

He passed the fleets test for the Naval Academy, only to learn two weeks later that he was a month too old upon entrance. He then requested transfer to the air department. Mr. Baldwin, his division officer, pushed through the transfer to the air group to up the USS *Hornet* (CV-8) in commission. He was made plane captain when Scouting 8 was formed. His first plane was a SBC, a by-plane with fabric wings. where two machine guns shot through the propellers. His pilot was Ralph Hovind; radio gunner, Charlie Lufburrow; second mech., Strickland; a better crew no one could boast. In April 1942 they made a run to Japan carrying the B-25 bombers with Lt. Col. Doolittle in charge of the bombing strike on Japan. Since this mission was highly secret, no one knew where the planes came from. President Roosevelt said that they came from Shang-ri-la; of course, word eventually got out that they flew off the deck of the *Hornet*.

Their next mission was the Coral Sea area but soon was ordered by Adm. Nimitz to proceed to Midway Island, where a large force of Japanese ships were headed. Engaging the enemy, the *Hornet* losses were all of torpedo 8 Sqdn. of TBDs except one pilot, Ens. Gay. Scouting 8 lost one dive bomber piloted by Don Griswald and radio gunner Ken bunch. He was the last man to talk to Don Griswald on deck as the chief asked him to "hook him up."

After Midway they again saw themselves in the South Pacific. In September 1942 the USS *Wasp* was hit by sub attack off their starboard side, blew up and sank. On Oct. 26, 1942, while holding the line for Guadalcanal, they too came under heavy attack soon

after they launched their strike against the Japanese carriers strike force. After their planes were launched he, Richard Marsh and Nettles sought shelter on the post forward cable net near the bow. A Japanese Kate piloted by Lt. Jiichiro Imajuku rammed into the port side just beneath him and his friends. The impact and explosion blew them in the air and burned them, but they had survived a very close call. The ship hit by two planes, the one under them and the one flown by Lt. Cmdr. Soki, into the after bridge and flight deck plus torpedo's and bombs, the ship was afire and the concentrated attack on the *Hornet* continued. Capt. Mason ordered abandon shop. He worried where Ralph Hovind and Charlie would land if they survived the attack on the Japanese ships.

He and Richard Marsh jumped off the port side when a destroyer cam in to rescue survivors. He believes the *Mustini* or *Hughes* saved them from a water demise. Many of his fine friends were lost but some weeks later Ralph and Charles showed up on their camp in New Caledonia, their plane, Old S-15, had been riddled with bullets. God love them! Ralph dropped her on the deck of the USS *Enterprise* just out of gas.

Ralph lives in Minnesota with his lovely wife, Mildred; Charlie died a few years back; but this team, "The Eagle and the Hawk" will always remain the spirit that keeps America strong. The old *Hornet* (CV-8) gone but not forgotten and the men that sailed her will live forever.

This old sailor, retired, lives on the bank of the Delaware River in upstate New York with memories of people and places dear to him.

JAMES E. SHACKELFORD, born Sept. 8, 1925, Hyanis, NE. Joined the USN Feb. 10, 1944; was assigned to the USS *Hornet* in August 1944; served as airplane handler; and achieved the rank of seaman 1/c. Participated in all action between August 1944-November 1945.

Memorable experiences include Hurricane Philip in 1944 and Okinawa in 1945.

Discharged Jan. 26, 1946. Received the Presidential Unit Citation. Retired AF, telephone company. Married Anna M. Pease in Miles City, MT, in 1952, and has two children.

HAROLD H. SIMS, born Dec. 24, 1924, Williamstown, PA. Joined the USN in June 1943; was assigned to the USS *Hornet* in December 1943; and served as gunner.

Memorable experiences include being on the ship when the typhoon hit on June 5, 1945; and the battles on Guam, Luzon, Okinawa and others.

Discharged De. 31, 1945, with the rank of seaman 1/c. Received the American Campaign Medal, Asiatic-Pacific Campaign Medal and WWII Victory Medal.

Married and has five children, 12 grandchildren, seven great-grandchildren, four step-children and 11 step-grandchildren. He is retired and enjoys hunting and working outdoors.

STEWART WESLEY SINGDALE, born Oct. 12, 1920, Brooklyn, NY. Joined the USN Sept. 10, 1940; was assigned to the USS *Hornet* in May 1955; stationed with VF-72; and served as power plant chief on the flight and hanger deck. Attended boot camp at NTS Newport, RI, 1940; served aboard USS *Idaho*

for transfer to Pearl Harbor to board the USS *New Orleans*, June 1940. The *New Orleans* had its bow blown off in 1944, by a torpedo from a Japanese submarine.

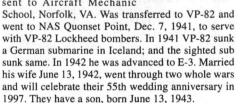

He was fortunate to have missed the Japanese invitation of Pearl Harbor because he was sent to Aircraft Mechanic School, Norfolk, VA. Was transferred to VP-82 and went to NAS Quonset Point, Dec. 7, 1941, to serve with VP-82 Lockheed bombers. In 1941 VP-82 sunk a German submarine in Iceland; and the sighted sub sunk same. In 1942 he was advanced to E-3. Married his wife June 13, 1942, went through two whole wars and will celebrate their 55th wedding anniversary in 1997. They have a son, born June 13, 1943.

Served in North Africa with the B-24 Liberators from 1943 to April 1945; transferred to O&R Quonset Point, RI. He had many other duties from 1945-55, and served aboard the USS *Leyte* during the Korean War. On May 4, 1955 he found himself on the USS *Hornet* for the Far East Cruise. He was in VF-72 Sqdn. Out of the 13 chief petty officers, they all went to shore duty; while at the same time he was also scheduled for shore duty, but the squadron needed a power plants chief, so after talking to his wife, he volunteered. He was top dog now and he was so glad he went on that cruise. He had good men and they asked him to go. He went with 20 F9F Panther Jets. He never had this responsibility before and the experience was wonderful to have complete charge. While on this cruise, they won the Atlantic Fleet Efficiency Award.

Besides having a wonderful cruise, the most important thing that happened to him was he adopted a five year old daughter. He retired from the USN in June 1960.

He finally got a position as a Naval Aviation Service Engineer, which instructing young sailors and marines to become aircraft mechanics. He held this position for 13 1/2 years and retired at the age of 55 as a GS-11. He is now retired completely at 76 years of age. Spends most of his leisure time collecting model cars and electric trains

TRAVIS J. SMITH spent four years in the USMC, November 1941-November 1945; was a USN gunfire and aerial spotter for the Guam and Okinawa invasions. Joined the USN in November 1946; was assigned to the USS *Hornet* after AUW School, July 1953; assigned to the V-6 torpedo shop, getting the civilian worker's to hang bunk's in the torpedo work room and later adapting the torpedo elevator to open the hanger deck torpedo hatch was very rewarding. Discharged in June 1962.

The food and around the world cruise was the most memorable of his 20 years career.

Worked on a college campus as electrician for 20 years. Married Helen and has four children and one grandchild. Has been doing commercial fishing the last 12 years.

WILLIAM J. SNOUFFER, born Sept. 4, 1923, Linworth, OH. He enlisted in the USN in November 1942 at Columbus, OH; went to boot camp at Great Lakes, IL; EM, AEM and Turret Schools at the 87th and Anthony Training Center in Chicago, IL. He was assigned to the USS *Hornet* (CV-12), V-2 Div., in July 1943. He then went to Creeds Field, VA, going aboard the *Hornet* in February 1944. After going through the Panama Canal the *Hornet* left Pearl Harbor in March 1944 and participated in all major campaigns until damaged in a typhoon in June 1945, going to Hunter's Point, CA, for repairs in June 1945.

Received the American Defense, Pacific Theater, Philippine Liberation and WWII Victory Medals, Philippine Presidential Unit Citation and Presidential Unit Citation. Was discharged in November 1945.

Married Marjorie and has two children and two grandchildren. He retired from Ohio Bell Telephone Co. after 38 years.

BUD F. SNYDER, born Dec. 16, 1920, Los Angeles, Ca. Joined the USN Jan. 8, 1942; reported to *Hornet* detail Sept. 1, 1943, after serving nine months aboard the USS *Bogue* (CVE-9) and advancing to AMM2/c. Plank owner of *Bogue* and *Hornet* (CV-12). Job on *Hornet* was PO in charge of fire fighters on the flight deck and jeep driver towing aircraft on respotting of aircraft.

Advanced to AB1 June 1, 1945. Transferred off the *Hornet* in September 1945. Served in all engagements of *Hornet* (CV-12).

Memorable experiences were the returns at night of aircraft from Turkey shoot; Japanese near misses of bombing and kamikaze's; three typhoons, the last that buckled the flight deck forward.

Served on six aircraft carriers in 20 years of Navy service. Retired July 9, 1921, rated ABHC.

Married July 1, 1946, and has two sons and two daughters. Resides in Oxnard, CA.

E.P. "GUS" SONNENBERG, born Feb. 15, 1920, Chicago, IL. Joined the USN in November 1941; was assigned to the USS *Hornet* in April 1944; assigned to VB-2 as a pilot; and achieved the rank of lieutenant. Participated in all action from May-October 1944.

Memorable experiences include ditching SB-26 at night on June 20, 1944; saved by gunner David Killary, who launched the raft.

Discharged in November 1945. Received the NC, Silver Star, Legion of Merit, Distinguished Flying Cross (3), Bronze Star, Air Medal (33), Presidential Unit Citation (2) and the Thompson Trophy in 1954.

Retired from the USAF as a colonel in 1970. He enjoys golf and traveling. Married Wilma Jean and has a son Bruce.

ROBERT C "BOB" SPIERS, born June 17, 1925, Boston, MA. Joined the USN in February 1943; was assigned to the USS *Hornet* Oct. 29, 1943; stationed as electrician on generators, fire room and engine rooms. Participated in action at all the battles from 1944 to June 1945.

Memorable experiences include being on the shakedown cruise and ran aground in the Chesapeake Bay.

Discharged Dec. 22, 1945. Received the American Area Service Ribbon, Asiatic-Pacific Area w/8 BSs and Philippine Liberation w/2 BSs.

Has been married for 52 years and has two children, five grandchildren and five great-grandchildren. Worked 36 years for General Telephone Co. before retiring.

WILLIAM "MICKEY" SPILLANE, born Oct. 26, 1945. Enlisted at NAS Alameda, CA, Feb. 16, 1963; assigned to the USS *Hornet* (CVS-12), February 1965-67, air department, V-4 Fuels Div., Airman ABF2. Went on Wespac tour, 1965-66, ASW Group One, the South China Seas and Yankee Station.

He participated in the shellback ceremonies, Operation Heritage, Sydney, Australia, CV-8 ceremony and the Apollo-Saturn 302 recovery.

Most memorable experience was the day the *Hornet* returned to Alameda from Hunter's Point from the salvager. opened during Fleet Week 95, the large public outcry to save the ship as a naval museum was wonderful.

Received the Vietnam Service Medal and National Defense Medal.

He is an inside wireman foreman in San Francisco. Married Janice Burke and has three wonderful children: Adam, USN Academy, 1995; Courtney Ann, Wheaton College, 1998; and Brian, California Maritime Academy, 1999.

JAMES ROBERT STAFFORD, born March 24, 1925, Ashland, KY. Joined the USN Aug. 18, 1943; assigned to the USS *Hornet* Nov. 8, 1943; and served as the ship's barber. He was assigned again to the *Hornet* Jan. 13, 1946. Participated in action at Luzon, Leyte Gulf, Midway, Siapan, Tinian, Northern Japan and the Bering Straits. He served with 18 other men from Paintsville, KY.

Memorable experiences include cruising through the Panama Canal; and liberty at Pearl Harbor.

Received the Good Conduct Medal, Presidential Unit Citation, Asiatic-Pacific Campaign Ribbon, WWII Victory Medal and 11 Battle Stars.

Married and has three sons, one daughter and four grandchildren. He is a member of VFW, PSO and is the county magistrate. Currently resides in Paintsville, KY.

VAN GORDEN STAUBER, born Jan. 24, 1923, Woodward, OK; moved to Hyattsville, MD; attended local schools and the University of Maryland. He joined the V-5 program in May 1942; entered active duty in December 1942; received commission and wings in October 1943; joined Air Group 2 in January 1944; assigned to Torpedo Sqdn in March 1944. Air Group went board the USS *Hornet* June 20, 1944, and flew night strikes against the Japanese fleet and dropped a torpedo on a Japanese cruiser. Landed aboard the USS *Yorktown* with aid of fleets' lights. The next day they returned to the *Hornet*. Made a water landing and were picked up by DD-400.

Returned to the States in October 1944 and was

assigned to Air Group 27, Sandford, ME. Air group went aboard the USS *Independence* and operated off of Japan until the war ended.

Received the Navy Cross, Distinguished Flying Cross and eight Air Medals. Retired from the USN in January 1983.

Married Dorthea Mills in November 1944 and has two daughters and a son and three grandchildren. He has been with J.C. Penny Co. for 35 years. He enjoys sailing.

DAVID SMILEY STEAR, born Dec. 11, 1920, Punxsutawney, PA; graduated from Concordia College, Fort Wayne, IN; and joined the USN in June 1942. He was commissioned an ensign and designated a naval aviator in 1943. He was assigned to the new USS *Hornet* in March 1944. During WWII he served two tours in the South Pacific and in August 1944 he was decorated with the Navy Cross by Adm. Marc Mitscher for distinguishing himself during the first battle of the Philippine Sea.

His naval career, which spanned more than 27 years, included flight instructor; commanding officer, FS-83; Attack Sqdn., commanding officer, USS *Forrestal* (CV-59); Air Group commander, COM CVG-7; commanding officer, USS *Paricutin* (AE-18); director of training, staff, CNATRA. His last tour was commanding officer, NAS Brooklyn, NY, from which he retired July 31, 1969. During this command, he was cited by the Jewish Welfare Board for "heroic and timely action in saving our Sacred Torahs (Holy Scrolls) from the flames when the stations "All Faiths" Chapel burned to the ground in December 1968."

In addition to the Navy Cross, he was awarded the Distinguished Flying Cross, six Air Medals, Presidential Unit Citation, Asiatic-Pacific Campaign Medal w/4 stars, Philippine Liberation, Japanese Occupation and the National Defense.

He passed away Sept. 21, 1996. His first wife, Charlotte, pre-deceased him in 1991. He is survived by his wife, Mary, daughters, Pamela and Davene, step-daughter, Deborah, and four grandchildren. *Submitted by Mary Stear.*

FLOYD STEELE JR., born Nov. 18, 1925, Joplin, MO; lived near Baxter Springs, KS, since 1937. Married Kathryn Lawhorn Nov. 6, 1943. Went to boot camp at Farragut, ID, February 1944; served aboard the USS *Hornet* May 1944 through November 1945. Assigned to arresting gear crew, V-1 Div. Principal duty was hookman, landing aircraft and helping to maintain arresting gear. He was a part of all battles and action during this time.

One day while landing aircraft, a Japanese plane slipped, undetected, into their plane's circle. As the Japanese plane lined up with the flight deck, as if to make a landing, he opened fire with his guns hitting a

20 mm gun tub on starboard side aft, killing a gunners mate, James Sperry, who reported aboard the *Hornet* the same time as he had. Anti-aircraft fire from the ship's in the task group was brought to bear on the Japanese Plane. Most shells exploded over and around the *Hornet*. Some shipmates working flight deck were hit by shrapnel from these guns. Some of their pilots had to make some quick moves to escape fire from their own ships guns. The Japanese plane escaped.

Released from active duty at NAS St. Louis, MO, in late January 1946.

Went to work under the GI bill in 1946 in a machine shop. In 1959 he became a part of the postal service for over 27 years, serving as postmaster for the last 13 years. He retired in 1986.

JAMES FREDRICK STEVENS, born Jan. 12, 1918, Forest, MS. Joined the USNR, V-6, in May 1941; was assigned to the USS *Hornet* ship's company in September 1941; was assigned SK3/c in payroll supply; and achieved the rank of SK1/c when the *Hornet* sunk. participated in the Doolittle raid, TF-16, battle of Midway, Guadalcanal, August 1942; sinking in the Coral Sea, Oct. 26, 1942; and was shipped back to Philadelphia Navy Yard to go aboard the USS *Princeton*. Discharged in November 1945.

Was on board the *Princeton* until MacArthur started to return to the Philippines, as the *Princeton* got sunk in the battle of Leyte. He was then assigned to the USS *Wasp* (CV-18) for the duration. *Wasp* was about 40 knots off Tokyo Bay when the first A-bomb was dropped. After the surrender of Japan they all came back to Boston Navy Yard.

Memorable experiences include two typhoons, one on the *Princeton* and one on the *Wasp* in January 1945.

Retired from New York Life Insurance Co. Married Katheryn Wells and has a son, W.F. Stevens and a daughter Karen Lasik; and six grandchildren.

WILLIAM L. STRAHAN, born March 8, 1918, Wadsworth, IL. Joined the USN June 2, 1941; was assigned to the USS *Hornet* Sept. 29, 1944; served as a VB pilot with Air Group 11. Participated in air strikes in the Philippines and the Formosa area.

Memorable experiences include perfectly coordinated air strikes; rescue submarine; Leyte landings; water landing, DD rescue, breeches buoy ride; flight back to *Hornet* alone after partial power failure; total exhaustion after bad winter weather strikes; kamikaze attacks; wounded and plane damage from heavy AA fire at Takao Harbor; landing aboard, out of gas, near dark, during storm; and finally the tour ended Feb. 1, 1945.

Discharged March 4, 1953. Received the Distinguished Flying Cross, three Air Medals, Purple Heart and Presidential Unit Citation.

Married Grace and has eight children: Kathleen, Janet, Priscilla, Gary, Joel, Paul, Will and Jonathan; and nine grandchildren. He is retired.

NEIL E. "RED" STUMMER, born Dec. 24, 1947, Goshen, IN. Joined the USN Aug. 7, 1968; was assigned to the USS *Hornet* December 1968; assigned to X Div. in the print shop; and achieved the rank of seaman apprentice. Their ASW chopper flushed a Russian submarine on the return trip from North Korean waters in April 1969. Also served a Wespac cruise, 1968-69.

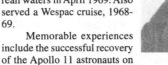

Memorable experiences include the successful recovery of the Apollo 11 astronauts on July 24, 1969, with President Nixon on board with other high ranking dignitaries; and the Apollo 12 recovery.

Discharged April 21, 1972. Received the National Defense Service Medal, Vietnam Service Medal w/4 BSs, Vietnam Campaign Medal w/60 Bar, Meritorious Unit Commendation Ribbon w/2 BSs, Navy Unit Commendation w/BS and Armed Forces Expeditionary Medal.

LYN A. "SWEDE" SVENDSEN, born in Cleveland, OH. Reported aboard the USS *Hornet* in the spring of 1957 after completing Electricians School at Great Lakes. In the true tradition of the USN, he was assigned as a machinist mate instead of an electrician when reporting aboard.

He was the mastermind of the famous "sink the *Hornet*" fiasco when he removed the cover plate on the sea side of a valve and let in the whole Pacific Ocean. He is one of a select few that served aboard both the CVA and CVS when the CVA was converted to a CVS in Bremerton in 1958. During at-sea refueling, he played the clarinet in the band that would entertain the refueling ships and also played for various functions in the ports that *Hornet* visited.

Upon leaving the USN in 1960, he completed college and is active in the industrial sales field. He is past executive director of the USS *Hornet* Club and a member of the board of directors of the Aircraft Carrier *Hornet* Foundation.

Married and has two children. He resides in Denver, NC.

HUGH MELVIN SWIFT JR., born Dec. 11, 1924, Los Angeles, CA. He entered the USN V-12 program on July 1, 1943, at the University of Redlands, Redlands, CA. Was commissioned an ensign through the Northwestern Midshipman's School (Tower Hall), Chicago, IL; then attended CIC School at Hollywood Beach, FL, and Fighter Director's School at NAS St. Simon's Island, GA.

Served aboard the USS *Hornet* (CV-12) in the Pacific as a CIC officer, and there after on the USS *Saidor* (CVE-117), the photographic ship at the atom bomb tests at Bikini.

Graduated from Stanford University with an AB degree, received a JD degree from Stanford University School of Law, and has practiced law in the greater Los Angeles area for over 47 years.

Married Jill Averill over 42 years ago, and they have three children: Julie Swift O'Connor, Diana and Molly. They reside in Tarzana, CA.

JOHN R. SZYMANSKI, born June 22, 1922, Wilmington, DE. He joined the USN Oct. 7, 1942, and was assigned to the USS *Hornet* Aug. 15, 1943. Arriving in Newport News he witnessed the launching of the ship and also was at the commissioning ceremony. He served on her entire war cruise, leaving her on Sept. 19, 1945, to be discharged Sept. 30, 1945. His duties on the ship were aircraft check crew.

Most memorable experiences to his estimation was the evening of the first battle of the Philippine Sea. That was the evening when their planes were returning from their strike on the Japanese Fleet, when the admiral wisely, even though putting their ship's at risk, turned all available lights on and firing star shells into the air to help guide their planes back. He was on the fantail at the hanger deck level watching as the pilot's tried to get back on deck. Some of the planes crashed had to be thrown over the side to save time and make room for another to come in. He really prayed for them and he is not ashamed to admit that he shed some tears for them.

He and his wife have five children and 11 grandchildren. He went back to his previous field in tool and die-making, formed his own tool and die shop in 1953 and in 1987 passed the business to his two sons. Retired to live in Owen, WI.

Awards include the American Campaign, Asiatic-Pacific Campaign, Presidential Unit Commendation, Philippine Liberation, Philippine Presidential Unit Citation and WWII Victory Medal.

RICHARD LINZEY TAYLOR, born June 18, 1935, Greensboro, NC. He joined the USN in June 1954, and learned leadership and responsibility on the beautiful USS *Hornet*. He served on the *Hornet* from March 1955-February 1956, when he was transferred to Submarine School. When he served on the *Hornet* they went to Korea, Okinawa, Hong Kong, Japan and Hawaii.

After his discharge in June 1958, he graduated from Guilford College. Carolina Ashe Davis became his wife Aug. 20, 1960. They have three children: Carolyn Linzey Taylor Johnson, Joseph Stephens Taylor and Cynthia Marie Taylor Martin Cave. They have four grandchildren: Anna Marie Martin, Megan Marie Cave, Meredith Ashe Johnson and Avery Phillip

Johnson. They have two step-granddaughters, Jessica and Mary Adkins. He retired from Sears in 1992 and presently teaches in Surry County, NC.

SPERGEON R. TAYLOR, born March 9, 1930, Des Moines, IA. Enlisted in the USN March 22, 1948; recruit training at NTC San Diego, CA, Honor Co. 90-48. Attended Hospital Corps School, USNH, San Diego, CA. August 1949, he was one of the first black's to attend Dental Technicians School, NTC San Diego, CA. Reported to the *Hornet* (CVS-12) in October 1963 and his tour ended in April 1966. Selected "White of the Year" for *Hornet*, 1963. He served as administrative assistant to the dental officer. Transferred to Fleet Reserve in September 1967.

Received the Good Conduct Medal (6th Award), FMF Force Combat Operation Insignia, 1st Marine Aircraft Wing Reinforcement, Navy Unit Commendation, UN Service Medal, Korean Presidential Unit Citation, National Defense Service Medal (2nd award), Korean Service Medal w/star and Vietnam Service Medal.

Graduated from Santa Ana College with AA degree and Pepperdine University with BS PPA degree. Worked for the US Post Office, Naval Regional Procurement Office and retired from Cal State University, Fullerton, CA, in 1989, as assistant to purchasing officer.

Married Eleanor G. Stewart, and they have one son, two daughters, four grandchildren and one great-grandchild.

THERON JACK TAYLOR JR., born June 20, 1921, Lewistown, MT; grew up and calls Cheyenne, WY, home. Joined the Navy aviation cadet (V-5) program in December 1941. Flight training, commission and wings at Corpus Christi, TX, November 1942. Served aboard the *Hornet* in VB-2 from March 1944 to November 1944. Selected Regular Navy in 1944; served aboard the USS *Princeton* (CV-37) and USS *Essex* (CV-9) in VA-55, Attack Sqdn. 55, during the Korean War, June 1951-December 1952. Attended Test Pilot School and test pilot, NATC Patuxent River, MD, January 1953-August 1955 and later as assistant director/director, Flight Test Division, September 1961-August 1963.

Med cruise on USS *Ticonderoga* as pilot in VA-66, September 1955-December 1955. Commanding officer, Attack Sqdn. 44 (VA-44), NAS Jacksonville, FL, January 1956-March 1957. Air officer, USS *Forrestal* (CVA-59), March 1960-August 1961. Naval War College, August 1963-June 1964. Commanding officer, USS *Graffias* (AF-29), Vietnam, August 1969-September 1971. Commanding officer, NAS *Atlanta*, August 1969-September 1971. Commanding officer, Navy and Marine Corp. Reserve Center, Portland, OR, October 1971 until retirement, March 1973.

Received the Navy Cross, Distinguished Flying Cross, Navy Meritorious Service Medal (2), Air Medal

(11), Presidential Unit Citation, WWII Victory, National Defense, Pacific theater Campaign and Service Medals, Korean Service and Korean Presidential Unit Citation and Vietnam Service Medals.

LEVERETTE GUY TERWILLIGER, born Jan. 15, 1919, Town Almond, NY. Joined the USN Feb. 26, 1941, and went through training at Norfolk, VA; Aviation Mechanic School; was assigned to the USS *Hornet* when it was commissioned. He was assigned to Fighting Squadron 8 and was with this squadron until the *Hornet* was sunk in the battle of Santa Cruz. He was on two converted carriers after Santa Cruz and wound up being assigned to the USS *Enterprise*.

The most interesting thing that happened to him was the commander of the *Hornet* Air Group wanted him to go up and fly with him in the plane called the C-Hag. The commander let him take a hold of the stick and fly the plane a little bit and it was quite an experience, as he was an on-board electrical maintenance on the fighters.

Because of ill health he was discharged on Nov. 13, 1944.

Married Phillis and has three daughters: Mary, Gail and Daisy. He is retired and living in Syracuse, NY.

LAWRENCE F. THOMAS, born Oct. 9, 1936, Minneapolis, MN. Joined the USN Jan. 23, 1955; assigned to the USS *Hornet* Jan 4, 1957; assigned to V-5; and achieved the rank of AO2. He left the *Hornet* Dec. 20, 1958, and went to the Reserves until retiring on Jan. 1, 1985.

Memorable experiences include two Wespac cruises and an overhaul in Bremerton, WA.

Retired maintenance man for school district #508, St. Peter, MN. Married and has two children and three grandchildren.

ALLEN TONSFELDT, born March 25, 1923. Joined the USN and left in 1942 to report to the USS *Hornet* to VF-11; then F6F fighters. Participated in strikes against Luzon, Formosa, Japanese fleet, Japanese convoy off Leyte Island, shipping in Manila Bay, Central Luzon, Yap Island, support for landing operations in Mindoro; strikes against Saigon, French Indo-china, Hong King, China Coast, Pescadres Islands; and Okinawa Jan. 22, 1945. Left the *Hornet* at the end of January 1945.

Received Distinguished Flying Cross for sinking a destroyer and Air Medal for destroying five planes on the ground. Received Presidential Unit Citation, Presidential Unit Commendation and Asiatic-Pacific Campaign Medal. Discharged in September 1945.

Married Luella Herman Oct. 6, 1946, and has five children: Pamela, Mark, Debra, Dale and Becky. They farmed until retiring in 1987.

LUKE TUSING JR., born Dec. 26, 1947, Berryville, AR. Joined the USN on July 15, 1966, Houston, TX; went to boot camp in San Diego, CA; assigned to the USS *Hornet* (CVS-12) on Oct. 29, 1966, Long Beach, CA.

While assigned to the *Hornet* they made two Wespac cruises, 1967-68. They were the prime recover ship for both Apollo 11 and 12 in 1969 (first moon landing). *Hornet* was sent to Korea after North Korea shot down US Recon plane in May 1969.

Sailed to Bremmerton, WA, for decommissioning in March 1970. Released from active duty in Bremmerton during decommissioning.

Graduated from Houston Community College in 1975 and University of Houston in 1980. Spent the last 26 years serving in the Houston Fire Dept. Currently driving an aerial ladder truck, and will soon be a fire inspector. Married 29 years to wife, Ann, and has two children.

JOSEPH FRANCIS UNDERWOOD, born May 4, 1923, Washington, DC. Enlisted in the USN May 14, 1941, and was assigned to the USS *Hornet* Dec. 9, 1941. He was assigned to the gas crew flight deck. He saw and was a part of all the action. Participated in the "Doolittle raid", B-25s off the *Hornet*, April 18, 1942; Midway Battle, June 4, 1942; Guadalcanal Campaign, 1942; USS *Saratoga* (CV-3) hit, Aug. 31, 1942; USS *Wasp* (CV-7) sinking; USS *Carolina* (BB-55); O'Brian DD hit by torpedo's, Sept. 15, 1942; Buin-Faisi-Shortland Island raid, Oct. 5, 1942; and survived the sinking of the *Hornet* in the Santa Cruz battle, Oct. 26, 1942.

Medals include the American Defense, American Campaign, Asiatic-Pacific, seven actions on the USS *Hornet*, seven actions on the USS *North Carolina* (BB-55), Commendation TF-16 Doolittle raid, EFATE New Hebrides, 1943, USS *North Carolina* (BB-55), 1944. He spent two years, nine months and 10 days in the Pacific War. Retired after 20 years in the USN, May 31, 1962.

He is a widower and has five children: Vickie, William, Edwin, Joseph Scott, Kristinia (Lynae). He finished the manuscript for his book about his time in the Pacific, serving on an island, the USS *Hornet* (CV-8) and the USS *North Carolina* (BB-55). He died following a stroke on October 5, 1998.

VITO W. VACCARO, born Sept. 2, 1925, Akron, OH. Joined the USN March 13, 1944; and was assigned to the USS *Hornet* the later part of December 1944; assigned to radio shack and copied coded messages. Participated in strikes on Formosa, Luzon, Saigon, Hong Kong, Tokyo, Chi-Chi Jima, Okinawa, Kyushu and a few others.

Memorable experiences include escaping the divine wind, pilots of Japan; and the typhoon of June 1945.

Discharged May 20, 1946, with the rank of RM3/c. Received the Presidential Unit Citation, Asiatic-Pacific w/4 stars, American Area Victory and Philippine Liberation w/star.

Married Mary Aug. 21, 1948; and has a son, Richard (June 1949), and daughters, Diane Adams (March 1958) and Mary Anne Causey (June 1959).

At the age of 72 he is retired and playing all the golf that he can.

RONALD T. VAIL, born Jan. 25, 1947, Montpelier, MS. Joined the USN in October 1964; was assigned to the USS *Hornet* in December 1965; served as coxswain; and achieved the rank of BM2. Participated in three cruises in Vietnam; one tour on the USS *Pine Island* sea plane tender.

Memorable experiences include picking up Apollo 8 space capsule.

Discharged in December 1967. Received three Bronze Stars.

Worked as a survey and tug boat operator for the US Army Corps of Engineers. He has one daughter. He also attended college at Mississippi State University and received his masters degree; has his USCG captain license; and an airplane pilot license.

ENSIO K. VAKKINEN, born Jan. 9, 1923, Finland. Joined the USN June 7, 1943; assigned to the USS *Hornet* (CV-12) in December 1943; and served in maintenance and repair, SB2C Helldivers.

Memorable experiences include the typhoon on June 5, 1945.

Discharged March 5, 1946. Received the Asiatic-Pacific w/9 stars, American Area, WWII Victory Medal and Philippine Liberation w/2 stars.

He is retired and living life of relaxation, recreation and opportunity.

JOHN STEVENS VAN DE MARK, born Jan. 10, 1926, Houston, TX. Enlisted in the USN on Feb. 16, 1943, Houston, TX; participated in V-12, NROTC, Rice University, commissioned, ensign, Feb. 20, 1945.

Reported aboard the USS *Hornet*, at sea, about April 15, 1945. Okinawa Campaign, Junior Gunnery Officer, 40 mm AA Quad Mount, Island Forward. Observed kamikaze attack, USS *Bunker Hill* (CV-17), TF-58 Flagship, May 11, 1945, while *Hornet* conducted refueling operations. Aboard when weathering typhoon, June 5, 1945. Heavy seas collapsed forward flight deck. Stern launch of aircraft, supporting Okinawa operations, unsuccessful. Watch officer, lookout crew, discovering detached bow section, heavy cruiser USS *Pittsburgh*, early morning, June 6, 1945.

Awards include Presidential unit Citation, Asiatic-Pacific Theater Medal and WWII Victory Medal.

Received BA degree, Rice University, 1947. Retired, General Insurance Marketing. Past member US Naval Air Reserve, commander. Resides in Houston, TX.

Originated negotiations Dec. 12, 1994, City of Baytown, TX. Proposed Berth for USS *Hornet* at Baytown Marina at eastern approach to Fred Hartman Suspension Bridge over Houston Ship Channel. Member, US Navy Memorial Foundation, Aircraft Carrier *Hornet* Foundation and USS *Hornet* Club, Inc.

RONALD "DUTCH" VELTMAN, born April 16, 1921, Brooklyn, NY. Joined the USN in June 1940; attended boot training, Newport, RI, 1940; Corp School, Portsmouth, VA, 1941; Newport Naval Hospital, RI, 1941; was assigned to USS *Hornet* Oct. 25, 1941, plank owner; assigned to H Div., medical.

Participated with the FMF 3rd Marine Div. in the invasion of Bouganville. The returned with two marines with severe leg wounds just above the left knees. Infection had already set in and they were going to amputate. One marine was dead set against it. They did what had to be done. The one marine that was not for it, never said a word, but if he had a gun he would have shot him. Called for a black cat PBY sea plane and took them to a base hospital at Tulija.

Memorable experiences include the Doolittle raid, April 18, 1942; Midway, 1942; Santa Cruz battle, Oct. 26, 1942, CV-8 *Hornet* sunk.

Married and has two older daughters, three grandchildren and one great-grandchild. He is retired.

RAYMOND J. VYEDA, born Oct. 4, 1934, Watsonville, CA. He enlisted in the USNR at the Receiving Station on Clement Ave., Alameda, CA, on March 19, 1952. In April 1953 he went on active duty at the NTC San Diego, CA, for boot training. In June 1953, he was assigned to the USS *Hornet*, Brooklyn Naval Yard, NY. The *Hornet* was recommissioned CVA-12 on Sept. 11, 1953. Took a shakedown at Quantonimoa Bay, Cuba. After that, took a world cruise to be reassigned to the 7th Pacific Fleet, TF Group 77.0. Rate aboard the *Hornet* was boatson mate seaman 1/c. In 1955, he was transferred to the NAS Oakland, CA, ASW Sqdn. VP-876. Upon his discharge in 1958, his rate was AE3.

Served as president of the USS *Hornet* Club in 1992 and in 1997. He is a trustee for the Aircraft Carrier *Hornet* Foundation.

His most memorable combat experience was engaging two Chinese aircraft in the Gulf of Tonkin.

Proposed to his wife, Molly, at Pier 2, NAS Alameda, CA, in 1954, which happens to be where the *Hornet* is docked at present. Married Molly on July 21, 1955. They have three sons: Tony, Ray Jr. and Ricky; and also a daughter, Lisa. In addition, they

have six grandchildren: Tonya, Anthony, Sarah, Danielle, Brittany, and a new arrival due in October 1997.

Retired as an electrical contractor from his own business, Anchor Electric. He was also a member of the Oakland Navy League, VFW, American League, USS *Hornet* Club and the Aircraft Carrier *Hornet* Foundation. He was very proud of the fact that he started the effort to save the *Hornet* on May 11, 1995. Ray passed away September 23, 1997.

GILBERT C. WAGONER, born Feb. 5, 1922, in Toledo, OH. Joined the USN Nov. 13, 1942, in Toledo, OH; attended boot camp at Great Lakes, IL and also Fire Control School there. Then Advanced Fire Control School in Washington SC; reported to the USS *Hornet* at Norfolk, VA Nov. 28, 1943, went on shakedown cruise; then through the Panama Canal, to San Diego, Hawaii and into action. Returned to the States for repairs from Leyte in the Philippines. When the *Hornet* docked for repairs in San Francisco summer of 1945 his fiancé came out. They were married by the Chaplain of the *Hornet*, Hugh Emory. Shipmates Jack Frild and Gene Mullen also attended.

Received honorable discharge in Toledo, OH Oct. 13, 1945, with the rank of FC2C. Awarded the American Theater, Asiatic-Pacific w/8 stars, Philippine Liberation w/2 stars, Presidential Unit Citation.

Attended Toledo University upon release, then went into various sales positions and had a home improvement business for 25 years, now retired. Married and has four children and four grandchildren. They recently celebrated their 50th wedding anniversary.

FRANK "MARINE" LEON WAHLER, born Oct. 24, 1918, in Wynne, AR and joined the USM Aug. 19, 1940, in Chicago. Assigned to the USS Savannah for two and one half years prior to being assigned to the USS *Hornet* (CV-12), Aug. 23, 1943, served as light anti aircraft gun; platoon sergeant, 20 mm gun; served in the third fleet operations during Philippine operations.

Memorable experiences were the battle of the Philippines when he was shooting down Kamikazes. Awarded the Good Conduct Medal w/Bar, Marksman Rifle, Excellent character of service.

Married with three grown children and five grandchildren. He retired from the city of Boston police department after 24 years. He and his wife reside in Boston.

PAUL H. WALDRON, born Dec. 9, 1920, in Kalamazoo, MI. Joined the USN Aug. 12, 1943, and assigned to the USS *Hornet* Nov. 28, 1943; served as an electrician. Participated in action in the Pacific area; Palau; Hollandia; Truk; Mariannas; Bonins; Yap; Philippines; Formosa; Luzon; China Sea, and Japan.

Memorable experiences were of the typhoon off the coast of Japan damaging the *Hornet*; "Hero of Guam", Radioman 1C Tweed brought aboard after 31 months in a cave during Japanese occupation. Discharged Nov. 5, 1945, with the rank of electrician mate third class. Awarded 13 Battle stars; Presidential Unit Citation and Pacific area March 29, 1944, to June 10, 1945.

Retired August 1980 as electrical supervisor at Allied Paper Co. Active church worker, serving on various boards, singing in the choir and enjoys masonic lodge activities.

Married April 1941; has two sons; David, who served in the Vietnam war as a helicopter pilot, now lives in the state of Washington; Mark, the youngest son, lives nearby. They have four grandchildren, ages five to 11.

FERMINE WALKER, born Oct. 9, 1924 in Lego, WV. Joined the USN Sept. 23, 1942, and assigned to the USS *Hornet* on Nov. 27, 1943; served as flight deck commander's talker. Participated in action from Nov. 27, 1943, to January 1946. Discharged Jan. 19, 1946, with the rank of AMM2C.

Married Doris Garrison and they have seven children, eight grandchildren. He is a barber by profession.

MURDOCK P. WALLEY, born Feb. 25, 1925, at Avery, MS. Inducted into the USN on Aug. 19, 1943. Attended boot camp, NTS Bainbridge, MD. He was immediately assigned to the USS *Hornet* at Newport New, VA "R" Div. where he worked as a plumber out of the carpenter shop achieving the rank of SF3. After christening on Nov. 29, 1943, trial runs in Chesapeake Bay and a grueling unusually short shakedown cruise, they weighed anchor at Norfolk Feb. 14, 1944 and set out on their momentous travels via Panama Canal and San Diego arriving at Pearl Harbor on March 4, 1944. Participated in numerous battle engagements for duration of war until ship was damaged by a typhoon. They were in San Francisco for repairs and he was home on leave when the war ended. After ship was repaired, they made several trips hauling troops back from the Pacific.

His most memorable experience while aboard the *Hornet* was the famous "Mariannas Turkey Shoot." They were notified on the PA by the ship's captain to come upon deck and observe these dog fights between US and Japanese planes - an awesome sight!

He was honorably discharged on March 12, 1946. Awards: Asiatic-Pacific Campaign Ribbon w/9 stars, Philippine Liberation Ribbon w/2 stars and Medal, American Campaign Ribbon and Victory Medal.

After a career with Gulf Power Company, Pensacola, FL, He is now retired and living on his pine tree farm in Lucedale, MS. He was married on Nov. 22, 1947, to Mabra Eubanks and they have one son, also a Vietnam era USN veteran.

HARRY J. WANDER, born March 30, 1933 in Emmett, ID. He served as the VS-37 flight surgeon during the 1960 Wespac cruise of CVS-12 and as the senior flight surgeon with CVSG-57 during the *Hornet*'s 1962 Wespac cruise.

He resigned from the Navy in 1967 after ten years active duty. He has been in the private practice of Pediatrics for 30 years. He joined the USAR and retired as a colonel, after commanding the 921st MASH (Mobile Army Surgical Hospital). His awards include the Army Achievement Medal and the Army Commendation Medal w/OLC.

His best memory is of his amazement at learning how the excellence of the training of several thousand men from many diverse backgrounds resulted in their performing so well that the ship functioned as one organism. His worst memories are of dealing with the injuries and deaths which inevitably occur during training and operational activities.

RAYMOND MARTIN WARE, born Sept. 22, 1924, in Owensboro, KY. Enlisted in the USN Oct. 27, 1941 at Louisville, KY. Boot camp at Great Lakes Naval Training Station. On Dec. 7, 1941, was waiting at the train platform for boot leave but was called back to barracks, sent to West Coast.

Assigned to the USS *Hornet*, CV-12, Nov. 1, 1943. When one is assigned a ship such as the *Hornet* there are many memorable experiences. Just being there is a class "A" experience. Squeezing through the Panama Canal, kamikaze attack just missing the flight deck, and shore patrol duty VJ night in San Francisco, these are a few of his most memorable experiences.

Earned all Medals and citations that ships company would have earned. Transferred off the *Hornet*, assigned to Great Lakes Naval Training Station for discharge effective Oct. 11, 1945.

Married Bonnie Bostic Ware, have five children, 13 grandchildren. Retired from Daytona Beach, FL fire department. Moved to Alabama in 1980. Now a gentleman farmer.

GEORGE W. WARREN, born March 2, 1927, Covington, Ky. Joined the USN March 2, 1944; was assigned to the USS *Hornet* Sept. 29, 1944; and was assigned to F6F as a fighter plane captain. Participated in all action in the Asiatic-Pacific Theater.

Memorable experiences include while operating deep within enemy waters in the South Pacific the *Hornet* was attacked by a Japanese bomber after dark. A decision was made to send up a F6F night fighter. He was instructed to climb in the cockpit and ride the brakes while the F6 was pushed in position for take-off. Once on the flight deck, but not yet in position, the Japanese bomber dropped flares which lit up the *Hornet*. Over the PA system came the order to "take cover." The crew that was pushing the F6 with him in it ran for cover. The *Hornet* made a high speed turn.

He was left sitting on the flight deck holding the brakes. He knew the F6 would roll overboard if he released the brakes, so he sat there for what seemed like an eternity. The Japanese faded from radar and the were secured from GQ.

Discharged May 19, 1946, with the rank of seaman 1/c. Received five Battle Stars and Presidential Unit Citation.

Married Juanita and has one son and four grandchildren. He and his wife are retired and living in Warsaw, KY.

WILBUR B. "SPIDER" WEBB, born June 14, 1920, Ardmore, OK. Joined the USN Oct. 1, 1938; was assigned to the USS *Hornet* in January 1944; assigned to VF-2 as a fighter pilot. Served with the USS *Colorado* and the USS *Oklahoma* in Pearl Harbor; USS *Hornet*, 1944, Mariannas Turkey Shoot.

Retired Oct. 1, 1958, with the rank of lieutenant and chief aviation pilot.

Married Clio and has a son, R.L. and daughter, Kathryn. He is retired.

HARVEY "SAM" LEONARD WEED, born July 8, 1940, Cornwall, NY. Joined the USN July 1, 1957; was assigned to the USS *Hornet* in December 1957; assigned to V-6 Div., electric shop; worked on flight deck; NCI driver; electric power to start planes.

Memorable experiences include three cruises; and almost crossing the equator, they were sent to the Taiwan Straits as a shoe of force, Quemoy-Matsu.

Discharged in June 1961. Received the National Defense Service Medal and Armed Forces Expeditionary.

Married to Shirley for 36 years; has a son Lenny; grandsons, Shane and Codie; and daughter-in-law, Pearl. Works for Orange County as a weigh-master in Newburgh, NY.

CHARLES F. WEISS, born Aug. 1, 1918, Spokane, WA. Joined the USN April 14, 1941. He was assigned to the USS *Hornet* in January 1945 as a fighter bomber pilot, VBF-17.

Most memorable experiences include being in an F6F waiting for take-off on March 18, 1945, when a kamikaze was blown form the air above their heads just before take off. On March 19, 1945, he took-off on a pre-dawn fighter sweep in Wakunee Air Base and was shot down and parachuted into Inland Sea. He was picked up be a Japanese fisherman the next day. He did not see the *Hornet* again until June 1997 at Alameda NAS.

Discharged Aug. 31, 1961, with the rank of commander. Received the Air Medal w/BS, Purple Heart and Presidential Unit Commendation.

After 21 years in the USN he worked as a NYSE firm for 24 years and retired in October 1988.

HENRY H. "HANK" WERTZ, born Feb. 19, 1919, Drain, OR. Enlisted in the USN Aug. 22, 1941, with basic training in San Diego, CA. Served aboard the USS Curtis before being assigned to the USS *Hornet* in August 1943. He was first with the 3rd Div. and then master-at-arms.

There were many memorable experiences, notably the kamikaze attacks and the typhoon which sent the *Hornet* back to San Francisco for repairs in July 1945.

Discharged at Treasure Island, Oct. 22, 1945. Received the Good Conduct Medal, American Defense, WWII Victory Medal, Asiatic-Pacific and Presidential Citation.

Worked mainly as a carpenter and cabinet maker in Chico, CA, and then in Santa Rosa. He and his wife have two children, six grandchildren and one great-grandchild. He is retired and spends time traveling in their motor home and gardening. They live in a small mountain community near Chico, CA.

JAMES R. WHALEY, born July 29, 1926, Covington, KY. Joined the USN March 4, 1943; was assigned to the USS *Hornet* November 1943; assigned to V-1 Div.; and achieved the rank of seaman 1/c. Participated in nine invasions and was on the *Hornet* the day it was commissioned until the day the war ended.

Memorable experiences include his friend,

Clark, has both his legs blown off; the typhoon was very bad, they lost the forward part of their flight deck and could not operate; picked up radioman "Tweed"; and the planes trying to come on ship after dark and the pilots were going in the water and finally the admiral turned on the search lights.

Discharged March 4, 1946. Received seven Battle Stars, Asiatic-Pacific Theater w/2 stars, Philippine Liberation and the Presidential Unit Citation.

Married Joanne and has two sons, James and Christopher; step-son, Brent; and step-daughter, Sue. Retired from Ford Motor Co.

RUSSELL WHEELER SR., born Oct. 18, 1927, Edenton, NC. In 1943 he joined the USN at the age of 15. After boot camp in Maryland he was assigned to the *Hornet* as a 40 mm anti-aircraft gun pointer. He participated in action at Formosa, Iwo Jima, Okinawa, Hong Kong, Luzon and Leyte.

The *Hornet* was awarded nine Battle Stars and the Presidential Unit Citation while he was aboard. He was discharged in 1946.

He has two children, Jo Ann and Russell Jr. He is retired from sales and currently resides in Edenton.

LAWRENCE PHIPPS WHITE, born March 22, 1916, Philadelphia, PA. Joined the USN in September 1934 as a naval cadet at Yale University. Was assigned to the USS *Hornet* Aug. 6, 1943-October 1945. Served in personnel, aide to executive officer, 5-2 division officer and radar watch officer.

Memorable experiences include making so many lifelong friends; and being aboard that famous and fabulous ship that deserved the Presidential Campaign Medal for valor.

Discharged December 1945. Received the American Defense, American Area Campaign, Asiatic-Pacific w/7 stars, Philippine Campaign w/star, National Defense and Presidential Unit Citation w/ star.

Married Helen and has three sons, one daughter and eight grandchildren. After 25 years as president of an instrument company he is retired; working in an antique store for charity; reads and writes a lot; and enjoys gardening.

BERT W. "BUD" WHITED, born Nov. 21, 1922, Fort Smith, AR. Joined the USN June 26, 1940 at NRS San Francisco, CA; attended boot camp at NTS San Diego, CA● served aboard USS Idaho (BB-45) in fire control, Oct. 10, 1940-Aug. 10, 1941. Served aboard the USS *Hornet* (CV-8), VS-8, beginning in Aug. 11, 1941. Served aboard the *Hornet* during the battles of Coral Sea, Midway and Santa Cruz where the *Hornet* was sunk on Oct. 26, 1942.

Retired from the USN as ADC USN on Jan. 6, 1960, after 20 years of service. Earned the Purple Heart, Good Conduct, WWII Victory, American Defense Service, American Area Campaign, Asiatic-Pacific Area Campaign and National Defense Service.

He has worked in accounting, field service engineer in electronics and cyrogenics. He is presently a Real Estate broker in Granthan, NJ. He and his wife, Barbara, have three grown children who reside in California.

JOHN T. WILLISS, born April 23, 1921, Baltimore, MD. Joined the service June 1, 1938. Commissioned ensign Aug. 1, 1943; was assigned to the USS *Hornet* in September 1944 with VF-11 as a fighter pilot; and achieved the rank of lieutenant. Participated in the battle off Formosa, Leyte Gulf, second battle of Philippine Sea and the action in the South China Sea.

Memorable experiences include the second battle of Philippine Sea; attacking enemy task force; large aerial battles off Formosa and Clark Field; major damage to his aircraft over Formosa and minor at Clark; and downing of two enemy aircraft.

Discharged July 1, 1962. Received the Distin-

guished Flying Cross, Air Medal w/3 stars and the Presidential Unit Citation.

He is completely retired except for tennis twice a week and working out three times a week. Divorced with two adult sons and two grandchildren.

EDWIN MARK WILSON JR., born June 8, 1918, St. Paul, MN. Joined the USN July 17, 1941, before Pearl Harbor to fight Hitler. After flight training he received his Navy Wings and joined VB-11. VB-11, flying Douglas Dauntless SBDs had its first combat tour at Guadalcanal in the Solomon Islands. Flying off Henderson Field, April 28-July 21, 1943 he got a bomb hit on a destroyer in Blackett Strait and in Kahili Harbor got hit on destroyer.

VB-11 flew Curtiss SB2C Helldivers on their second combat cruise aboard the new aircraft carrier, *Hornet*, Sept. 29, 1944-Feb. 1, 1945. Lt. Wilson led every third attack group off the *Hornet*. He got bomb hits on destroyers off Okinawa, Formosa and Leyte; and on a cargo shop in Manila Bay. On Nov. 5, 1944, had tailhook shot off at Clark Field, Luzon, and crash landed aboard the *Hornet*. Next day, Nov. 6, 1944, portion of tail shot off at Clark Field, ditched, and picked up off raft by destroyer Mansfield (DD-728). Two days later he and his radioman/gunner, Harry Jespersen, were back on the *Hornet*.

Received three Distinguished Flying cross, three Air Medals and other Medals.

As a "weekend warrior" he flew prop fighters, F6Fs and F4Us; jet fighters, TV-1s and F2H-2 Banshees, in the USN Air Reserve. In 1962 he was selected for captain in the USNR. In January 1971 selected for rear admiral. Represented commander, Naval Air Reserve Forces on the West Coast until retired in February 1978. At his retirement ceremony he was awarded the Meritorious Service Medal.

He is regional vice president of the Association of Naval Aviation. on Jan. 17, 1986 a brass plaque was unveiled at NAS Alameda honoring RADM Wilson for his "Outstanding Service to Naval Aviation." At the ceremony he was called "Mr. Naval Aviation of the San Francisco Bay Area." He is a widower with three grown daughters and a son. Member of the *Hornet* Club; plank owner of the USS *Hornet* Carrier Museum.

VINTON J. WOGAN, born Dec. 22, 1944, Morris, MN. Joined the USN May 12, 1964; assigned to the USS *Hornet*, 1966-68; served as HS-2, jet engine mechanic; and achieved the rank of E-4. Attended boot camp at San Diego, CA, and was stationed at Ream Field, Imperial Beach, CA.

Discharged May 9, 1968. Received the National Defense Service, Vietnam Service Medal w/3 BSs, RVN Campaign Medal w/Device and Presidential Unit Citation.

He is a truck drier and resides in Alexandria, MN.

ELMO M. WOJAHN, born March 2, 1924, Brown County, MN. Joined the USN Aug. 19, 1941; attended boot camp Great Lakes, IL, Co. 136, 1941; was assigned to the USS *Hornet* Oct. 20, 1941; assigned to V-2 Div., hanger deck and control phone talker; and achieved the rank of ADRC. Action while at sea: deliver Doolittle raiders to Tokyo; Coral Sea; battle of Midway; Solomon Island raid; battle of Santa Cruz.

As a 17 year old farm boy from Minnesota, everything was very impressive. Seeing the *Hornet* for the first time, "She was big and beautiful?" Little did he know where history would take them.

Memorable experiences include after abandoning the *Hornet* he was making his way to the USS *Mustin* when the Japanese came back for another attack. The destroyer moved full speed and caught him in its wake. He felt like he was in a Maytag washer. The destroyers came back after the attack and he was picked up by the USS *Morris*.

Discharged July 19, 1962.

Married Avis Gaustad, Nov. 14, 1948, and has six children, 16 grandchildren and two great-grandchildren. He is a retired farmer.

SAMUEL W. WOODS, born Oct. 25, 1922, St. Joseph, MO. Served boot camp at Green Bay, WI; boarded the USS *Hornet* (CV-12) at Newport News, VA, with the Douglas Dauntless Dive Bomber Sqdn. in the latter part of 1943, where they put her in commission.

His most memorable experiences were the Okinawa turkey shoot; crossing the equator; and the typhoon, where they lost 25 feet of flight deck; becoming the second ship in history to launch planes off the fantail.

While aboard the *Hornet* he received the National Service Medal (2 awards), Asiatic-Pacific Campaign Medal, Philippine Liberation Medal, WWII Victory Medal, American Theater Medal and the Presidential Unit Citation. Was discharged Nov. 11, 1945, at Terminal Island, Long Beach, CA.

he and Yrene have four children. They are retired and live on a small avocado grove in Lakeside, CA.

FRANK A. WOOLSEY, born March 10, 1924, Troy, NY. Joined the USN April 13, 1943; transferred from the USS *Lexington* to the USS *Hornet* in late in 1944; served as aviation ordnance man mostly on the flight deck.

While aboard the *Lexington*, took a suicide plane in Island Structure that killed 45 men, injured over 100, on Nov. 5, 1944. Also watched the sinking of the Princeton on Oct. 4,

9144. Last action aboard the *Hornet* was bombardment invasion of Iwo Jima after the Philippine Sea Battle.

Discharged in December 1945. Received the Philippine Liberation w/2 stars, Asiatic-Pacific w/3 stars and WWII Victory Medal.

Married to Irene Cusack Woolsey and has two sons, Frank A. Jr. and Timothy Paul. Worked 40 years with his own insurance agency; has a Real Estate License; and works with mutual fund sales. He retired in 1988 and the travel as often as they can. He will attend his 55 year high school reunion in September 1997, Troy, NY.

JAMES GORDON WORLEY, born Nov. 27, 1932, Sparta, TN. Joined the USN March 19, 1951, Nashville, TN, and attended boot camp at NTS San Diego, CA. Served at Mare Island Naval Shipyard in Vallejo, CA, 1951-53. Served aboard the USS *Hornet* (CVA-12) beginning in September 1953 until March 1955.

Most memorable experiences were the 1954 world cruise and on July 26, 1954, the *Hornet* was a part of the task force TG-70.2, searching for survivors of a downed British airliner tat was shot down by the reds in the China Sea. Plans from the task force were attacked by two Chinese fighter planes. Both Chinese planes were shot down.

Discharged March 11, 1955. Received the National Defense Medal, Navy Occupation (Europe) Service Medal, China Service Medal and Good Conduct Medal.

He and his wife Clata have two grown daughters and one teenage granddaughter who resides in Tennessee. He is president of the Oak Ridge Machinist Union. For the past 20 years, has been serving as a member of the Anderson County Election Commission. Worked as a machinist 35 years at Lockheed Martin Y-12 Plant, Oak Ridge, TN.

RONALD P. WRIGHT, born Aug. 27, 1932, Granttown, WV. On March 18, 1951, he joined the USN and went to boot camp at Great Lakes. Upon graduation he was posted to NAS Anacostia DC in the Security Div. In 1953 he was transferred to the USS *Hornet* (CVA-12), in V-7 Div. To recommission the ship; shakedown cruises to Cuba and Haiti; steamed back to New York; and left for a world cruise, stopping at ports in Lisbon, Naples, Ceylon; crossed the equator June 24, 1954; then on to the Philippines, Singapore, Hong Kong, Japan, then to Hawaii and San Diego.

Discharged in March 1955, then home to begin his acting career, on stage, movies and television. He is now retired. Married to his wonderful Christine for 32 years until she passed away in 1933. His years aboard the *Hornet* were the greatest. He has two children and four grandchildren.

DENNIS P. YANNONE, born Jan. 18, 1947, Burke, SD. Joined the USNR March 1, 1964, Fremont, NE; attended boot camp, NTC San Diego, CA; Reserve cruises, NTC Great Lakes, IL, port. Entered active duty at Treasure Island, July 7, 1965. Reported to the USS *Hornet* (CVS-12) at Long Beach, CA, August 1965. Served two Wespac Far East cruises, 1965-67. Operation Heritage Cruise to Sidney, Australia, 1966.

Received National Defense, Vietnam Service w/ 3 stars and RVN Campaign Medals.

Transferred from the *Hornet* to, and released from active duty May 15, 1967, Treasure Island, CA. Honorable discharged March 1, 1970. Upon release returned home to Fremont, NE. Married and has two children. Employed with the Department of Utilities as a distribution electrical engineer, June 26, 1967, to date.

BENJAMIN L. YOUNG, born Sept. 28, 1930, Greenwood, MS. Enlisted in September 1948; attended boot camp at NTC San Diego, 1954, as a SK1. Flew from San Diego to Brooklyn and joined the *Hornet* and sailed to Norfolk. Embarked on a round the world cruise through the Suez Canal. Their weapons space was air conditioned so they seldom left them so as to avoid the heat.

Crossed the equator and became a shellback. Red Chinese air liner over Hanian and *Hornet* pilots then shot down two Chinese fighters. Cruised through Wespac and returned to San Diego. In 1955 he joined the *Hornet* as a SK1 in the supply department. He served in the supply office maintaining all departments. Enjoyed the Wespac cruise and returned to San Diego. In 1956, while the *Hornet* was in Bremerton, he was selected for OCS. Commissioned ensign in August 1956 and retired as commander in 1976.

Married Connie Swift and have two children, Benjamin and Russell and two grandchildren, Shaun and Erica. Enjoy living in Las Vegas.

RAYMOND L. YOUNG, born April 15, 1933, Medford, OR. He joined the USN in October 1952 and served aboard the USS *Hornet* from October 1954-October 1956 as cook in the chiefs mess and later as night cook.

Many of his experiences aboard the *Hornet* were memorable. He remembers when the *Hornet* lost a propeller off Okinawa and entered Yokosuka's dry dock to replace it. When the *Hornet* returned to Bremerton, WA, he stayed aboard while she was converted into a super carrier. He was discharged in October 1956.

Married Roberta three months before he boarded the *Hornet*. They have three sons: Raymond Jr., Rory and Ricky. They own and operate Glen's Bakery and Restaurant in Crescent City, CA. His father opened it in 1947.

ALLAN ANDREW ZAUN, born March 6, 1911, Milwaukee, WI. Joined the USN April 20, 1942; was assigned to the USS *Hornet* Nov. 13, 1943; and served as chaplain. On Sept. 22, 1944, the ship was strafed by a Japanese Zeke and it was shot down.

Memorable experiences include June 19, 1944, the Mariannas turkey shoot. As chaplain aboard the CV-12, it was his esteemed privilege to offer her commissioning prayer on Nov. 29, 1943, at Newport News, VA. He remained aboard until their return to San Francisco, July 11, 1945. A portion of that prayer was: "Bless, O Lord, guide and protect the way our ship and planes shall go. may every battle further subdue the enemy, and hasten the day when peace shall once again bless the world. Bind us to one another and to Thee in a loyalty that shall know no end."

Discharged Jan. 25, 1946, with the rank of lieutenant commander. Received the WWII Victory Medal,

American Defense Service Medal, American Area Campaign, Asiatic-Pacific Campaign, Presidential Unit Award, National Defense Service Medal and Letter of Commendation.

Married to Helen and has three daughters, three grandsons, one granddaughter, two great-granddaughters and one great-grandson. He is parish associate of First Presbyterian Church, Gainesville, FL.

JOHN ANTHONY ZINK, born Aug. 18, 1921, St. Marys, OH. Joined the USN in June 1942; was assigned to the USS *Hornet* in October 1944; and was assigned to VF-11. Participated in raids against Okinawa, Formosa, Luzon, Leyte, Mindoro, Hong Kong, South China Sea and Manila.

Memorable experiences include the strike against the Japanese fleet; five airborne victories (three from the *Hornet*).

Discharged in September 1945. Received the Distinguished Flying Cross and Air Medal w/3 stars.

Married and has four children and two grandchildren. He is a retired oral surgeon.

ROBERT F. ZUTIC, born Oct. 2, 1932, Jersey City, NJ. Joined the USN April 2, 1952; and was assigned to the USS *Hornet* in the spring of 1955 to VF-72 as a technician. He was discharged in June 1956.

His tour of duty in the USN was a wonderful experience for him. The cruise to the Far East instilled a love for travel. While he loved the sea he also enjoyed flying and earned a private pilot license.

He traveled a great deal as sales manager for the Aroma Chemicals Div. of Haarmann & Reimer in New Jersey. He resided in Kinnelon where he was a familiar sight running at the high school. He had a son and daughter and three granddaughters. He passed away July 28, 1996.

HORNET BUZZ

VOL 2 NO 6   14 May 1954

ARMED FORCES DAY 1954

BY THE PRESIDENT OF THE UNITED STATES OF AMERICA

To the Navy, Marine Corps:

On this, the fifth annual Armed Forces Day, we of the Navy and Marine Corps affirm anew our pride and satisfaction in serving with the Army and the Air Force in our nation's great defense team. Backed by their vital reserve components, the Navy and the Marine Corps stand ready to insure that America's control of the seas will always be a powerful weapon for freedom. With surface, subsurface, amphibious and naval air forces, we are proving daily the value of sea power for peace.

Charles S. Thomas
Secretary of the Navy

Approximately 757,000 men are on active duty with the Navy at present. Navy warships in commission include 14 large carriers, 8 escort carriers, 4 battleships, 19 cruisers, nearly 250 destroyers and more than 100 submarines.

The world's first atomic-powered submarine, the USS Nautilus, has been launched, and another, the USS Sea Wolf, is under construction.

Two new attack aircraft carriers, the USS Forrestal and USS Saratoga, now are being built, and the Navy will gain additional strength from two cruisers now being converted to guided missile ships.

Our nation's power for peace lies largely in maintaining its fighting forces fully ready to meet promptly and decisively every challenge to our security.

Lemuel C. Shepherd
General, USMC
Commandant, USMC

WHEREAS the members of the Armed Forces of the United States have constantly demonstrated their loyalty and devotion to the service of their country; and

WHEREAS the men and women of the Armed Forces are actively engaged, at home and overseas, in upholding and defending our democratic way of life as opposed to ideologies which seek to destroy the basic principles of freedom cherished by this Nation; and

WHEREAS it is appropriate that on a special day each year our Armed Forces demonstrate to the people of the United States and our friends overseas their increased teamwork and efficiency and their technological advances; and

WHEREAS it is fitting and proper that all our citizens devote one day each year to paying special tribute to our fighting forces as the protectors and defenders of our Nation:

NOW, THEREFORE, I, DWIGHT D. EISENHOWER, President of the United States of America and Commander in Chief of the Armed Forces of the United States, do hereby proclaim Saturday, May 15, 1954, as Armed Forces Day, and I direct the Secretary of Defense and the Secretaries of the Army, the Navy and the Air Force, as well as the Secretary of the Treasury on behalf of the Coast Guard, to mark that day with appropriate ceremonies and to cooperate with civil authorities in suitable observances.

I invite the Governors of the States, Territories, and possessions of the United States to provide for the celebration of the day in such manner as will pay suitable honor to the members of the Armed Forces.

I also call upon my fellow citizens not only to display the flag of the United States on Armed Forces Day but also to manifest their recognition of the sacrifice and devotion to duty of the men and women of the Armed Forces by attending and participating in the local observances of the day conducted by the Armed Forces and the civil authorities.

IN WITNESS WHEREOF, I have hereunto set my hand and caused the Seal of the United States of America to be affixed.

DONE at the City of Washington this twenty-fifth day of January in the year of our Lord nineteen hundred and fifty-four and of the Independence of the United States of America the one hundred and seventy-eighth.

(SEAL)

DWIGHT D. EISENHOWER

Armed Forces In "Age Of Peril"

Saturday, May 15, will be the fifth annual Armed Forces Day. It is the day set aside each year on which the nation inspects its defense team. Citizens, including servicemen and women, have the opportunity to see how the U.S. is maintaining power for freedom and peace.

Most military installations, both in the U.S. and overseas, throw open their portals to exhibit their fighting equipment and their ability to use it to preserve peace of this country and the world.

This year's observance is of special significance because the threat of communist aggression is still very much in existence. The communists have not shown, either in word or action in the past year, that they desire real peace.

In Korea the preliminary negotiations for a peace conference have dragged on, making it clear to those nations concerned that the Reds do not want a peace conference at all.

Germany Still Divided

Almost nine years ago WWII ended but Germany is still divided and occupied by foreign troops. This situation is necessary because the Soviets still refuse to accept the conditions (free elections throughout Germany) by which the country could become free and united.

Within the Soviet Union itself there are no signs of peace. The Reds are not relaxing their arms build-up. Today the Red Army has 175 divisions and about 70 more in its satellite countries.

The Soviet air force has about 20,000 operational planes, of which a large portion are jets.
Continued on Page 3

1903-1998

This book is dedicated to Rear Admiral Clifford H. Duerfeldt, USN Retired, first Executive Officer of the USS HORNET, CV-12 and first President of the USS HORNET Club, Inc.

Rear Admiral Duerfeldt passed from this life on September 8, 1998. He was a key player in life and history of the HORNET and the HORNET Club and will forever live on in the memory of his shipmates.

HISTORY OF THE USS HORNET CLUB, INC.

1949 was a great year! Four years earlier, newspaper headlines across America proclaimed "Japanese Surrender! World War II Ends!" and the world entered a new era of peace. Historians would agree, the "flattops" of the Navy were a decisive factor in attaining this peace. The thousands of men who served aboard the USS HORNET, from her commissioning on October 20, 1941 through decommissioning in 1970, would surely agree.

1949 was a great year! For the seed of the USS HORNET Club had been planted two years before in Arlington, Virginia. Then Captain Roy Johnson, Air Group Commander and Executive Officer on CV-12, had been holding get-togethers at his home for former shipmates. His guests included Admiral A.K. Doyle, Kenn Henderson, Bob Neuhauser, Captain Curtis Myers, Harold Neubig, Captain Clifford Duerfeldt, Larry White and Dr. Frederick Hartman.

These Charter Members decided to hold a reunion of all "alumni" they could locate, at the Mayflower Hotel in Washington, D.C. on May 7. 1949. Even they couldn't envision what the next 50 years would entail! Many of you first heard of this reunion on Arthur Godfrey's radio program. The "USS HORNET CV-12 CLUB" was born that year with Rear Admiral Clifford Duerfeldt elected President and Commander Curtis Myers as Toastmaster. Many of you have the original member card signed by the Admiral. At early reunions, Admiral J.J. "Jocko" Clark and Admiral William F. "Bull" Halsey could be seen reveling amid the crowd. The Hornet Club was to hold reunions and elect officers each of the next 50 years.

In the early days of our club, the wife of each years elected president assumed the many secretarial duties for that reunion. The fourth reunion, held at the Brooklyn, New York Park Sheraton Hotel in 1952, advertised a party package price of $20.00 per couple, dues at $2.00 and a hotel room rate of $10.50! "Television in each room-No Extra Charge, Air Conditioned Meeting Rooms and ... babysitters available"!

In 1977, Mary Prophet, whose husband, Tom, had been President four different years, was elected our first permanent Secretary/Treasurer. In the 8 years Mary served with dedication, our club grew to 250 members from CV-8 and CV-12. During these years, Mary kept our member information organized on 3x5" index cards!

On May 9, 1983, the "USS HORNET MEMORIAL CLUB" was incorporated in Boston, Massachusetts with "Jake" Catterall, President; Al Masse, Vice-President; Peter Pinocci, Secretary and Fred Tamburino, Treasurer for the sole purpose of raising funds for donation to the Pensacola Museum. The club raised $23,500 from our membership and donated "in memory of all ships HORNET."

Mary Prophet was Honored in 1985 at our 37th reunion, and her Assistant Secretary, Connie Masse, was elected Secretary/Treasurer. Connie, helped by Mary Basile and other wives, over the next decade, would nurture the USS HORNET CLUB to over 1,000 members. These members now included shipmates from CVA-12 and CVS-12, Associate Members and a new segment of our club, Sons and Daughters of the Hornet (now called Family of HORNET). Al Masse, CV-12, had become our memorabilia collector and Ships' Store coordinator, and originated the idea of supplying photographs for sale.

Our reunions echoed great exploits of the past: Doolittle Raiders, Battle of Midway, Truk Island, Santa Cruz, The Marianas "Turkey Shoot", Leyte Gulf, Korea, Hainan, Vietnam's "Passage to Freedom", Matsu, Subic Bay, Tonkin Gulf, Apollo 11 and 12! Our membership kept expanding.

In 1995, Connie retired after 7 years as Assistant Secretary and 11 years as Secretary/Treasurer. Eighteen years of devoted attention to all HORNET CLUB members! Carla Svendsen was elected Secretary/Treasurer, in September 1995, for our Jacksonville and San Jose reunions. All will remember the energy of our 1997 President, Ray Vyeda and wife Molly, in their efforts to help "save" the USS HORNET. Our Executive Director, Lyn Svendsen and Carla would undertake a giant step forward for our club by upgrading us into the computer age and produce our first membership directory. They also published newsletters called "The HORNET BUZZ". We became a non-profit veterans organization with our Incorporation in 1995 as The USS HORNET CLUB, INC. Because of Lyn's employment responsibilities, Carla and Lyn resigned on October 1, 1997. Connie Masse came out of retirement, at the Board of Director's re-quest, so the planning of our 50th Anniversary Reunion could continue. Reunion President, "Swede" Hedenberg, Connie, and our Board of Directors, along with a "ship-full" of helpers have worked countless voluntary hours to make this Anniversary Reunion a success!

The USS HORNET earned many nicknames during her lifetime. "Mighty", "Shangri-La", "HORNET+3", "Three More Like Before" and "Gray Ghost". Our membership has grown to well over 1100 members, covering 3 continents, 5 countries and the United States from Hawaii to Maine. The HORNET has gone through many eras. From her 1st Commander in 1775, Captain William Stone through World War II to Flag Ship for Commander Antisubmarine Warfare Group Three to her final Commanding Officer, Rear Admiral Carl J. Seiberlich. She rested for many years then was brought to Alameda Naval Air Station as the xCVS-12 under Captain James Dodge. Finally, on May 26th 1998, The Honorable John Dalton, Secretary of the Navy, awarded the USS HORNET to the Aircraft Carrier HORNET Foundation and designated her a National Historic Landmark!

As Jerry Lutz, of the Aircraft Carrier HORNET Foundation said recently, "Without ALL who served aboard the USS HORNET, she would not be called MIGHTY! Without ALL of the USS HORNET CLUB, she would not be SAVED!"

Today's USS HORNET Club thrives due to energetic Board of Directors members, Officers, dedicated committeemen and women, and, especially, due to a membership of loyal shipmates and their spouses! To YOU, we dedicate this reunion and may God Bless all those who've gone on before us!

Respectfully submitted,

Roni Massé, Secretary/Treasurer
USS HORNET Club, Inc.
P.O. Box 7189
North Port, FL 34287
Phone: (941) 423-4547
Fax: (941) 423-9536

INDEX

*Biography entries do not appear in the index since they are in
alphabetical order on pages 56 through 91.*

– A –

Adams 30
Agana Bay 15
Akagi 10, 48
Akigumo 11
Alabama 11
Alameda 10
Aldrin, Edwin "Buzz" 24, 27
Alicia 9
Anderson 11, 31
Anderson, Jack 32
Andes, Ivan F. "Ike" 36
Antietam 23
Apollo 11 24, 27
Apollo 12 26, 27
Apollo 3 23
Argus 8
Armstrong, Neil 24
Arnold, Jack 15, 16
Attu 22
Aubel 30
Aubel, Richard Glen 32
Avant, Joseph 9
Averitt, G. 40

– B –

Baker, Fred J. 33
Balcome, Rog 33
Barnard, Lloyd G. 16
Barton 52
Bataan 16, 20
Bayers 30, 31
Bean, Allen 26
Beck 47
Beckwith 30, 31
Beebe, Marshall "Marsh" 20
Bell, Gordy 30, 31, 33
Belleau Wood 16, 20
Bennett, Floyd 44
Bennington 20, 23, 24, 27
Berry 31
Berryman 18
Bethel, John Huston, Jr. 30, 31
Bilbao 30, 31
Blair, F.K. 16
Blair, Frederick James Campbell
  31
Boineau, G.M. 30, 31
Bon Homme Richard 27
Boring, W.H. 30, 31
Bourne 30
Boyer 31
Brandt, Donald 15
Branham, Clint 36
Brash, Duane Frederick 32
Bratcres, Charles Ray 31
Brewer, Charles 16
Bridget 44
British Guiana 8
Bronstein 44
Brookens 31, 42
Brouillard 31
Brown 30, 31, 47
Brown, C.R. 22
Brown, J.S. 31
Browning, Miles R. 13, 14, 15
Browning, Mrs. 14

Buckling, "Pop" 41
Buell, H.L. 16
Bunker Hill 14, 18, 20, 21
Burgess, Robert 33
Burton, Robert E. 37
Butterly 31
Byerly 30, 31

– C –

Cabot 14, 19, 20
Cady, Gordon Duward 31
Calypso 9
Campbell 30
Canaan, Gerald 26
Canberra 31
Cardon 30
Carey, William Peter 32
Carl Vinson 29
Carmick 14
Carr, George 16
Cassano, Nickolas 36
Castro, Hank 40
Chamberlain 30
Chapman 30, 31
Chase, Kenneth 31
Chauncey, Isaac 8
Chleborad, Paul 33
Clark, J.J. "Jocko" 14, 15, 17, 19,
  36, 45
Clements, Robert E. 30, 31
Clouser 30, 31
Coats, Robert C. 20
Cocks 30
Coeur, G.A. 30, 31
Collins, Michael 24
Coln 47
Congress 8
Conrad, Pete 26
Cooper 30
Copile, Joe 40
Corry 14
Cox, D.L. 13
Cox, Robert Ronald 32
Cramer 40
Crawford, Robert 32, 33
Crehan 30, 31
Crowder, Cynthia 43
Crowder, Melvin 40
Crowell 30, 31
Crowley 30, 31
Crusoe, K.G. 31
Culver, William Saylor 32
Cunningham, Charles H. 33
Curtis 20
Cyr, R.F. 30, 31

– D –

Dance, Robert Christian 31
Davidson 44
Davis, Harry R. "Stinky" 37
Dayhoff, Nelson Woodrow 31
Dehaven 22
DeRolf, Warren 31
Dewey, George 13
Dewitt 30, 31
Dickhoff 30, 31
Dittmar, G. 40

Dodge, Jim 28, 29
Dolphin 8
Donaldson 31
Doolittle, James H. 10, 40, 46, 47
Dow 47
Doyle, Austin K. 16, 17, 22, 36
Dubois 30
Dudley, T. 40
Duerfeldt, C.H. 92

– E –

Earl 30
Eaton, General 8, 31
Eccles 30
Eccles, W.G. 30, 31
Edling 30, 31
Edwards 31
Eft 30, 31
Engle 30, 31
Engmanson 30
Enterprise 10, 11, 12, 14, 18, 20,
  24, 28, 41, 42, 46, 47, 48, 50, 51
Eolus 9
Erwin 30
Essex 12, 14, 16, 18, 20
Evans 44
Evans, John Ward 33
Evans, Samuel 8

– F –

Fairfax, Eugene 30, 31
Farley, R.P. 30, 31
Faulk, Glenn 33
Flagler, Henry M. 9
Flanigan, R. 40
Flath, R.N. 30, 31
Fone, Al 40
Ford 30
Forrest 14
Fowler, Klein 40
Fox, Carl 37
Franklin 9, 18, 20, 21
Franklin D. Roosevelt 23

– G –

Gallant, E.W. 49
Gallatin 30
Garlic 30, 31
Gartman 41
Gay, Ensign 50
Gay, George H. 10
Gelblat, Laura Joan 43
General Ernst 18
Gerry, George 44
Giarraputo, D.A. 37
Gibbo 40
Gillette, Norman C. 26
Gluck 31
Going, Frankie 40
Goldberg, Samuel Elsworth 31
Gordon, Richard 26, 27
Graebner, William Herbert 32
Grau 30
Griffin 30, 31
Griffith 30
Grosso 30, 31
Groves 30, 31

Guffa, G. 40
Guggenheim, Harry 44
Guinan, George 40

– H –

Haley, Claude E. 33
Hall, John Phillip 31, 32
Halsey, Admiral 10, 18, 21, 41, 42
Hamaker, Dowd 33
Hammar, Barbara 43
Hammond 49
Hampton 31
Hancock 18, 19, 20
Hardy, L.S. 30, 31
Harvey, Frederick G. 37
Hayes 30
Hayter 30, 31
Helgerson, Edward Erwin 31
Helm, James H. 9
Helmuth, Lawrence "Larry" 30,
  32, 33
Higgenbottom 30
Hintze 30, 31
Hiryu 10, 48
Hist 9
Hobson 14
Holloway, Robert 43
Holloway, William Fred 39, 42, 43
Holsclaw, Clyde 40
Holt 30
Hopkin, Esek 8
Hopkins, Jack 40
Hueston, Edward 40
Huiner 30
Hyland, Joe M. 30, 33

– I –

Independence 19, 20
Intrepid 18, 20, 23

– J –

Jacobsen 30, 31
James, C.W. 30, 31
Jeffers 31
Jenkins 44
Jensen, R. 40
Jesmer 30, 31
Jessen, Robert 40
Johnson 47
Johnson, Andrew 9
Johnson, Edward Harold 31
Johnson, Homer R. 33
Johnson, Roy L. 14, 15
Jones 30
Jung 47

– K –

Kaga 10, 48
Karr, Kimberly 43
Kater, Fred Homer 32
Kearns, W.E. 31
Kearsarge 11
Kennedy, John F. 23
Kenney 30
King 30, 31
Kinkaid, Thomas 18
Kissinger, Henry 24

Kitty Hawk 23
Knott 30, 31
Knox, Frank 14
Knox, Mrs. Frank 9, 13, 14
Koressel 30, 31
Kroeger, Edwin John 32
Kroger 30
Kurita, Takeo 18

– L –
LaChapelle, W.H. 40
Lady Sterling 9
Lake, Kenny "The Kid" 37
Langan, Lieutenant 36
Langley 20
LeBlanc, Fritz W. 33
Lee, Leon Edsel 31
Lepianka 30, 31
Lewis 30, 31, 42
Lexington 10, 14, 16, 18, 19, 41, 48, 50
Lindesmith, George Edgar 31
Lindsley 47
Liston 31
Lizotte, W.E. 30, 31
Logan 30
Long Beach 27, 44
Lynch 30

– M –
Magariello, John 40
Maier, Willie 30, 33
Makigumo 11
Mangini 31
Mann, William Manniere 31
Manning, S.J. 31
Manthe 31
Marias 22
Maring 30, 31
Marz, Gayle 32, 33
Mason, Charles P. 9, 11
McBride, R. 30, 31
McCain, Admiral 24
McCampbell, David 16
McCarron 30, 31
McDonnell 47
McGowan, Edwin W. 33
McKinney, Robert A. 33
McReynolds, R. 30, 31
McVeigh, John James 31
Meade 30, 31
Meyer 30, 31, 42
Micheel, Mike 44
Midway 23
Miles 30, 31
Miller, Earl L. 45, 48, 50
Missouri 23, 39
Mitscher, Marc Andrew 9, 10, 11, 16, 17
Monihan 36
Monterey 14
Montgomery, A.E. 14
Moore, H.H. 30, 31
Moranville, H. Blake 30, 31
Morgan, Norman E. 33
Morris 51
Morris III, A.W. 31
Morriss 30, 31
Moss 47
Mossey 47
Mudd 30, 31
Musashi 18, 21

Mustin 11, 51
Myers 30

– N –
Nagumo, Admiral 49
Nashville 41
Nautilus 8
Nelson 27, 31, 40
Newkirk, Stanton R. 43
Nicholson, John 8
Nickerson 9
Nimitz, Admiral 15, 48
Nishimura, Shoji 18
Nist, Joe 40
Nixon, President 26, 27
Norfolk 10
Norris, Otho 8
Northampton 11, 41, 51
Nowlin, T.H. 30, 31

– O –
Oakely 30
Oberg, Burton T. 33
Ogish 30
Ogle 30, 31
Oklahoma City 22
Olson, J.B. 30, 31
O'Neill, Edward 40
Onion 30, 31
Ooghe, Thomas William 32
Operation Blackjack 23
Operation Gold Ball 23
Operation Magic Carpet 23
Oriskany 12, 27
Ozawa, Jisaburo 16, 18

– P –
Paine, Dr. 24
Palella, L. 40
Papen, George William, Jr. 32
Parsley, C.L. 30, 31
Patterson, Jonny Wilson 32
Pavela, J.V. 31
Peacock 8
Pfluger, R. 40
Picirilli 47
Porter 51
Powell 47
President 8
Princeton 18
Prothra 47
Ptacek, Henry 32

– R –
Ramsey, J.W. 30, 31
Randolph 20
Ranger 24, 28
Reagan, Ronald 26
Reese, Edward 40
Regan, Frank 36
Reick 31
Reiserer, Russell 16
Reynolds, Albert F. 44
Rhode Island 9
Richardson 30, 31
Richfield 30
Riera, R.E. 18, 30
Riffel 47
Riley 47
Rivers, William Malloy, Jr. 32
Robcke, J.H. 30, 31
Roberts 30, 31

Robertson, Gordon H. 44
Rodger, John 8
Rogers, F.J. 40
Roland, Virgil David 32
Ronsville 30
Roosevelt, Franklin D. 10, 11, 21
Roosevelt, John 21
Rouse 31
Rowland 30, 31
Russell 30, 51
Ryder 31

– S –
Saggau 30, 31
Sahm 30, 31
Sailor, Warren James 32
Saito, Yoshitsugu 15
Salamaua 22
Saltonstall, Commodore 8
Sample, William D. 15, 17
San Fillipo 47
Sanson, Admiral 9
Saratoga 10, 50
Sarratt, C. 40
Satterlle 30
Savage, Jimmie "Doc" 30, 31
Saville 31
Sawyer, Laurence E. 33
Schaeppekotter 31
Schiller, Laurence C. 33
Schmitt 40
Schrader, Frederick R. 18
Schwab 30
Sebec 22
Seiberlich, Carl J. 24, 26
Self, Chuck 29
Shangri-La 10, 22, 23
Shaw 51
Shultz 30
Sieg, R. 40
Sims, John Peek 30, 31, 32, 42
Sisley, W.R. 30, 31
Smith 47, 51
Smith, C.D. 30, 31
Smith, Dean Harvey 40
Smith, H.E. 30, 31
Smith, Lieutenant Commander 44
Smith, Lloyd Addison 32
Sobiar 30
Sorenson 47
Soryu 10, 48
South Dakota 51
South, M.P. 30, 31
Spreckner, Eddie P. 33
Spruance, Raymond 15, 16, 21
Steed, Clint T. 33
Stimpson, Charles 30, 31, 33
Stingray 15
Stone, William 8
Stonewall 9
Strahan 30
Stratton, Doc 44
Suddreth, J.M. 30, 31
Swaim, Joyce Eugene 32
Swope, James 30, 31

– T –
Taylor 44
Taylor, Jack 15
Tegge 30
Teony, R.E. 40
Theimer 31

Thresher 10
Ticonderoga 24
Tidwell, W.A. 40
Tillar 30
Tiller 31
Tonsfeldt 30, 31
Traveller 8
Trendall 30
Trout 10
Truman, President 21
Tuscaloosa 40, 43

– U –
United States 8
USS HORNET Club, Inc. 93
USS Hornet Historical Museum Association, Inc. 27
Ussery 31

– V –
Valdespino, H.C. 40
Vance 30, 31
Vinyard, Tex 37
Vraciu, Alex 16
Vyeda, Ray 28

– W –
Waldron, John C. 49
Walker 30, 31, 44
Warren, Thomas Jack 30, 31, 32
Wasp 10, 14, 16, 18, 20, 50
Watson 31
Webb, Wilbur "Spider" 16
Welder 30, 31
Welfelt 30, 31
Wenke 47
West, O.H. 30, 31
White, Henry S. 30, 31
Widhelm, Gus 41
Wiley 30
Wilkinson, James 8
Williams, T.St.C. 30, 31
Williss 30, 31, 42
Wilson 30, 31
Wilson, Richard Everett 32
Winner, William H. 33
Winslow, John 11
Wise, John 39, 47, 50
Wolfe 30, 31
Wompatuck 9
Woodward, Mr. 13
Woolsey 31
Work, D.T. 30, 31

– Y –
Yamamoto, Admiral 48
Yamato 21
Yoder 30
Yorktown 10, 12, 14, 16, 20, 41, 42, 48, 49, 50
Youmans, Kermit "Dipsy" 44
Young, Marion Russell 32

– Z –
Zaun, Chaplain 14
Zellin, W. 40
Zink 30
Zink, J.A. 31
Zoecklein 30, 31
Zuikaku 16

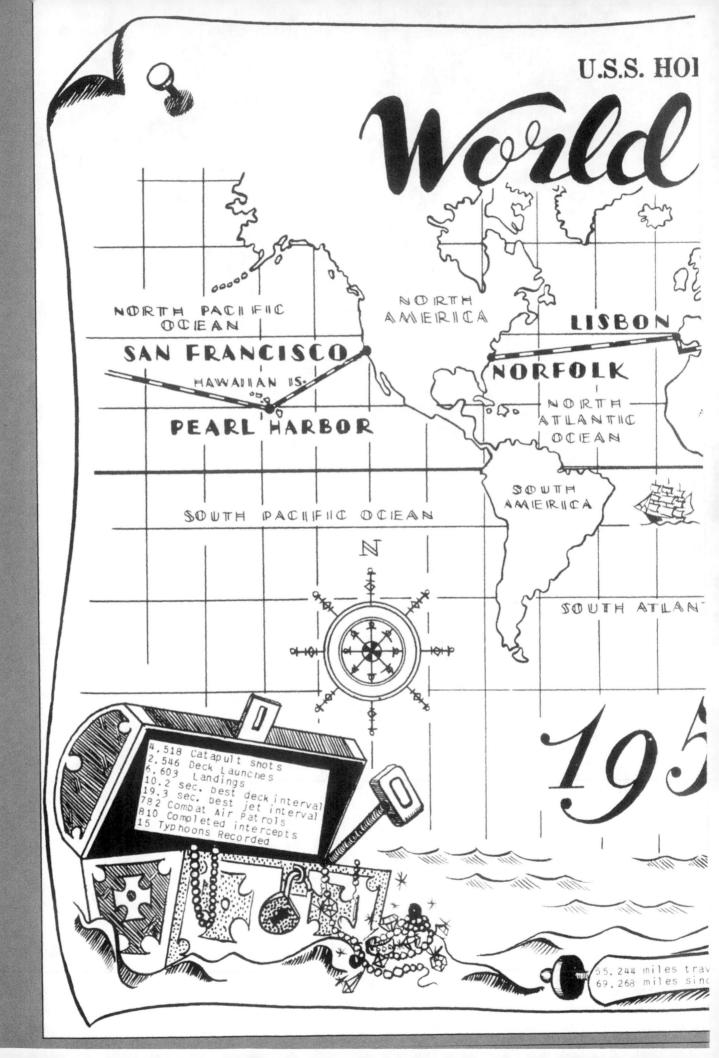